IN THE SHADOW
OF THE REICH

IN THE
SHADOW
OF THE
REICH

by Niklas Frank

*Translated by Arthur S. Wensinger
with Carole Clew-Hoey*

Alfred A. Knopf

NEW YORK

1991

THIS IS A BORZOI BOOK
PUBLISHED BY ALFRED A. KNOPF, INC.

Copyright © 1991 by Alfred A. Knopf, Inc.

Originally published in German as *Der Vater: Eine Abrechnung* by
C. Bertelsmann Verlag GmbH, Munich, in 1987. Copyright © 1987 by
C. Bertelsmann Verlag.

Library of Congress Cataloging-in-Publication Data

Frank, Niklas, [date].
[Vater. English]
In the shadow of the Reich / by Niklas Frank; translated by
Arthur S. Wensinger, with Carole Clew Hoey. — 1st ed.
p.   cm.
Translation of: Der Vater.
ISBN 0-394-58345-0
1. Frank, Hans, 1900–1946. 2. Frank, Niklas, 1939–
3. National socialists—Biography. 4. War criminals—Germany—
Biography. 5. Fathers and sons—Germany—Biography. 6. World
War, 1939–1945—Atrocities. I. Title.
DD247.F62F7313   1991
943.086'0922—dc20
[B]   90-53425
CIP

Manufactured in the United States of America

FIRST AMERICAN EDITION

IN THE SHADOW
OF THE REICH

A Bloody Footnote
to the History of
Our Times

She had no orgasm when you came—when I came.

    She had no lofty sensations when you were lying on top of her, fat as you were—not even at the time you were siring me. You never knew that. I got it from Aunt Margot. "Can't imagine what men find in all that," Mother would say in astonishment— and then she would have one unsuccessful pregnancy after another. (Were you always the father?) Yet she bore me for you, the Minister of the Reich without Portfolio, the President of the Academy of German Justice, the Governor General of Poland, and today a bloody footnote to the history of our times—executed, thank God, cremated and scattered in the Konwentz Brook at Solln near Munich, your ashes mixed with those of Göring, of Streicher and Ribbentrop, of Jodl and Kaltenbrunner, of Frick, Keitel, Seyss-Inquart, of Sauckel and Rosenberg—a nauseating mess.

    Your final photograph is on the table in front of me. There you are, still fresh in your death, at rest on your blanket, with your neck snapped, your eyes closed, your mouth half open, your full lips maybe just a touch too pale—did you bite your lips under your black hood at the moment of your plunge?

    Such beautiful hands, the fingers so long. One might easily imagine them practicing mazurkas, études. And they're so elegantly arranged—it is almost as if at the very moment the trapdoor opened, you were about to snap them at some headwaiter, imperiously requesting your dinner check.

But that image won't work. At the time of your death, your hands were tied behind your back, your feet strapped together at the ankles. The suit in which you dangled out your life is really quite becoming. Or did they put it on you after the fact? Was it when they wiped the blood from your lips? As you were falling through the trapdoor, did you strike your chin on its wooden edge on the way down? Was that the reason for the blood? How unfair it would have been if the blow had knocked you out. You deserved to enjoy, in full awareness, every last millimeter of rope, right up to the final jerk. All right, I admit it: Woods, the American hangman, *was* a miserable executioner. No real feeling for details, such as the correct measurements for a trapdoor.

How happy Mother was when she learned of Hangman Woods's demise in 1951. It happened when he was testing out an electric chair. Both Mother and I drank a cup of coffee to celebrate (real ground coffee it was, too; we had so little, but this was a special event). "Now if that's not a sign from Heaven!" Mother exclaimed, calling upon the Lord God to wreak vengeance for the Nazis.

When I first saw the photograph of your dead body I was shattered. Now it only makes me sick, that dead face of yours on which the imprint of your lies still lives.

Do you still remember? October 6, 1946, ten days before your final photo opportunity? I was sitting facing you, in the Nuremberg prison, on Mother's lap. You were next to an American GI wearing a glossy white helmet; there was a pane of glass between us. I knew that you would soon be dead. But still you had to lie. You said we would soon be celebrating Christmas, all of us together at the Schoberhof, our house on the Schliersee in Bavaria. And even at that tender age I was thinking to myself, Why is he lying like that? He knows he's going to be hanged, doesn't he? As I was climbing down from Mother's lap and about to leave with her, you cracked some stupid, familiar joke: "And then Tony Huber came along, too, shitting all over the woods. . . ." That was not enough of a final message for me to leave with, let me tell you. Why didn't you say, "My son, you are seven years old. You know that I'm going to die. We shall never see each other again. I am condemned to death by hanging. The punishment is a just one. But, son, I am so very frightened of dying"? And then perhaps after that a little word of advice for me to take with me through life, like: "Never throw away paper clips!" Or: "Just forget the first stanza of 'Deutschland über alles'!"

No, instead of that you had to bring up the only funny story you ever knew, about Tony Huber shitting in the woods because he was so frightened of the robbers—and he such a thief himself. In the old days you used to tell it while we listened to a recording of the overture to Auber's *Fra Diavolo*.

But that was no record player the GI with the white helmet was holding in his lap.

As a young boy I absorbed, and was absorbed by, your death; I made it a part of me. I had to do that, because I wanted to live. Do you understand that—do you hear me? And I made it; I'm the one who is alive! And I'm older now than you were able to get to be. That is something I aimed for. That is something I swore I would accomplish, even as a child. Even if it would be only one moment older than you were at your death.

The nights just before October 16 were the holiest ones in my rituals of release. I took almost physical pleasure from your dying. I would begin to see you: There you would be, walking back and forth in your jail cell, your fists pressed against your eyeballs, moaning, muttering to yourself some preposterous military regulations about bearing up heroically in the face of death, then sitting down again and listening for them to come for you. You're familiar by now with all the different sounds. You have been sitting there long enough in that room with the bars; your pulse beats rapidly, you force yourself to look once more at your final letters home to your dear ones (noting perhaps how hollow and false and pious

they sound?), and then get up again, clasp your hands, nervously
intertwine your fingers, pull them apart again, open your fly; you
have to pee again; but only a few drops come. You know that
people piss and shit when they die, and you want to be clean in
your death, at least down there. I can feel your panic in death,
now, as footsteps approach your cell. You cringe against the rear
wall, staring at the door, your eyelashes fluttering, and let out a
whispered, strangled "No!" The bolts. The locks. The door is torn
open; guards leap upon you, chain your hands and feet. And
between your guards you toddle off with tiny steps down the long
corridor, to the gymnasium. (What an exercise in stretching awaits
you there!) The sweat is running down your back between your
shoulder blades, down the crack of your ass; the chains at your
ankles make your gait ridiculous; and they're holding you by both
of your upper arms, the way guards have done since time began,
as if from the moment of your arrest on, you had forgotten how
to walk. The door to the gym opens; you see the tall platform,
on it three gallows, curtained beneath by black cloth; will it be
the curtain at the left, in the middle, or the one to the right that
will conceal your fall from the eyes of the witnesses? You see them
now, perhaps recognize some of the German witnesses—Hoegner,
for example, the Premier of Bavaria. Oh, how the entire Frank
family hated him from that moment on; they said he was a traitor,
just because he had been "in attendance." Is it possible that you
have one more thing to tell me? Here is your opportunity now.
For even in your case the executioners insist on honoring that
foolish old tradition and letting you—you dreadful blabbermouth—say a few final words. Well, get to it: Let's have a last
greeting for your son. Maybe now is the time for that word of
advice about paper clips; or maybe you could say, "Christ, how
you make me want to puke, all of you!" or "Hello there, Herr
Hoegner—my wife will never be able to forgive you for being
here!" or "What a life that was, and what a death!" But no; you
just had to remain a bastard to the very end, for the present and

for the hereafter. And so you say: "I thank you for your kind treatment during my incarceration. I pray that the Lord God may receive me in His grace and mercy."

The only thing that makes any sense about that sentence, Father, is its grammar.

They said you whispered those words. And then they led you up the thirteen steps (symbols are essential), slipped the hood over your head, the noose around your neck, and away with you into Eternity. These images were my attempt to exorcise you, the devil that haunts me.

I flew to America, to get eyewitness testimony and other firsthand information. Father Sixtus O'Connor, seventy-two years old, living in Albany, New York, was the first to destroy the joy I used to get out of my fantasy of your death. When they opened the door of your cell, he said, there you were, kneeling on the floor. Amazing. Your hands were folded in prayer. O'Connor approached you; you looked up at him and said—he swore you said—"When I was a little boy, every morning before I went off to school my mother would make the sign of the cross on my forehead. Please, Father, do that for me now!" And so he did it. What a scene that must have been. You son of a bitch. Who would expect someone to be kneeling on the floor of a cell when you open the door? What a fantastic scenario—absolutely perfect for the tragedy of a ham actor like you.

"And then we walked between the guards to the place of execution," the pious man in the U.S.A. tells me.

"Father O'Connor," I say, "did you pray with him on the way there?"

"No, we just talked."

"About what?" I ask him, for it was a long walk to the gallows. It was shortly after one in the morning; the guards were quiet; I wonder if it was possible for there to have been one final honest bit of conversation between the two men. "What did you and my father talk about?"

"Oh," answers this splendid specimen of a Franciscan, "about this and that—I can't remember any longer, to tell the truth."

Damn it all, why did such a mediocrity like you, my father, choose to live with nothing but other mediocrities right up to the very moment of your death?

This man of God clearly had other things on his mind at the time. Proudly he continues, "And the last words your father spoke were 'Jesus, have mercy.' I heard it with my own ears."

I become embarrassed. (I think to myself, Is it conceivable that your piety was real, after all? Did you really find your way to the bosom of the One and Only True Church after your arrest?) At that moment I am actually ready to place my blind trust in your newly found faith, prepared to believe you had converted like some modern Saint Paul, and that you were no longer just some sanctimonious faker at the end.

O'Connor saves me from my delusion. "I begged your father to . . ."

"To what?"

"To say 'Jesus, have mercy.' And he did say it. Those words were on his lips when the trapdoor opened under him. I heard it clearly: 'Jesus, have mercy.' "

The man of God was clearly pleased. You, too? Were those words your ticket to Paradise?

The noose took your breath away even before the fall—the very second before, when you were standing up there, high above the others, your head in the black hood, your heart a high-pressure pump, your body stiff with the frenzy of fear. Yes, Father, it is a goddamn shitty shame to die completely awake and conscious, the picture of health, having been tested and declared by the officials at Nuremberg to belong to the highest of the three echelons of Nazi criminals, well fed while all of Europe is famished—and then for you to give in and in a loud whisper say, "Jesus, have mercy"!

"I heard him say it with my own ears. Before the snapping sound. That, you see, was the terrible thing about your father's death, that sound of his neck cracking. You could hear it all over the gymnasium." I weep, Father, I weep. Why do I weep? What was the snapping like? Like a cork being pulled from a bottle? Like the sound of a willow branch breaking? Like the splitting of kindling? Like clicking your tongue against the roof of your mouth?

It was the last sound you made; the only thing that followed was the death fart. You're hanging. You dangle there now. It is a fact. You are swaying gently back and forth. The doctor—*two* doctors listen with their stethoscopes, and before they confirm your death, O'Connor scurries up, for now is his chance, the payoff for the Church, to follow through with the deal he had prearranged with the authorities: that there would be a little hole cut in the black hood, a hole right at the forehead, specially cut out so that you could receive extreme unction quick as a wink before it was too late. The priest makes the sign of the cross on your brow with the holy chrism. He's got what he came for. Bye-bye, baby, and Amen.

You probably were no longer aware.

The end of a criminal, a big shot gets hanged, a thoroughly cultivated German, someone who had known the truth of poetry and music and who sold out for big expensive limousines, a Horch, a Mercedes, and a private railroad car.

Three Fathers
Too Many

Your betrayal assured me a regal childhood in the Third Reich. I had everything. At night snuggled up under luxurious blankets on the backseat of a mammoth limousine, green and red lights on the dashboard, next to me my nursemaid, in front of us the chauffeur with his uniform and cap; me dozing, filled with wonderful food. Life for me was meeting illustrious guests in halls lighted by chandeliers. I would be passed along—"Now make your little bow to the gentlemen, and kiss the ladies' hands." I was still only a child, and for me the Third Reich was little more than being surrounded by formal military breeches and tight-fitting ladies' gowns covered with glitter and usually stretched to the bursting point by the fat thighs beneath them.

I can see myself holding a diamond-studded sword with both hands and whacking off the tops of nettles, until it is taken away from me ("No, no, that's much too valuable for such things"). Where did that sword come from, Father? I can see myself, the object of benevolent smiles, playing hide-and-seek among the tombs of the Polish royalty in Cracow, up at the castle, the Wawel. I see myself, guarded by SS soldiers, splashing naked in the pond at still another castle, Kressendorf; see myself eating noodle soup with the SS guard. I think what the Third Reich meant above all for me is crying and running around the big round table in Belvedere Castle in Warsaw, running around and around after you, and you making fun of me: "Well, now, where do you suppose he is, our Little Stranger? You don't even belong to our family, do you? Well, what do you want then, Little Stranger?" And all the while the only thing I wanted was to be in your arms, and I cried until my tears dried up—until they were as dry as your ashes were, later. Today I thank you for that.

Perhaps I really was the "Little Stranger." Ten years old in 1949, I had enough sense to understand the rumors whispered by our relatives that insinuated I could make my choice among three possible fathers. One of them was you. The second was Karl Lasch, your friend, the one you liked to call "my blond rascal," the man with the two doctorates—not surprising, considering the fraudulent way the two of you cooked up at least one of them. You, the President of the Academy for German Justice; he, your director there. Later you brought him to Cracow and made him one of the governors under you. He, the handsome Lasch, the dream of illustrious ladies, also loved her—your wife, my mother.

Am I the secret child of their love affair?

"No," said Frau K., your secretary, whom I visited decades later. (She had peered out through the curtains of her little one-family house, watching me come up her garden path to visit her.) "No, there's no resemblance at all to Lasch!" Would I be happy if there were? They say he was friendly to animals, this handsome SA chargé.

If the rumored affair with Mother was in fact true, you had your sweet revenge. You did not so much as lift a finger for your own governor when he was about to be murdered by the SS. Or were you too frightened? I believe you were. He did nothing different from what you did. He, too, made a personal fortune for himself, just as you did—even though you passionately denied any such thing right up to the bitter end.

Poor Lasch, the little potentate. He had a fancy photograph taken of himself at his palace in Lvov, festooned with his medals like some big shot, looking into the camera with those bedroom eyes that no doubt dressed and undressed Mother. He scarcely had time to warm up his governor's chair before his body was cold. And all that only because he had emulated the behavior of the other German Lords of the East. He, too, sent truckloads of fabrics, furs, foodstuffs, home to the Reich, wheeled and dealed in luxury automobiles bought in Holland with government money and then shipped illegally to Poland for resale. (What bum luck that his father just happened to be sitting in one of the trucks when the SS stopped it at the German border.)

Like so much else in that life of yours, the history of this betrayal ran its predictable course. Lasch, embroiled in an affair with some secretary or other, had managed to get yet another secretary into his bed. That naturally put the first one's nose out of joint, and so she promptly alerted the SS to the details about the next shipment, let them in on when a truck loaded with loot was expected to be on its way to Germany from Poland for the war profiteers. Or do you suppose Mother tipped them off about Lasch? You know how she could fight. Even Father O'Connor knew that about her: "Your father, you know, was still scared of your mother, even when he was in prison in Nuremberg."

Here, then, is one possible scenario: Mother had palmed me— Lasch's brat—off on you. Do you think she was going to put up with two more of the "blond rascal's" floozies? Or could it be that she was already fed up with him, especially after she got word of his marriage plans? In fact, he did get married. So if it was Mother who betrayed him (and I like the idea of her doing that), she was quick about it. Lasch and his bride did not so much as get a chance to hop into their marriage bed; the only thing he could manage was some final letters to her, in 1942—pious, slobbering letters like your own four years later, from your cell in Nuremberg.

Lasch was your first murder—among your friends, that is. When they came to get your governor, there you were sitting quiet as a mouse up at your castle. After the war those who knew him did not wish to have their own honor tainted by such an association, not unlike the situation with our family. So they invented a fairy tale about how Lasch had to die because he had helped rescue so many Jews in Poland that they were nearly obliged to put the gas-oven workers at Auschwitz on a half-time schedule. It was on Himmler's orders, they said, that he was forced to leave this vale of tears so suddenly—almost as fast as the way you got your hands on many a valuable antique. Himmler had a pistol put in Lasch's cell, so the story goes, and so naturally Lasch, the man of honor, shot himself right in the forehead ("the spot of the brave," as the chroniclers of kitsch call it). None of it is true. Daddy Number 2 surely had no desire to knock himself off; so two SS characters took care of it for him, presumably in a prison in Breslau.

I didn't know him during those days of might and glory, any more than I knew my Daddy Number 3, Carl Schmitt. Did you, Father, happen to know about Mother's relationship with that gentleman? Mother's chauffeur used to complain bitterly about having to wait for hours outside the restaurant in Berlin where he and Mother would secretly carry on in a delightful *chambre séparée*. That was Schmitt. He was the great expert in constitutional law, as it is called these days, the same one who concocted the legal cover-up for Hitler's murder of Röhm and the SA men in 1934. He lived on much longer than I had realized.

In fact, it was not until 1985 that I read of his death in the newspaper, old as Methuselah. I had an urge to salute the memory of Daddy Number 3, and so I went to Plettenberg. He was to be buried that afternoon. (He had been forbidden to teach after the war—one of a very small number, it must be added. Despite that, he managed somehow to see to it that his apostles, in the spirit of their former master, muddled the minds of their students in the next generation.) In the morning I went to the cemetery, where I found myself alone. I went as far as the mortuary hall but did not have the courage to enter. A man came out, a gardener perhaps, and asked me what I wanted. I said I would like to see Herr Schmitt's coffin, but he didn't understand me; he shouted that he was hard of hearing and I shouted that I wanted to see Herr Schmitt. Yes, he shrieked, he was in there. I roared back that I—no, that my father—had been a very close friend of his, of Herr Schmitt. Aha, he screamed back, a friend, then, and said that I should come with him, which I did. Inside the hall the man's voice reverberated as if he were standing at the walls of Jericho. There was the coffin, inside it my Father Number 3. I assumed the reverential posture, hands folded over my private parts, where-upon the man shouted, "Would you like to see him one last time?" I nodded, and we stepped into the niche where he lay. "Unscrew the top on your side and I'll do it over here," he bellowed, and I unscrewed the two bronze bolts. I was frightened of my first confrontation with the man who was responsible for fashioning the will of the Führer into law. The gardener heaved the coffin lid up, and there lay . . . Gerhart Hauptmann, that famous writer—at least he looked just like him, my Father Number 3: ivory-white hair, red eruptions on his face from lying so long in the hospital, fingers intertwined over his chest, bloodless, alabaster, so appro-priate to this Christian lying-in-state of an old Hitler fan, his fingers so white, their contours so vague, that they all seemed to blend into one. The hands looked like a pair of pale, webbed flippers. There was no smell about him. I thought to myself, I have never seen this man before, in the flesh; the least I should do is touch him once. The gardener heaved a great sigh. "The lid is heavy," he shouted in a voice loud enough to wake the dead. (It occurred to me that it was somehow appropriate for them to hire deaf people here.) I laid the tips of the index and middle fingers of my right hand on his brow. Light as a feather, his head waggled back and forth once, saying "No, I am not your father." He was already way beyond rigor mortis, this nearly ninety-six-year-old gentleman, over whom we now lowered and fastened the wooden coffin lid. In a loud voice I thanked the gardener for my first and final tête-à-tête.

A Million Gallows
Along the Autobahn

I would have liked him, that Father Number 3 of mine—just as I liked them all, your comrades-in-battle from the GG, the Government General of Occupied Poland, those at the Justice Ministry, all those old men and women, those of them still alive in astonishingly good physical shape today, bright as buttons, witty. They were always delighted when I made my appearance among them. "Do you realize how really *outstanding* the bureaucracy in the Government General *was?*" one of them said to me not long ago, with pride in his voice. "You can still tell that from the splendid positions all of us have now in Germany."

Well, Father. I've got to congratulate you on the creation of a postwar Germany, a new country in your spirit. Five years and three months of bureaucratic training and practice in a raped land; that is why it has worked out so well with putting those constraints on civil rights in Germany today. Yes, indeed, it's getting to be more and more a state created in your own spirit.

Once again, a choking, suffocating, putrid mantle of political self-glorification has settled down over Germany. The arrogance of power is on the march just as you were then. They have your same shameless, sordid manner; they manipulate the law, they disdain the average citizen. No, your times were not swept away with your ashes in the waters of the Konwentz at Solln. Your goddamned ashes fertilized far too many plants along the edge of that brook; they germinated again. Because of people like you, your Eternal Germany is threatened more from within than from without, and its conscience is like yours—which is to say, it does not exist. One fateful initiative, one evil impulse, coming from almost anywhere, and you can take over the reins once more, you and a thousand others like you.

You know, we've got that same old itch once again. But this time we've got it good. Reunited. Seventy million Germans equals seventy million times that clammy, secretive urge for aggression. When is that bottled-up power, lying in ambush, growing by the day, going to be let loose again? How much do they want for Eastern Europe? Isn't it ours anyhow? What do we care about the West? To be German means to be free, no bridle, no boundaries, unlimited freedom.

I have wicked fantasies lodged in my brain, one of them an image of millions of gallows erected along the autobahns right after the war; of the American hangman Woods driving slowly past them in your confiscated Maybach, and releasing the trapdoors one after the other. What a wholesome chorus of cracking necks would have resounded over Germany, the snapping neck bones of all those judges, lawyers, industrialists, guards, wardens, and informers. Not one of you had the right to go on living. The ones who managed did so underhandedly. The minute the war was over, your beloved judges and public prosecutors, for example, issued themselves their own certificates of purity, denazified themselves, 99 and $^{44}/_{100}$ths percent pure. By adding nothing more than the prefix "democratic," they went on judging and prosecuting in your spirit. In that sense you have every right to be satisfied. Your Societies of the Upholders of Justice, your League of Lawyers, your Union of National Socialist Jurists, your Academy of German Justice, have survived you. The recipients of the Nazi Blood-Order of German Justice brought your immortal thoughts with them right into our successor state. At many a trial they're suddenly radiant again. It is then I know that you have returned to dwell among them, you perfect exemplar from the underbelly of today's herd of former fellow travelers, still drooling with lust for the old pomp-and-glory days. I run into your sort more and more frequently these days.

After the war, Mother used to like to sit with a copy of the membership roster of your Academy of German Justice on her lap and take malicious pleasure in putting little checkmarks in front of names she had come across in newspaper obituaries, or in news reports about this or that person having been promoted to lofty, sometimes even to the loftiest, positions as judges or other high officials. In Mother's own personal checklists many a patriotic career appeared a good deal different than in today's official versions. She had known many of them personally. "That one!" she'd say. "He couldn't find enough boots to lick."

Imagine for a second that you survived, you the prototype of the German criminal, the man who began his career with doctorate in hand, ran his own law firm, and was an assistant at the Munich Institute of Technology, you who never actually bumped anyone off personally, but who certainly saw to it that when it was done, it was done with great precision. A career that began that way would have fit well into the new Germany. After a bit of denazification, your metamorphosis from Nazi to good Christian Democrat would have taken place without a hitch. With that gift for speech-making of yours and with that folksy way you could shift into a Bavarian dialect with farmers and others, you were ready-made for a seat in the Bavarian parliament or even the Bundestag in Bonn. Spiced with a few Latin phrases, your inspiring voice would reflect your ardor for the new democracy and your condemnation of the brownshirt dictatorship, to which, alas, you had fallen a helpless victim; for, as everyone knew, you had submitted your resignation as Governor General of Poland to the Führer over and over again.

Almost as if Hitler wanted to safeguard my youth, he refused to accept your ridiculous attempts to resign. Admit that you bent and twisted these rejections into proof of how much love and trust Hitler had in you, and you swallowed this fiction yourself.

The appeal for clemency that your lawyer, Seidl, submitted just before your date with the gallows—I still tremble at the thought that it might have succeeded—is something you claimed not to want. You were placing your hopes in Pope Pius XII. You would have enjoyed the wording of the appeal. The way you altered your confession of guilt at Eastertime of 1946 to the evasive qualifications of that following autumn, the way you began to balance the crimes of the Germans against the crimes of the Allies, was just like the arguments of that crafty lawyer Seidl. He said that the legal decision had been rendered, the verdict that you were to be executed; but the question as to the *political* wisdom of actually carrying out the sentence was another, and more dubious, matter. Struggling to keep your neck out of the noose, he then began to list your arguments, those that have become the foundation for the subsequent German politics of psychological repression: that whole business about the terrible crimes perpetrated by the Eastern powers . . . the Red Peril . . . and the bombing of Dresden . . . and how restless the German people were . . . and how the Western world needs them . . . and that Hans Frank alive would be of much greater use to the victors than as fish food in the Konwentz Brook . . . and . . . well, you know all the sorts of things one has to write for such an amnesty appeal—you were a lawyer yourself. But the whole attempt did no good.

Just imagine if it had worked. You would have ended up hanging out with Hess in Spandau, well nourished and ancient (because there would be nothing there to wear you out). Then there would have been a big stink if I as your son had refused to go along with President Weizsäcker's plea for your release, my grounds being simply that to have you constantly muttering and justifying yourself in the same house would have been too much to bear. Praise be to the Soviets for refusing ever to let Hess out of Spandau and for the fact that he had to shuffle his way through the prison yard for the rest of his long life until he died. He was another one who through his dedication, his speeches, and his acts made it possible for us to commit the most insane crimes in all of human history.

And even if I should be overcome by pity and find myself picturing an old man, totally isolated, waiting for his death, all I have to do is quickly change the slide in the projector I have in my head, and just as intensely summon up the image of a Polish, Russian, or Jewish mother (here come the clichés) who sits hunched over holding the crumpled photo of her only son whom we have shot to death, beaten to death, gassed, whose brains we have dashed out against a wall—all those things one does when one wants "to give culture a shot in the arm," as you once so delicately defined one of the goals of the war.

The Gallant
Herr Hitler

The snapping of your neck spared me from having a totally screwed-up life. You certainly would have poisoned my brain with all your drivel, the fate of the silent majority of my generation, who did not have the good fortune of having their fathers hanged.

That's why I'm happy to be your son. How poor by comparison are all the millions of other children whose fathers spouted the same garbage filled with deceit and cowardice, with bloodthirstiness and inhumanity, but who were not so prominent as you. Their tirades were not worth recording, their journals not worth preserving. I have it good. I can scrape together the festering scraps of your life in the archives of Europe and America. I am able to examine them with no fear of being molested by that buddy-buddy bullshit and lying by your family and former associates. No matter how often I try to get to the root of them, with scalpel or hammer, the same typical German monster emerges.

There is no doubt about it: you will also lose the second Nuremberg Trial, this mini-trial with your son as prosecutor, judge, and hangman in one. Yes, I know, that is not in the spirit of the separation of powers, but it is difficult to find enough players to fill these roles. Almost every person who has ever spoken with me about you has had a remarkable urge to defend you to me and has been horrified when I said, "My father was a criminal." They told me this was utterly appalling and kept insisting on the virtue of filial piety—a virtue that evidently is meant never to be consumed, not even by the flames of the ovens packed with Jews. They told me in conclusion, holding out little hope for reconciliation with them, and adding a word or two of course about the Allied bombing of Dresden, "You don't understand that time, because you weren't really old enough."

On the contrary, Father, now I do understand it. That is why I am dragging you up out of the void, out of your cauldron down there in Hell, where I've pictured you ever since my childhood.

For years I've hunted down everything there was to know about you, beginning each new encounter with a polite introductory sentence: "I am the son of Hans Frank, Governor General of Poland, executed at Nuremberg. As far as I have been able to discover, you were the head of the ———— in Cracow." Not everyone was prepared to speak to me. Some tested me first with questions. "What was the name of the Frank family's dog?" Tommy. "Who was Frank's closest administrative assistant in Cracow?" Secretary of State Bühler. "When did your good father leave Cracow?" January 17, 1945. Once I had passed the test, the worst part began. They began to mourn for you, to lament your fate, to say how sorry they were for me because of my ruined life; for themselves, because of the brevity of their glory days in the Third Reich. And I had to put up with all that crap, unable to get a word in edgewise and say that as far as I now knew, you were a real asshole of a human being. If I had managed to get that in, that would have shut them up, scared them into making the sign of the crooked cross.

I wanted to learn everything there was to know about you. I was prepared, as your son, to let mercy temper justice. But the more I learned about you, the more I read about you, and the more I came to recognize the new self-satisfied, reactionary conformity in Germany—the more you came to life, and the more I hated you.

I reach down into the pile of rubbish that was your life left to me in the form of documents, letters, photographs, written testimony by those who knew you; and I continue my endless search for further evidence of your cowardly existence.

After your death Mother rarely spoke about the great and glorious life the two of you had together. Had it become a painful memory for her? There were only two stories that still seemed to please her. One of them was about gallant Herr Hitler, whom she had once had the honor of sitting next to at Bayreuth. Her program fell from her lap. "Just imagine! Adolf Hitler bent over and he picked up that program, kept it for himself, and gave me *his very own* to keep. The Führer was such a gentleman!"

The point of her second story was the underhanded remark made by a diplomat, which, of course, Mother, lamebrained as she was in those things, never caught on to, and took as a genuine compliment. François-Poncet, the French ambassador to Berlin at the time, turned to your wife, his dinner partner at some state function or other, and, having endured her inane chatter throughout the meal, said to her, "Madame, how much better it would have been had *you* become the diplomat."

Needless to say, those are pretty pathetic memories of a life, Father. She never once told me about her expeditions to the ghettos in Warsaw and Cracow, about her avaricious and intimidating raids on the Jews there, deprived as they were of all human rights. I had to learn that elsewhere. That research cost me plenty in flowers, pretense, and trickery with relatives, acquaintances, and Mother's women friends, before I began to realize, even vaguely, for how many human beings the Franks were angels of death and objects of justifiable hate.

Eighteen Thousand Marks
for Frank Memorabilia

What were the things of yours I possessed before I set out on my search for you?

A rubber stamp which if you pressed it down on a piece of paper would produce the beautiful and appropriate words "Property of Reichsminister Dr. Frank."

A card (elegant, heavy paper stock) on the back of which a list has been written in Mother's hand. It runs from "coffee warmer," "31 new napkins," "silver and red foxtails," "French silver brocade," "1 decanter with silver stopper" to Item Number 31, "porcelain chandelier." And on the front, the card says, "Sincere Christmas greetings, Heil Hitler!" And then your signature, "Frank," and under that, "Governor General." Eventually I was able to determine that the list was of valuable objects that had been plundered from our home after the humiliating collapse of the Frank family. Yes, yes, Father, relax; I know, it lists only the *tiniest part*. On the other hand, didn't we plunder all these things ourselves in the first place?

And I was bequeathed a bust of Mother's head, in plaster of paris, a mighty flattering portrait, too, like the ones you see in palaces.

I also have twenty-three postcards showing Kressendorf Castle, our weekend home near Cracow. (Numerically they are the most impressive part of my legacy from the family's days of grandeur—except for the photographs.) Mother must have sent dozens of these cards to those friends from earlier years, the ones who didn't make it and got stuck in the plebeian flatlands. The typical message on the cards was probably something like "As you see, I have moved."

And I own your prayer book, the little slender one in which you wrote me one final farewell the evening before you called out your "Jesus, have mercy." That final word from you to me made me furious because you misspelled my first name; you put a *c* in it. I remember thinking at the time, people shouldn't do things like that, not at the hour of their death.

"To you, my dear, good Nicki," you wrote, "I dedicate this little prayer book in heartfelt love. May your life be lived under the merciful protection of God! May God guide your steps to His peace and grace! My prayers are with you forever, my Nicki. Your Daddy." Too late, too late, too late. You did not seize even this opportunity to say something to me. And all that about praying for me forever is pure crap. In the first place, you had only a few hours left on earth to do that. And as for the Great Beyond . . . let us just suppose for a second that you are in Heaven—there you can intercede for me directly, no prayers needed. In Hell, on the other hand, where I think you are, you would get a good rap on your knuckles from old Lucifer if you should try to fold your hands in prayer on the rim of that cauldron. Even when you died and I was only seven I was not much impressed by the idea of those hands of yours clasped in prayer, trying for all the world to imitate Dürer's engraving.

Today I possess more than these bits of rubbish. The legends about your pious and brave life have scattered like dust. Your sentence of death was a just one. Yes, I don't wish away those terrifying final days, nights, hours, and seconds before your death.

You deserved them, if only to experience a tiny bit of the appalling fate that we Germans inflicted on so many, many millions of others.

Did your death serve any purpose?

In 1984 I, an anonymous customer, could have bought the following Hans Frank items from a Munich dealer in Nazi memorabilia: a white silk jacket with a red swastika woven into the upper part of one sleeve; a little watch ("Hitler presented it to him personally"); an oil painting of a bunch of real sharp soldier boys on guard duty; your military ID with photograph from 1918 (you're staring out of the picture, cheeks puffed out, ignorant of what the war is all about); another ID, this one from 1942, giving your permanent address as Fürth, oddly enough; and a guest book that clearly had nothing to do with you or your family. Everything together: eighteen thousand marks. "If you took that to the U.S. to resell," the young salesman's pitch went, "you'd make a huge profit—they're nuts for stuff like that that belonged to famous Nazis." So, a group of Hans Frank relics is worth eighteen thousand marks nowadays in respectable circles, are they? If only Mother could have lived to see that!

But my greatest treasures from you are your statements. Statements you made in public. In front of educated Germans. Who applauded you for them. Sentences that I could repeat verbatim when I was a child, like:

"After the war is over they can make mincemeat out of every Polack, as far as I'm concerned."

Or this one: "If I were to have one poster printed for every seven Poles I'm going to have shot, all the trees in Poland couldn't provide enough paper."

Now that sentence has a breathtaking élan about it; even something of a punch line, because it gets to the point by clever indirection. One can even sense the cultivated drama connoisseur behind it, the one who later actually recommended that his American interrogators read Schiller's *Love and Intrigue*. The point of that, to be sure, was to provide these gentlemen (who would then be tutored in at least one of the German classic texts) with the background sufficient to appreciate how you had become the victim of the Nazi equivalent of Schiller's villain, Secretary Wurm: Heinrich Himmler.

About Grandpa
and the Protein Shock

There really were advantages to growing up in the Federal Republic as the son of a major Nazi war criminal. Your help was especially beneficial when it came to hitchhiking. Who was it, after all, who had the first civilian cars after the war? Former Nazis, of course. They were the ones—you can feel their presence in our new government—who were still young in the years right after the surrender, the ones so full of the old Nazi piss and vinegar, people like you, forty-six and full of fight. From the moment somebody stopped to pick me up, my path to success was assured. All I had to say after a couple of kilometers was, "Do you happen to realize that I am the son of the Minister of the Reich without Portfolio and Governor General of Poland, executed at Nuremberg as a major war criminal?"

Even as a small child I was able to reel off your titles, and as a teenager my success with them was still considerable. It wasn't long before the driver indulged himself in glorious reminiscence (omitting all mention of his somewhat lesser crimes); for as a soldier, either on the march to the East or on the way back, he had crossed through your kingdom, through your Government General. Then came the inevitable moment I would be waiting for, the moment when his emotions would be deeply touched, when he lamented the unjust sentence that ended your life, and

said it was so obvious that I, skinny little fellow, was now so bereft
and impoverished, and when you think how the English had
bombed Dresden, and that he himself had seen how two SS men
had dragged a wounded American GI out of the line of fire at
Monte Cassino and taken him to a German doctor, and that really
the Jews were to blame for what happened to them because it
was true that *everything* had been in the hands of the Jews, and
just take a look at this marvelous autobahn we're driving on, my
friend—may I call you that? in memory of your father?—the Führer
built this autobahn, and now I have to get some gas and you're
going to get a fine lunch, on me.

Only one person, Father, only one solitary postwar German
automobile driver in all those years of hitchhiking (it was in 1953,
near Osnabrück), turned onto the shoulder of the highway and
without saying a single word, in silent disdain, let me out of the
car. The memory of that still makes my ears burn. I wonder if he
is still alive. Democrats usually die so young.

When was your death? The first time you heard Hitler speak?
Or was it at the November 1923 putsch in Munich, when you
were still putting up all those revolutionary posters around the
city, even after Hitler had given up on the effort? You had to leave
Germany for a while, stayed away for half a year (something you
never talked about); but you returned with an amazing command
of Italian—that was something Mussolini really admired about you.
Were you touring the North Italian lakes as someone's Ganymede
then?

Funny, I wouldn't mind a bit if that were true. The court
psychologist at Nuremberg, Gilbert, later certified that you had
latent homosexual tendencies. Did they ever actually break out?
You were really handsome as a young man, no rough edges, beautiful head of hair, a very gay lad.

Oh, if only you had found your lover for life at that time!

This goddamned "if." If, instead of dying quickly and relatively
painlessly at the end of a rope in Nuremberg, you had only died

slowly and painfully like Hitler's enemies on a butcher's hook in Plötzensee prison in Berlin. If you had only been a stowaway on a freighter to Sweden in 1933. If you had only poisoned Himmler with a bit of strychnine in his wine, that time he visited you in Cracow. Mother left me the photo; I'm looking at it now. You're sitting at a table with Himmler, up at the castle, wine glasses in front of you, Himmler with a cigar in his hand, a jovial-looking fellow in spectacles. You hated him, yet kissed every last square inch of his ass. Why aren't you, the "man of justice," as you loved to call yourself, also a man of the justifiable crime? One second after this photo was taken, why couldn't you have thrown your tie like a noose around his neck, dragged his strangled body through the corridors of the castle, and then hitched him up to my little pedal car for me?

What a colossal pension we would have had! "Just like all those Stauffenberg relatives," as Mother used to say so longingly about the relatives of Count von Stauffenberg, who, as you remember, in 1944 tried to assassinate Hitler.

No, there's no pension. All that is left instead are quotations and sentences of yours. And clever puns on your name, like this one from Berlin: "*Im Westen liegt Frankreich; im Osten wird Frank reich.*"*

That one is easy to understand if one appreciates what a poor little critter you were as a child.

Even your father was a deceitful lawyer, disbarred in Munich— that was something they never told me. I loved Grandpa a lot, as you know, because he could balance a beer glass on his bald head. For me he was the love of life incarnate.

I was mad as hell in 1944 when you wouldn't let him be my godfather, too. That was when the Soviets were threatening your Government General and you were beginning to cast pious glances again at the sanctuary of the One and Only True Church and had

---

* France lying in the West; Frank lying—looting—in the East.

to begin finding some safety nets for the family. So it was off with the youngster into the arms of the Catholic Church. That way I got a lovely ceremony at the Schoberhof back in Bavaria from the good Father Haas, who splashed water on my forehead and put salt in my mouth and I rejoiced in my holy state. You and Mother couldn't quite reconcile yourselves to the fact that this antiquated faith might be seen entering our exemplary National Socialist household, and that's why you got yourselves a priest from outside the community.

Grandpa balanced his beer glass on his head for me and marched around in my honor.

Long before Hitler, Grandpa used to have a regular seat in the Schelling Salon, a typical old Munich tavern, where he could always be found. He was known to be something of a two-bit lawyer and used to put together legal documents and petitions and write letters for working men, tenants, and farmers.

At noon you used to leave grammar school and go directly "home" to this tavern, where you would get your hot meal of the day. Your mother had run off to Prague by this time, a fabulous woman. Did she perhaps have an inkling that she had given birth to Rosemary's Baby? She lived in Prague with some professor or other, a sensual, irrepressible woman of old Bavarian stock from the Lenggries Valley. She hated Mother and loved Lilly, your childhood sweetheart and later your mistress. In her mind's eye she saw Lilly installed in the Government General as the new and true mother of the people for her boy Hans, to whom she came crawling when she heard about your great ascent to fame and fortune. For me, Grandma was a witch. Mother drilled it into me. "Never go up there—that's where the wicked woman is." Whenever she came to the Government General on a visit she would always stay on the top floor of Kressendorf Castle. Sometimes I would sneak up there, and I would race away, my heart beating like crazy. Those corridors were wonderful for running.

It could not have been easy for you, born in 1900, to grow up in a tavern in the Schellingstrasse. Shall I try to pinpoint for you the very moment in your young life when you might have decided to set out on the pathway to crime? Was the stench in the Schelling Salon perhaps too much for you, and you decided then and there to become the lord of a castle, to live in noble and lofty halls? Or did you take an oath in the presence of Kathi, the serving girl: "I shall never go hungry again"? However it was, you lived out your short life replete and satiated, right up to gallows-time.

Or did you vow silently to yourself, "No more chickens in the kitchen!"? Family rumor has it that they had free run in Grandpa's little second-floor apartment on the Barerstrasse, so that he would have all the fresh eggs he could eat during World War I, and you, too. The diet made a strong and feisty man of you. Maybe the two of you ate too many of those eggs. But even that's not enough to turn someone into a criminal, is it? One can hardly account for the following words spoken by you by claiming they were the consequence of protein shock suffered in one's youth. Anyhow, this is what you said as a forty-three-year-old Governor General on the twenty-fifth of January, 1943, at the Belvedere Castle in Warsaw:

"There is no reason for us to be squeamish when we hear about seventeen thousand people being shot. May I remind us, everyone gathered together here, that each and every one of us already has his place on Roosevelt's roster of war criminals. I have the honor of being Number One. We are all, as it were, accomplices, speaking from the perspective of world history."

Are Grandpa and the Schelling Salon really to blame, twenty years after you left them, for your having spoken the following words at a governmental session at the castle? Each of them individually is, of course, just an "innocent" word. But the way you strung them together makes it almost impossible for me to read because of the anger and bitter shame I feel. Yet I read them over and over again:

"Now as to the Jews—and I am telling you this quite candidly—

there must be a stop put to them, one way or the other. As far as the Jews are concerned, I shall henceforth use as my one guiding principle the assumption that they are to disappear. . . . We must obliterate the Jews wherever we find them and whenever the opportunity is afforded us, in order to uphold the unity and integrity of the Reich. . . . We cannot shoot these three and a half million Jews, we cannot kill them with poison; but we can proceed with the necessary steps that somehow or other will lead to their successful extermination. To put a point to it, this can be done within the context of those measures taken in the interest of the welfare of the Reich as a whole."

Lord God,
Send Us the Man
Who Will Bring Us Order

How do creatures like you get their start? From the rubbish pile of your life I fish out your diary. An intimate document—and an honest one, I hope. Let us see. Can I discover entries here that may have been decisive in delivering you up to the hangman three decades later? Here you are, eighteen years old. Your first entry reads: "Today I mustered in as a recruit, one of the generation born in 1900. Having been declared fit for active service in the infantry, I was assigned to the imperial regiment. Today, for the first time in my life, I learned from personal experience how crude the executive mind of the Prussian military system really is, that compulsive outgrowth of pedantic discipline in the spirit of Frederick the Great. We Bavarians, members of a genuine Germanic race, have been armed with a powerful sense of free will; only with the greatest reluctance and under duress do we tolerate this Prussian military dominance. It is this fact above all that constantly renews for us the symbol of the great, unbridgeable dividing line made by the mighty Main River, which separates South Germany from the North. To our way of thinking, the Prussian is a greater enemy than the Frenchman."

You were making such pleasantly unpatriotic noises back then, in those last gasping days of an empire that had but a few more days left to squawk. But it is another entry you made the very next day that demonstrates something I have noticed over and over again during my search for you. You were too much of a coward to face reality, and you kept retreating into the role of sentimental visionary. "Today I took a train to Wasserburg and from there walked to Zell, to see a peasant family I know, and to dedicate myself to a few days of repose. But I also wished to take advantage of the opportunity of observing and getting to know the Bavarian peasantry at close range."

Kiermeier was the name of the family you wished to "observe"—as if they were dung beetles. What came forth out of all that observation, you master of kitsch, was something you could just as easily have written in the city, seated before a painting by Spitzweg, our equivalent of the Americans' Norman Rockwell. "I feel at ease with these people, in their tidy home close by the River Inn. They know only their own never-ending work, and had the war not interposed itself—the war that called their sons, Blasius and Isedor, to arms and that was to blame for their very first exposure to newsprint—they would not have been interrupted in their idyll. At present they have their two sons at home on leave, strong, well-built fellows—and of course that only increases their feeling of contentment. When the entire family gathers about the big table in the evening by cozy lamplight, I retreat into a shadowy corner in order to observe them. I would only disturb them if I sat among them at their table! They present an image of the profoundest contentment. How much happier are these simple people—those who can see the wheat for their own bread growing in their own soil—than we city-dwellers, we victims of insatiable, proliferating materialism."

Early expressionism, naturalism, realism, all those exciting movements in the arts and letters of your day, simply passed you by, you an honors student of the humanities. You read what the representatives and practitioners of these movements wrote, but you understood none of it. Your conception of the world was already so askew by the time you were eighteen. (By the way, Grandpa didn't instill any of that in you, I'm sure of that.)

"People of Germany," you wrote in your very next sentence, "return to your roots, as long as there is still time. Preserve your ideals. With all your might, pull yourselves up out of this swamp of speculation and materialism that threatens to seduce and engulf you. Return to Nature, return to your own soil. Only there will the healing process you so badly need come to fruition."

Oh, Father, what nonsense. There is no flavor of Grandpa's Schelling Salon in that fluff. Colorful characters, real people, hung out there. Just to study Grandpa, that charming deceiver and marriage swindler, would have been enough for a lifetime. But no, that was not for you. Here is what you wrote in April 1918; you were a senior in high school, and the only thing that really reaches into your thoughts is the Great War. Monday, April 8: "The most glorious spring weather—made for the delight of mankind. And all the while the bloodiest battle in history is being fought out."

Damn it all, your diary touches me. It does. From 1918 to the mid-twenties you were occasionally capable of truly effervescent sentences, and there are even some that I believe. But where, I ask you, did you get that blindly prejudiced deification of the German people? "Have we not taken up the Greek ideals and fostered and enlarged them? Is not German science the science of the whole world? Is there another land that has its Kant? Is Goethe not the greatest poet of all the nations? (Shakespeare is rarely his equal.) Even though our literature has not attained the unity of the French, our heights and peaks rise up over the heads of all the others! Has any other music ever begun to approach ours? No!—Given these circumstances, it is a great consolation to know that we share our tragic destiny with the ancient nations of im- memorial fame."

It is easy to make an anti-Semite out of someone who thinks like that. By the time you were eighteen you already had the infamous German arrogance in you. And you had the drive to get to the top, to get away from all the simple folk in the Schelling Salon.

"Once again the story of Napoleon's life, which I am reading now for the third time, touches me profoundly. Whence comes this compelling urge in me to pattern my life after this man's? It must be truly glorious to rise in dizzying flight to such heavenly heights, no matter how great the fall that must follow. . . . The desire to experience these heights burns like a fire within me. But my path shall go, not like that of Napoleon, over the bodies of those cursing and seeking to destroy him, but instead past the milestones on the way to the liberation of humanity. A united and free World Reich will then be the ultimate creation of the Germans."

If only you had stuck to those milestones along the way to human liberation. You would have followed a difficult road; it would have led you into exile, to the underground, to the butchers' hooks—but not onto the gallows platform with all those other big shots.

Your imploring prayers for a powerful savior can probably be found in endless diaries kept at the time by the patriotic nationalists of the middle class in Germany. Here you are, December 19, 1918: "Lord God, send us now the man who will bring us order!" I thought when I first read that, Oh, no, you don't suppose he means himself? On the thirty-first of that same month you get pretty close to saying so: "When I observe the life of the masses here, I cannot believe that I am the worst son of Germany." Not yet you weren't, Father; that came a bit later—and you were only *one* of the worst, anyway.

"I wish for our nation," you continue, "men who can once again restore it to universally acknowledged prominence, while keeping it firmly anchored within. We must succeed in this!" You did, old chap; and so you did. On January 2, 1919, you planted your radiant visage into the diary when you wrote, "With shining eyes I look to the future." It's not surprising that you followed this the next day, after the usual lamentations, with your solution to all our travails: "Proud Germany, whither has your greatness gone? Dispersed is your might. We are doomed to be the slaves of the earth, for our nation of today is incapable of constructing a state able to flourish. And here am I in its midst. Am I truly alone in my dismal anticipation? Shall I be the one to lead the revolt of the slaves? By God, I will!" Not a bad prediction—only you have it backwards. You led people *into* slavery.

A few days later you were again calling upon yourself: "What is important is the man's intelligence. Let us have a man now, *the* man! And yet, the time is not quite ripe."

What exactly are you planning? "People of Germany"—in your diary you are shouting for the attention of sixty million German people, January 15, 1919—"People of Germany, all my life of action belongs to you!"

You fulfilled that promise, even though nothing good came of it for your People of Germany.

There are two passages in your diary of this period where I find you particularly revolting. On the fifteenth of December you rise up in indignation: "A nauseating and unfortunately typical scene in a cafe. A Frenchman—surrounded by flirtatious German females entertaining him with their foolish giggling. Is that not a mockery of our people, our nation? Unconscionable!" And just after the murder of Eisner, the first Bavarian Prime Minister after World War I, and the first elections in the new democracy: "While the proletariat was carrying on with its preposterous demands, splitting into factions, fighting, the true German arose in the background— blond, blue-eyed—and with mighty hand seized command of the regiment."

Well, there you are, hatched out in your true colors, you little Aryan, enemy of everything foreign. And you scream out your stupendous ode: "Oh, what energy is locked up within me! I sense my will, filled with restless urgings. I glow with the need to be the pilot of this ship! A great new Germany will arise from these ruins, a Reich that will signify a world of civilized culture and whose founder will be crowned with the diadem of a liberated humanity! [*Father, that turned out differently: it was a Germany devoted to the destruction of culture, full of hate and blood lust.*] I am replete with joy when I realize I can work without letup sixteen hours at a stretch. That is a capacity I shall soon have need of. [*As a Nazi big shot, Daddy dear, you were a lazy bum.*] Humanity, awake! Let yourself finally be aroused! Cast aside the mundane rubbish that encumbers you. Why do you dwell in the depths when you have seen the heights? It has now become impossible for me to forgive the enemy. There is but one goal remaining: Germany, the heart and the brain of the world! [*No, wrong: Germany covered the world with its filth; that's what you mean, Father.*] I no longer mourn. Henceforth I observe what transpires here with the eye of vengeance. Vengeance will raise us high above our tormentors. [*You did, in fact, take revenge, first on your compatriots who thought differently from you, and then . . .*] I believe in the German spirit. It will pluck us from the misery into which the barbaric, mindless rabble would plunge us. [*The German spirit was busy most of all with systematically exterminating human beings.*] By God, this mob will easily be brought under control. [*And that, Father, became reality. And when I first read the following threat, it made my scalp crawl.*] Only through dictatorship—but not that of the proletariat!—will Germany be saved." *You really had no sense at all of the emerging Weimar democracy, did you? None of the classics was of any use to you there; and Heinrich Heine—the mere thought of him must have enraged you.*

A boyhood friend of yours confessed to me that he always had the impression you were merely "accumulating" bits of education in order to show off. You must have been one hell of a windbag. You certainly did not *understand* anything. In the words from *Faust* (almost) your heart was shut, your brain was dead, even when you were eighteen, nineteen. With that sort of education, with that gift for oratory, with that way of thinking, the only possible end product was bound to be something dangerous.

And here is another sentence of yours that, perfidious though it may be of me, aches to be turned against you. On March 15, 1919, in your crazy fabrications, you posed the question: "Is Western humanity to be extinguished?" Yes, evidently so. And you are in large part responsible for the fact that the German banner was to be emblazoned with the word "Inhumanity." But what do I read now? "Our future is the future of the world, and the German nation is the savior of mankind." This savior, Father, was a mass murderer, and you—incensed at the conditions laid down at Versailles—thrust the sword of vengeance into his hand. "Now be steadfast, all you who are German on God's wide earth. We are enslaved, we are reviled. From the suffering that awaits you, people of Germany, subtract that portion for which you are to blame—the rest will more than suffice for our retaliation at the everlasting court of universal justice."

Mother must have laughed scornfully when she read the following sentence, this one connected with the business about enslaved mankind—which you also translated into reality. (As you well know, she swiped this diary in order to use it against you at your divorce trial in 1942–43 and to get bits of it into the hands of Hitler's camarilla.) "The mark of the man is to be unconditionally the master," you wrote. "Weak men are worse than women, for when they are weak they are cripples."

I stand in utter astonishment at this diary of yours—and helpless, too. How is it possible that anyone ever took you seriously? Or that stupid, braggartly attitude of yours with which you as a young man said farewell to the arts: "Mark you well, the art of today is like all the other vacuous posturings, empty and affected, puffed up. There is nothing in it of the truth of life, which one cannot create, which one can only feel and *live!*" And where is it that you found your truth? "I read Rosegger's *The God Seeker* and am shattered. Religion, so deeply thought through. Humanity, so deeply sensed in all its misery. I am filled with bitter premonitions about our immediate future. How far—in his modest and mature depth of feeling—how far Rosegger stands above the literary insanity of our times, aesthetically and expressionistically depraved as they are."

No thanks. Even if the common room were filled to the rafters, I wouldn't take an empty seat next to a student like you. Not even if you promised, with your prissy mouth, to share further tidbits from your diary such as: "One thought fills me with ardor today: The statesman must be a priest among the people." Or: "Be sufficient unto yourself in true and virile humility, and strive for perfection. Behold, well-being must needs then be yours." If I had to listen to that, I'd have to dump my stew all over that beautiful full head of hair of yours.

On March 26, 1919, Wednesday, you did a bit of self-analysis: "Two different natures are within me. The one appears to me in the form of a sovereign queen, who, cool and secure in her power and might, causes me to gaze down upon my certain victory; yes, who compels and urges me forward, who makes me quiver aloud at the thought voiced within: You, do you see, yes, you of all the millions, are the one who will accomplish the great task!" "Quiver aloud," Father? How do you do that? Forget it. Now on to your second nature. "And opposed to that, my second nature, the one who makes me so self-conscious before my fellow man, who keeps pushing me along, saying: 'Look, bow down before this one, the one who knows more, can do more, understands more.' Hand in hand with this goes doubt; oh, this dreadful doubt of mine! The battles that arise from this confrontation! Really and truly, I shall either ascend to the heights—or go mad. Perhaps both?"

Let me tell you, it was this second nature of yours that was victorious, the lickspittle one. For not only was there Hitler to contend with, but also a number of others whose hands you kissed, whom you came sucking up to. It makes me want to throw up

when I read about it. On March 18, 1921, you made your last
entry for a long while—until the eighth of October, 1925. The
years in between brought you your chances for advancement. You
had the opportunity to study at the university. You chose the law,
and enrolled at Munich and Kiel, where you wrote your dissertation. And what does the freshly baked law grad write into his
diary on October 8, 1925?

Pretty disconsolate stuff—stuff that makes me think for a moment, damn it, maybe he'll be able to steer a straight course after
all: "Before me, a picture of Caesar's bust. Above me on the wall,
Bismarck and Frederick the Great. Between them, a picture of a
woman. Spirits that are so near, and yet I cannot reach them. To
think that I have had the boldness to write this down in this book,
in all my poverty, in the chilly, empty space surrounding me. To
think that in all my unspeakable worthlessness I still have dared
to ally myself with a movement that supposedly has brought me
to the heights, that has presumed to guide me by its self-inspired
thread of conviction along the Alpine path [*Father, you're beginning
to jabber again. Drop it. Come down from your rostrum and be honest*],
that has indicated to me time and again, through hope and trib-
ulation, that I am the one who is being called. [*Well, so it is you I
have this remarkable superiority complex from; it was with me as early as
my hitchhiking days. Once, in a cozy circle of old former Nazis, someone
said to me, "You grew up as a child in a noble household. You lived in
beautiful surroundings. We were all looked after; we had servants. We were
somebody—and that feeling will stay with you the rest of your life!"*] Oh,
I am the loser, the vanquished. With all my titles, doctor of laws,
man of aspiration, husband, I have been inexpressibly ineffectual.
While earlier the saps and juices of abundant youth watered the
fruits of the wellspring, I rattle like dry bones now. While earlier
my resilient stride was quick and fresh, I now have nothing to
record: no works, no fruits, alas, not even seed for the future."

After reading passages like this one, I can't imagine how you
could possibly have had anything against expressionism.

Come along now, let us leave your pathetic little office on Munich's Gabelsbergerstrasse and go out into the streets. Let us begin from the very beginning again. You could become an advocate for the "rabble," as you referred to them. Or you could emigrate with me. To do that, bring along your good and fruitful wife, Brigitte—you are not yet parents. And I shall forgive you that little vain and macho lie that you added with a tragic sigh that same day in your diary: "Gertrude has been rejected; I have swept Brigitte into my arms." Tell the truth. You know that Brigitte swept you into *her* arms. It was in that artist's studio in Schwabing where you fell into the trap of a cool, calculating lover.

Come on, then—let loose a little bit more of your youthful despair. The Weimar Republic is already six years old. Yes, true, things are pretty rough in Germany; but for the bourgeois middle class, the one you belong to, life is a bit more decent, and you have prospects. You're good-looking. You are an incredibly gifted windbag, and educated besides. Come on, let's go join up with the socialists, or go to Berlin and avenge the murder of Rosa Luxemburg. You could learn a little from her prose, too.

"Hitler,
the One and Only"

You did none of the above. Instead you closed your diary and went out into the streets—but in quite a different direction. May you be cursed for that. May your great good fortune be cursed for having brought you to "the One and Only," as you phrased it in a singularly repulsive passage you wrote years later, on February 19, 1937, in the very same diary. You're thirty-six years old now. If things had gone according to the way I would have liked, you would already have perished in the concentration camp at Dachau. Why? Because for four years you would have been a courier for the Social Democrat or the Communist underground, or even the Catholic underground. You would have become a good friend of the great Father Rupert Mayer, who, archconservative old dog though he was, never once put up with anything the Nazis tried.

But where do I find you messing around instead? Read it yourself, Father: "This evening I was with Lasch at the great festival concert which Furtwängler conducted at Philharmonic Hall for the German People's Winter Benefit for the Needy. It was a powerful, profound, thrilling experience to hear this true giant of a conductor re-create the overture to *Der Freischütz*, Brahms's Fourth Symphony, and Beethoven's Seventh. A magnificent evening of consecration. With indescribable emotion I felt the years I have experienced pass before

me, accompanied by this glorious music—the magical fabric of my
destiny knotted together on the loom of time from one momentous
point to the next. [*What's going on, Father? Were you listening to the
Maestro, or were you busy with your shuttles, weaving the images of your
past life?*] Those sounds surging up from the depths made me shiver
in the ecstasy of youth, strength, hope, and gratitude. There in
the loge sat the Führer flanked by his two most faithful companions,
the Soldier and the Orator, Göring and Goebbels. All the famous
of Berlin were there. The leadership of the Reich was vividly
present, in celebration and resplendence. Representatives from all
the states, the bearers of names known to the world. And I amongst
them as a Minister of the Reich—and the youngest of all. I was
borne up by the swelling sound. Eternal Germany, now you live
again. Glorious Reich, now you are saved. Immortal nation of the
German *Volk*, dwell in Fortune's eyes! The Führer was radiant. And
I was struck silent [*just as well—Furtwängler wouldn't have put up for
a second with your gushing interruptions*] in contemplation of our
blessing: That He, the Führer, was meant for us. Oh, God, what
ineffable joy to be able to call this one greatest man in the history
of mankind ours! Generations to come will envy us for having
been His contemporaries. And to me was given the task of being
even more to this Man: I can know myself as His true fellow
worker."

You jubilant jerk. Let's hope you're red in the face with embarrassment down there in Hell.

So that's what became of you in eleven short years—a totally
uncritical, sweet-talking slimehole of a Hitler fanatic. The Communists and the Socialists, like the first Jews, were already locked
up in the concentration camps, you guardian of German justice.
That was your world—and I sit there in the Philharmonic Hall
like an evil little sprite on your rounded shoulders (you already
had that greasy look that came upon you with the years, already
fat and paunchy)—I sit like a sprite on your shoulders with not
a thought in the world for Meister Furtwängler; and I whisper in

your ear: "Father, you have only nine more years to live. This neck of yours that I'm holding tight between my little legs . . . in exactly 3,567 days the sound of its snapping will reverberate through the gymnasium at Nuremberg. And your dear friend Lasch, my Daddy Number 2, who's sitting there beside you, your 'blond rascal,' he will be dead in only five years."

Something like that must have gone through your mind, too, when you reread your diary later, for just above this jolly, insipid passage you added in about 1944, "Lasch was shot to death May 6, 1942, on the command of the Führer."

You forgot to add: "*I was partly responsible for that. I let him be bumped off, because I was scared to death of Himmler. At that time I was in a lot of political hot water because I had been stuffing my own pockets in Poland. I'm sorry, my blond rascal; times were hard then. It just happened to be you and not me in that cell. You must have been very surprised to look up and see those two SS men. They came right in without knocking. One of them held you tight while the other one shot you in the head. May God have mercy on your soul, my blond rascal.*"

God? Your "God," at least back then, on February 10, 1937, while you were writing your entries at your official villa in Berlin-Dahlem—that "God" was a different one. "I return now to this diary. I intend to resume my writing at this point, so that it may be witness to the unity of my expectations, faith, hope, knowledge, and battles. So that I may describe how it was that the young fellow with conflict and hesitation in his heart and in his life became the Minister of Justice, for Adolf Hitler. [*Father, I'm reading this, but it so happens that I now know a great deal more about you than what is in these notebooks; and the truth is that at this point you were sitting on the bench, politically speaking. Not a single one of the bigger shots took you seriously, not in the slightest. Justice (with your help) had already become injustice. But at least you finally had your Horch limousine, the one I loved so much; and your Maybach, too; and, in third place in my opinion, your Mercedes.*] And in order to demonstrate that even with all the grandeur of my titles and offices I think of myself as a humble soldier and servant of the communal whole—a knight of the order of the National Socialist German Workers' Party. I hereby swear my fidelity to the task. Down to the very last and most secret fiber of my being, I belong to the Führer and his glorious enterprise. Even a thousand years from now each German will proclaim the same. [*Jesus, Father, guess again!*] I herewith make my confession of my faith. To serve Germany is to serve God. No Christian confession, no Christian faith, can be as strong as our conviction that if Christ were to reappear on earth, He would return as a German. [*Whoa there, Father—wait a minute! Thirty-six years old and so much of your mind already lost?*] In truth, we are God's weapon for the destruction of the evil powers on Earth. We battle in God's name against the Jew and his Bolshevism. May God protect us!"

Here for the first time in your private diary you confess your anti-Semitism. But admit it, you never really were an anti-Semite. Simply because it was expected of you, you instantly agreed to be one. What do those parasites on the great German body politic want anyhow, right? We'll just have to exterminate them, if that's what's wanted, right? This is not contradicted in the slightest by the following excerpt: "I bear witness to my deed, my task. German justice is the strong weapon for the securing of our nation's people's communal life. May the law of our land be ever protected with might and be a powerful defense for honor, race, soil, freedom, and the work of our people and our Reich. Our law stands forever—and it stands engraved in eternal bronze. It demands vigilance, strength—tempered and firm forevermore. The Party and the Reich must be as spirit and body to our nation. Be ever mindful of the Führer, you generations to come, and of his vanguard. Follow steadfast the example we set. Never falter! Be never forgetful! Be always firm but unassuming, clear in mind, bold in heart, united and strong! Then posterity will say: Hitler's battle was the decisive battle for all that is Germanic and German—and it was victorious!"

Your drivel on that February evening was not to be stopped.

You took stock, retrospectively: "On December 9, 1918, I began this journal with the formulation of a special wish, 'Let me serve my people in some way, O God! . . . I shall await my call.' [*A damn lie, Father—this "first" entry was added by you long after its fictional date.*] The call came on the day I first met the Führer. It was in June 1919 at the university, at a lecture by Feder given to the 'Cultural Attachés' of the Munich garrison, to which I had been sent as representative of my squadron."

Strange, Father—there is no entry at all in your diary for that day, none that might have immortalized the encounter.

I have to hand it to you, though, Father—you were good at adding fraudulent entries after the fact. Beginning in March 1942 you went back and put in comments here and there for the earlier years, such as "Oh, my Lilly!" and similar gushy bits of nonsense, simply in order to pull the wool over the eyes of your rediscovered first love—make her think you had never forgotten her. That didn't fool Mother for one second.

Your words in that February diary entry strut back and forth in your mind; you were proud as a peacock. "I was part of the movement beginning in 1919. From then on I revealed layer after layer of myself: from university student, to SA man, to law clerk, lawyer, assistant in jurisprudence at the law seminar of the Munich Institute of Technology; in 1930, Reichsleiter; March 1933, Bavarian Minister of Justice; June 1933, President of the Academy for German Justice, which I founded. Also in 1933, Reich Commissioner for Justice. In 1927, Reichsführer of Jurists. December 1934, Minister of the Reich. . . . Thus has been the course of my life; thus has been my active career."

Can you at least appreciate now how bloated that sounds? Why don't you add (it is your private diary, isn't it?) that you remained Bavarian Minister of Justice only up to the completion of the *Gleichschaltung*, the "forced centralization of justice" in the Reich at the end of 1934, and that in gratitude for your activity as a lawyer during your "time of battle" they gave you the job as

Minister of the Reich (don't forget "without Portfolio") as a sinecure? Furthermore, you were Reich Commissioner for Justice
only until "justice" in the various states ceased to exist. And that
preposterous Academy for German Justice was totally insignificant.
That, indeed, describes the course of your life, but your "active
career" was a fantasy.

With all the time you used to spend in the john, you would
have had plenty of opportunity to work your way up to being a
mole for the Resistance instead. I remember clearly how you would
spend hours on the toilet studying the entire output of the foreign
press, from the London *Times* to the *Neue Züricher Zeitung*, from
Figaro to the *New York Times*. How was it possible to sit there and
shit away so much of the truth?

"O God, you who have shaped my destiny in so wondrous a
way, who have permitted me to ascend to the pinnacle—God,
help me to the end of my days. Give me strength for my work.
Give me the trust of my Führer."

What "work" are you talking about, Father? Listen to me, you
had nothing to do. One solitary piece of legislation was brought
for your signature, the one having to do with the reinstatement
of military conscription. Even at Nuremberg you were still so proud
of the fact that your name was on it. Why so proud? Didn't you
know that every army in the world harbors the germ of criminality,
as was proved all over the map by the Wehrmacht in the Second
World War—with its plundering and hanging and shooting and
killing of defenseless noncombatants?

"Eternal and glorious God, I bow down before Thee, seized by
profound emotion. Let me be Thine! Receive the sacrificial tribute
of my labor! Help me, O God, to strengthen in the heart of our
people their faith in Thy justice!" Two years earlier the Nuremberg
laws on racial purity had been promulgated—no doubt in the spirit
of your stupid God, right?

I now read the conclusion of this incredible bombast of yours:
"The night is silent roundabout. My path has brought me hither,

where now I dwell—where now I meditate. I am aglow for you, my Germany!" Others are soon to be consumed in that glow of yours, others whom you first gassed, who tried to reach the ceiling of the darkened room, scrambling up through the bodies piled on top of them, screaming. Zyklon B has a way of filling a space from below. The last to die were the strongest, who fought their way up through the piles of collapsing bodies, who finally died themselves with their noses pressed to the ceiling of the gas chambers.

You precious little Nazi glowworm, you made it. Your most fervent wish was fulfilled, the one you uttered a thousand times from 1925 to 1933: "A thousand marks, Brigitte! A thousand a month. That is what we've got to aim for."

And Mother's eyes would glitter.

What a sly little she-devil that one was. You never knew it, but early on she had her sights set on the future. She vowed, "By the time I'm thirty I've got to be married!" And she was five years older than you. Time was passing. She was a secretary at the Landtag [the Bavarian State Parliament] and at the Institute of Technology. She typed ridiculous doctoral theses for candidates. You came into the office once, and Aunt Margot, who was also a secretary there, was the first to see you. With a knowing wink at Mother, that adept sharpshooter, she passed you down the line. Your fate was sealed. Mother took your manuscript, engaged you in conversation, did her little Circe act on you—and *poof!* Soon you were invited for a little *souper à trois*, the third being a painter in Schwabing Mother knew. He, of course, had been bribed to let her have his studio for the night. And what happened after that, you know better than I do. You arrived with flowers. Mother put on her coy look, said that unfortunately the artist friend would not be joining you after all. (I used to know his name, but Aunt Margot is dead, Mother is dead, and I just can't remember.) After a cold supper and some fiery Italian wine, she gave you no other choice but to mount her. In matters pertaining to lovemaking, she was an experienced woman, orgasm or not. You were proud as a foolish peacock afterwards, and by the very next day it was clear that Mother was not letting you go. Again, you had no other choice: you had to propose.

Mother, you made it, barely eight months after you had set yourself that goal.

She was twenty-nine, you a lawyer without hopes or prospects.

And who was it who paid for your wedding trip? Naturally Herr S., the shipping magnate's son from Hamburg. He was Mother's lover, but out of consideration for his Hanseatic interests, he neither would nor could marry her. Instead, he used and abused her according to the practice of his class. It was usually at Lake Starnberg, where he owned a house; sometimes Tuesday evenings, occasionally Thursdays; mostly, however, on weekends.

Yes, your life was hard before Hitler. But the one who pays sets the rules. Herr S. went along for the honeymoon, you spineless jerk. Your lovey-dovey snapshots from Venice have an added touch of irony for me because I know who was behind the camera. Mother looks impressive to me, and Herr S. from Hamburg does, too. You were clearly the fool.

The whole affair still put you in a sour mood whenever you thought about it in the Nuremberg prison. "My sorrows began as soon as we went on our honeymoon, the three of us! With Hans S., Brigitte's friend," you wrote. You also complained about Mother's little ruse at the artist's studio in Schwabing; said that in retrospect it was nothing more than "a momentary erotic intoxication," and claimed that in the last analysis you married Mother out of some kind of crazy whim of the moment and that ever since you had been living in a kind of "mental slavery."

Father, old chum, all this lamentation certainly caused quite an explosion at home. For as you are well aware, all these quotations come from a letter meant for your mother which your lawyer sent by mistake to your wife. After reading it she practically broke into the Nuremberg prison in her rage. Since she couldn't tear down the walls, she went into one of her fits of stubbornness, called her marriage quits, which made you write another letter to your mother: "No wife, no children, no Lilly. I am plunged into darkness. [*Wait just a bit longer and your hood will really make things dark.*] I could weep when I think of all the things I have done in absolutely the wrong way during my life, I, the number-one pupil at the gymnasium, number-one student at the university, a Ph.D. summa cum laude, festooned with medals and titles—and now, nothing left for me at all." Wrong, Father: A noose is waiting for you.

Even in her honeymoon photos Mother has that loose, fatty flesh of certain thirty-year-old women who can't control their weight. From Venice on, that flesh was your meat course. Later on, you had separate bedrooms. In the morning you would trudge across the hallway to Mother, bare-chested, not a rib to be seen under all that flab of yours. Nursemaid Hilde was witness to these plodding, dimwitted sexual excursions. Aunt Margot told me that Mother would groan aloud to her, "All he has to do is walk past me and I'm pregnant."

One noontime, when you were doing the deed with Mother, Aunt Margot stumbled in on you accidentally and shrieked at the scene before her. You rolled down off Mother, shouting, "These shit women!"

You were right, of course; but consider the situation: Aunt Margot had a right to a career at Mother's side; she was the one who got the two of you together in the first place. And Mother was not going to let you tell her what to do. She kept faith with her friends, she did. That's why she had to have the big open Mercedes. There would usually be five other women passengers along with whom Mother, every time in a new outfit, rode through the streets of Munich or Berlin as the wife of the Minister of the Reich. Mother loved the power she suddenly had over the other secretaries. She loved it when you became the Bavarian Minister of Justice and then Commissioner of Justice for the Reich, when you finally had money and status, all coinciding with the time during your official career when the first victims were dying in the concentration camp at Dachau, as people did later by the millions in your Government General in Poland. Above all, Mother loved her power over you, over the personnel, over the Jews in the ghetto—right up to the unconditional surrender, an event that for the rest of her life she considered to have been rash and unnecessary.

Swastika with Twuzzie

Your road to "power" began with an obsequious letter to Hitler on March 5, 1925.

"Most esteemed Herr Hitler!" you wrote in that goddamn illegible old-German script of yours. "Ever since the day I began to wear my swastika along with my [*and here there's a word I can't make out; it looks like "twuzzie"*] from my 1918 uniform . . ." You should have written more clearly so that I could understand what is going on with your "twuzzie." Was it like a scarf? Or was it a medal from the First War? If that was your twuzzie, you must have stolen it, because you never got anywhere near the front lines.

Whatever it was you wanted to tell Hitler about your twuzzie, I can't make it out at all. I'll be hanged if I can—oops, sorry; that was a bit tactless, wasn't it? Anyhow, you continued like this, a little more legibly: "Ever since those days . . . [*twuzzietwuzzie*] . . . and somewhat later [as] a member of the National Socialist Party, I have known but one problem: Down with Marxism [*Father, you idiot—what you mean is "goal," not "problem." And now come two more indecipherable words, something like "Cover new."*] I was silently with you and walked behind you to the Odeonsplatz" [*during the attempted putsch in 1923*].

That, of course, is also pure nonsense. It was, naturally, a bitter disappointment that Hitler did not once look around to see who was with him on his infamous march to the Feldherrnhalle. If he had, he would surely have noticed your twenty-three-year-old full-moon face. He might also have noticed your twuzzie and asked, "Say, where did you get that beautiful twuzzie?" And then you would have stopped to explain the whole thing and interrupted the march for a while. And then if you had stopped the march, the police would have had a chance to position themselves better, and maybe one of the officers could have picked both you and Hitler off with one shot. But the whole stupid affair was fated to take place as it did, despite your twuzzie. And the only thing that came out of it for you was a shabby Minister of the Reich job (without Portfolio, or any real function at all)—and even that you had to fight for with letters like the one we're in the middle of . . . which goes on: "As a result of my arduous work, I have managed first to recognize and then to research what socialism is, from both a practical and a theoretical standpoint . . . as a lawyer hrunt" [or is it "hrus"? That makes no sense. Tell me, were you drunk or what?].

Yes, okay, you were a "lawyer" for some dubious little film workers' union. I have not been able to find out more about that, but my bet is that they threw you out pretty quick—anything that had to do with the real working class was not your mug of beer. Don't you think that even a madman like Hitler would have seen the contradiction in your letter? On the one hand, you say you want the overthrow of Marxism more than anything else, and on the other, you tell him you were a union lawyer? But you probably analyzed the situation correctly and realized they were happy with any ass-kisser they could get hold of, especially one who was a lawyer and could finagle things so that Hitler's thugs would not end up in jail. You continue: "Grant me now the opportunity to struggle *and to strangle* in the service of our holy cause."

All right, I'll take "and to strangle" back; that's my own little alliteration—but you have to admit that there is something to it, you throttler of justice, you slime.

Now let's have the two final paragraphs. The first goes: "I am prepared. I sense the imperative: to serve you."

What nonsense. In the first place, you were hardly prepared; you were mostly broke in those days. Mother had opened up a questionable little business in furs. You had to appeal for state assistance to get you out of financial trouble. And then, you were living with her on the third floor at Grandpa's place—I can just imagine the chickens running around, and I hear there was a rabbit there, too. It might actually have been fun for me to develop that minor chapter in your lives if it were not for the corpses strewn along your subsequent path. You were still in legal training and knew perfectly well that both the Reds and the Blacks, the Socialists and the Conservatives, could use people who knew what they were doing. But that was not good enough for a clever braggart like you. You already had it figured out that those with shirts of another color, the brownshirts, presented a rare opportunity. Anyone could tell from observing their meetings that they were crazier and more out of control than you were.

Here is the last paragraph of that love letter of yours to Adolf: "Grant me, then, the opportunity to present myself in person to you. Dare I hope? With a loyal Heil! [*That's a new one on me; I've never read that one before or since. "With a loyal Heil" indeed.*] Your Hans Frank."

Not even this willingness to be the ass-kisser ended in success. It wasn't until a full moon later that someone who merely signed himself "B." bothered to answer you. "Dear Sir, The communication you directed to Herr Hitler has been forwarded to us. We gather from it that it is your intention to take on an active role as co-worker within our movement."

Those bastards, right?

And the way the letter continued—saying that you should report to the party office in Schwabing—was really nothing more than a ploy to get rid of you. Whoever or whatever it was, though—whether it was that God you were always jabbering about or some Bavarian wood sprite—someone or something gave you another chance. You took a trip to the South Tyrol, where you managed again to analyze a situation in completely the wrong light. But somehow or other you interpreted a few facts correctly. For instance, you saw that the Italians, who had raked in that part of the Tyrol after World War I, were treating the Austrian Tyrolese just as horribly as you later treated the Poles and Jews (with the minor exception that they were not being executed and gassed). Anyhow, here is your letter about that experience. I can actually make out the first word despite your awful scrawl. The word is "profoundly."

You write: "To the National Socialist German Workers' Party, Munich. Profoundly shocked, I have just returned from our German South Tyrol. Italian fascism reveals itself there in its very action as the most terrible kind of cultural vandal."

There follows some blahblah. Then you actually pay Hitler back for his earlier rejection of you. In that period, August 1926, you were still showing a few rays of promise as a lawyer. "I know fascism [*from a few hikes in the Austrian Alps?*] . . . and I am therefore obliged to point out that in fundamental ways Hitler's statements about the South Tyrol are incorrect."

The basis for your assertion, to be sure, is preposterous: "Italian fascism functions as a southern European ethnocentric act of violence that will *never* have any contact with our Germanic culture, unless it be on the field of battle."

I have spent hours sweating over your old German script, always with the hope of discovering something that might speak to me in a human way, something that might arouse in me one iota of love for you, something that might begin to explain to me why you were what you were. In vain. What comes out is never much more than the drivel of a numbskull. (What, I wonder, must the children of today's politicians have to put up with? They'll have a big problem, too, when they have to pull the plug on their fathers and their slippery lies.) Anyhow, after several more featherbrained and empty-headed sentences, you deliver your punch line: "On the grounds of principle, yet altogether amicably, I must withdraw from the party to which I was devoted body and soul, but to whose most recent changes in direction I cannot subscribe. I return my party card enclosed."

Father, how about joining up now with one of the socialist parties, or the Communists, and taking me with you by the hand? No, nothing came of your great political insights. You slipped right back in—in fact, you were in a better position later on. You became a Nazi lawyer, a revolting loudmouth, especially for anyone still capable of thinking democratically. Now you were in a position where you could submit wholeheartedly to your "imperative" of serving Hitler for the rest of your days, a spineless, flabby-assed Nazi.

Why do I drag you verbally through the mud? It makes me feel like a rebel. It makes me feel young again. It makes me feel ex-hilarated, as if I were twelve again, in the Bavarian Alps, and sticking out my tongue at that God hiding behind the peak of the Brecherspitz. I feel proud of myself for being brave enough just to stick out my tongue at that deity of the Schliersee and that village of Neuhaus. I have the same feeling about you. And so, of course, it is your victory over me. You are lodged deep in my brain. But someday, maybe when I am very old, I'll have the upper hand. I'll win the victory. The sound of your neck snapping will be only a little sound in my head by then.

Here's the way your account of your second try at fame and fortune in the Party goes. (It's from your memoirs written in your prison cell in 1946, *Face to Face with the Gallows*. That's the title someone else gave it, not you. You still believed you would just be staying on in prison.) "After I passed my examinations in 1926, I settled down the next year as a lawyer in Munich. In July of 1927 I was also hired under the civil service as an assistant professor for commercial and business law at the Munich Institute of Technology. It then transpired that the clock of destiny suddenly began to strike in its mysterious way. [*That's your sentence, not mine!*] In October 1927 I read by chance a copy of the *Völkischer Beobachter* in my apartment. [*Don't make me laugh! "Read by chance"? Friend, you were not only a subscriber but even owned a piece of that Nazi-battle-cry rag; it arrived regularly in the mail.*] There I saw a notice that read: 'Lawyer sought to take over the defense of poor, unemployed party members in court trial. No remuneration. *Gau* Berlin.' " You took over the case and got them off with minimal sentences. From then on, you gradually became a leading Nazi lawyer. And lo and behold, your reputation took on a very different complexion. Brownshirts from all over sought your counsel in their defense. Then one day "Herr Hess and one of his co-workers arrived at my apartment, completely unannounced. [*You don't say! Not even a little bit announced? Cut the crap!*] They brought greetings from Herr Hitler, who had received a report from Goebbels about my legal activities in Berlin. He said he wished to have his personal gratitude extended to me. And at the same time he wanted me to assume responsibility for the Party in a major case coming up in Darmstadt. I said, 'But I am not a member of the Party.' That, said Hess, was completely beside the point; all that mattered was that the legal interests of the Party be represented. And I agreed" . . . and renounced justice forthwith.

And so you soon became the Advocate and Champion of the Nazi cause, Frank the Second, the one at the Reichswehr trial in 1930 in Leipzig—how stupidly proud you were of this accomplishment up to the very end—who extracted the oath of legality from the witness Adolf Hitler. Hitler vowed then and there that his struggle for domination would be based *only* on democratic principles.

Grandpa
and the Milk Cow

Prior to your period of grandeur, which began in 1933, there
had been some pretty low stretches in your life. It's time for
me to summon Grandpa now for this account, and also (are you
twitching in your cauldron?) to call on Creszentia Breitschaft. The
other conniving members of the party were Mother and, in an
especially repulsive way, you, naturally.

You will recall a letter written to the Honorable Frau Minister,
your good wife, by a certain Frau Elise Lutze. Right? That name
makes you tremble, too, doesn't it? Yes, she was the matchmaker,
the marriage-arranger, who collaborated with your father—my
same old grandpa with the beer glass balanced on his bald head.
She would steer a variety of unmarried or widowed women between the ages of forty and fifty in his direction, provided they
had substantial savings in the bank. Then Grandpa would turn on
his charm and fleece the stupid geese. So then . . . (I just can't
type fast enough on this machine. It is the same one, by the way,
that Mother used for her correspondence during the Time of
Grandeur and then later in the new West Germany, when she
would peck out her pathetic letters of supplication to any fool
who let himself be taken in by the tragic story of your execution.)
Creszentia Breitschaft was the name of one such poor creature—

literally poor, that is, after she had fallen into the hands of Grandpa, Mother, and you, through the good offices of Frau Lutze.

Frau Lutze gently recalls those earlier days in that letter to Mother, asking the Honorable Reichsminister's wife to put in a few words with Minister Frank on behalf of her husband, "in order that he might again find some modest government job or other." She continues, "At the same time I should like to tell you how often I have admired that marvelous photo-portrait of you on the Theresienstrasse and how sorry I was to see that it is no longer on exhibit." (Father, I have to tell you how great I think it was that, as a brand-new Nazi big shot's wife, Mother arranged to have her photograph put on public display.) After delivering herself of this bit of flattery, Frau Lutze gets down to brass tacks: "How are you and your splendid husband? Since the first of September I have been living on the Weinstrasse . . . I simply could no longer raise the rent for the apartment on the Thierschstrasse. There is so much more I could tell [*this is the decisive sentence, Father. You must have noticed it yourself and decided to placate the good woman by an act of great kindness*], so much I could tell you about the dreadful conditions under which we are now living. But I must not take up too much of your valuable time. In closing I should merely like to ask you once again not to forget me in my sad situation. . . ."

There is no doubt at all that Frau Lutze could have recited chapter and verse about the rotten way the three of you swindled the Breitschaft woman. Following Frau Lutze's tip, Grandpa had ferreted her out. She was the owner of the railway-station restaurant in Leutkirchen, and her husband had died only a short time before. Grandpa lost no time in launching an affair with her. He had a way of getting experienced women into the sack; somehow or other he could sweet-talk them into it with his clever chitchat about being a lawyer, at the same time he was taking off his skivvies. That seemed to impress them. For him to have mentioned anything about being disbarred would have been to insult his own honor.

Anyone who got involved with the Frank family was caught like a fly in a Venus's-flytrap. And that is what happened to the young Widow Breitschaft. Her own mother smelled a rat from the beginning. In a deposition she swore that Grandpa, still married at the time, had promised to marry her daughter Creszentia (known as Zenzi). She recounted his lies one after another, and ended her written statement: "Herr Frank has therefore treated my daughter in a false and wicked way and has been the ruin of my sweet child." This innocent "sweet child" touches me more deeply than anything you ever put in writing—for one simple reason: it is genuine.

Grandpa takes Zenzi for everything she has, and keeps on postponing his divorce. Then he falls in love with the gentle but extraordinarily tough Fräulein Donauer.

For years, statements fly back and forth.

Zenzi's mother about Grandpa: "The man has been exploiting my daughter financially and is going to ruin her."

Grandpa about himself to you: "Today I was at a wedding in a Protestant church, and the deeply religious and pious ceremony had a profound but also fortifying effect on someone like me, someone who has been dealt such hard blows by fate and been so little appreciated by his family. I was made to feel that my trust and my only consolation rest in the hands of the Heavenly Father, to whom I prayed that He might awaken in your hearts the willingness and capacity to be mindful of your own father and treat him in the manner he deserves after a life of such self-denial, one filled with sacrifice and renunciation."

Zenzi to Grandpa: "Are you finally and sincerely willing to marry me, as you said you would, before I leave for Hof?"

Grandpa to Zenzi: "I am at a very low point in my life and am living in primitive circumstances. If you were personally to bring me some money, I will accept. I will go to the Bamberger Hof at 6:30 exactly and look around in front, right and left. If you are there, it will be a sign to me that . . ."

Zenzi to Grandpa: "I am ashamed of your degrading treatment of me. No man worthy of trust and admiration would ever act that way. . . . You once said that I was a woman without self-esteem. Now I am going to prove to you that my pride is stronger and more dignified than you ever believed it was. The goodness I have in my heart is something you have never valued or even understood; and you have killed it."

Grandpa to "My dearest Zenzi. I am now at the extreme point of emotional confusion, filled with the profound seriousness of our recent talk. On my knees, I beseech you: Have patience with me, I am an unfortunate man who has caused you great suffering. Please, please, let me pull myself together, for if I don't I shall perish."

You to Grandpa: "Dear Father, I beg you either to call or to come to me today concerning the Breitschaft affair. I would finally like to put an end to this dreck."

"Dreck"—that is a word that Lasch used when he was sitting in his death cell. It is a word that must often have come to mind for you and those like you. Dreck is what all of you shat; dreck is what you yourselves were. It is why the word is stuck up there inside your brain. I now understand why it was that in later years, when you were racing through the countryside in your Mercedes and your Horch, Grandpa became so adept at jumping into the roadside ditches near Neuhaus and hiding in the weeds for fear you might catch him.

Meanwhile Grandpa must have stood up bravely to the Widow Breitschaft, for she writes him in a rage: "What on earth can you be thinking of to suggest that I should now be put to the test, I who have had to put up with a man who has been living with his mistress now for four years? You are with her every day. It is out of the question for me to put up with that any longer. . . . I will not endure such outrages, and I regard this demand as nothing more than a prolonged postponement of our marriage agreement."

Why did Zenzi put up with such treatment by the Franks? You

know why, Father. It was clearly nothing more than an obsession on her part to be connected with a family that, thanks to you, was suddenly becoming more and more prominent. Poor Frau Breitschaft. Incidentally, however, she must have known something about your and Grandpa's dirtier secrets. At least she hints at that in a letter, where she says it would be "in the interest of Grandpa and his family to pay more careful attention." To what, Father? What kind of skeletons-in-common did you have in your closets?

Zenzi to Grandpa: "You want the Donauer woman for your heart and the Breitschaft woman, me, for your material interests. Let me put you straight once and for all: I am not your milk cow."

And yet, again and again, Grandpa won her over and then left her dangling, until she exploded: "I am not going to be cheated and deceived all on account of a rotten, stinking female who has nothing and is good for nothing."

And so she threatened Grandpa with litigation, accusing him of false marital intentions, sexual intercourse resulting from illegal methods of seduction (Grandpa was sixty at the time!), and embezzlement. Grandpa must have done a lot of scratching of that bald head of his, for as an ex-lawyer he was perfectly well aware of the applicable laws and the penal consequences of breaking them. At that time the *Bürgerliches Gesetzbuch* was still in force, the Civil Code which became the object of your unending derision.

We Franks counterattacked. With Grandpa (who was still legally married to Grandma in Prague) and Mother, you hatched a first-class plan. In its coagulated German officialese, it read as if its purport were to assist Frau Breitschaft in her fervently pursued marital plans—or so she was made to believe—whereas in truth it was tantamount to her ruination. "The undersigned herewith declares that on the day of the legal revocation of his marriage he will pay to his then legally divorced wife, Magdalena, the cash sum of 1,200 reichsmarks and thereafter a monthly sum of 50 reichsmarks, the payment to begin on the first day of the month following the divorce as legally granted. Munich, December 8, 1930. Signed: Karl Frank."

So far, so noble. But then comes the print mark of your devil's hoof (poor Frau Breitschaft!): "For the legal obligations of Herr Karl Frank, as set forth above, I stand surety and am guarantor, beginning on the day of our marriage (which must take place on or before February 1, 1931). Munich, December 8, 1930."

Frau Breitschaft signed, and when the divorce was granted, coughed up the 1,200 marks like the good woman she was—and continued to wait in vain.

Then she reverted to the formal form of address in her communications with Grandpa, to whom she wrote: "For years I have borne up under the almost inhuman treatment suffered at your hands, most especially during the past year. I have now twice lost the very roof over my head. I am without a home."

Were you sorry for her? You were? Then please explain to me her next sentence: "Another thing, your good son also refuses to repay me the 500 mark debt he owes: 280 marks for the rent I paid for him and the rest for moving expenses."

And then please explain these sentences I find in a letter you wrote Zenzi on your pompous official stationery (by this time you were a Nazi representative in the Reichstag): "My dear Frau Breitschaft, I ask you for a great favor. Constituents of mine in Silesia have suffered enormously in consequence of the ban on the publication of two newspapers, the *Schlesischer Beobachter* and the *Schlesische Tageszeitung*. I, too, have suffered serious personal loss. Would you help out just one more time? You know, of course, that you are my only creditor, and also that all banks are closed to us. Grant me a final one-year loan of 1,200 reichsmarks. I shall then pay it all back in regular monthly installments. You would be doing us a huge service. The battle is difficult, but Germany must be free! Can you send the money—1,200 reichsmarks—directly to my address at the Reichstag, Berlin. This will be the last time—help once again. You have always been a good person. Heil! Your Dr. Frank II."

You bastard. Tell me, how could Germany become "free" with the loan of 1,200 marks from Frau Breitschaft? How often did that woman help you out? I puke on you for having taken such disgusting advantage, behind Grandpa's back even, of that woman, Zenzi, who was really never up to dealing with you two bastards.

Frau Creszentia Breitschaft never received anything in return for her kindheartedness. Grandpa married the Donauer woman. He had met her one evening while he was sitting at the bottom of the staircase in the entrance hall of her building, drunk. Later on, after they were married, he was again seated in the same place, again drunk, the one difference being that this time he had a different lady love in his arms. His gentle but tough wife went on such a rampage that he didn't dare do anything like that again. It seems that the only pleasure left in his life was to take a good shit out of doors. As you know—it was the reason for your great embarrassment as Minister—this practice of your father's was, as far as he was concerned, the finest pleasure life could now hold. Whenever he went walking with his wife and came upon a forest clearing or an open field, he would march right to the center of the place (it had to be dead center); the Donauer woman would hold his overcoat like a curtain around him; and Grandpa Karl the lawyer would shit and piss into the dirt to his heart's content. (By the way, it occurs to me that Grandpa was obviously the model for your stories about that prodigious bowel-mover Tony Huber, whom I have mentioned before.)

The good man died in 1945, just soon enough not to have to endure the ignominy of the hangman's rope that dispatched his son a year later. A scoundrel himself, he saw through the crooked regime of his scoundrel son. Nevertheless he exploited with zest the opportunities opened to him—to the extent that you permitted. You probably know what happened to Frau Creszentia Breitschaft. I do not. For me, she lives on in the sentences she wrote to Grandpa, such as: "You certainly cannot imagine that I am going to put up with another year of your fooling around, you clown." Or the well-considered threat: "Get your life in order and don't force me to have a letter written to Hans—because if you continue to cause me problems, no one can prevent me from sending a letter addressed directly to your son Hans at the Reichstag."

And she lives on in the scenes she made for Grandpa's edification. Zenzi had finally resorted to counterattacks; every day for a while she would wait in ambush in front of his Munich apartment, or she would take him by surprise in the taverns where he went for his relaxing glass of beer—paid for with her money, of course. Once she turned up at the Goldener Stern with a five-tail whip that she cracked over the table, screaming at him all the while, "Now I've got you again! There he sits with his floozie! And his pal, the head bastard, is there too!" The floozie was the Donauer woman. Who the head bastard was cannot be determined. At first, I thought it might be you; but that would not make any sense (for a change).

I like the whole scene: Zenzi swinging her whip over her cowering Casanova. Only a few days after this, he had another heated encounter with her, as he told the court in mournful tones: "Last Thursday as I was coming from Fräulein D.'s home on Herzog-Heinrich-Strasse—it was six in the evening, and all sorts of people were out walking—she shouted curses at me, right on the street, and called me a 'damn pimp'—in a voice that everyone could hear."

I love Frau Breitschaft for that. How I should have preferred living with her kind, instead of with the pimps, the cheats, and the traitors in lawyers' clothing, the big shots, the collaborators, the murderers.

For a long time I puzzled over Grandpa's description of the threats Frau Breitschaft came out with. They all, he said, "were based on the fact that she—and after all, over the years she was in a position to get to know a lot about family business and such through me and my son—that she said she would be generously rewarded and honored if only she would reveal these family stories and the like to the *Munich Post* or to Jewish attorneys." Now I ask you, Father (and cross your cold heart), what could a woman like that discover in so honorable a lawyer's home that might be of interest to newspapers or attorneys? I know already what an enormous number of dirty skeletons you have in your closet—and yet it would appear that they are only a small part of the filth you took with you to your grave.

If only the Breitschaft woman had told the press what she knew. The fourth estate was still functioning in Germany at the time. But she never did. What finally happened to the woman? Eventually she had to swear an oath of disclosure and declare personal bankruptcy. She already had heavy debts before she was tricked into paying the entire costs of your mother's and father's divorce. She was sent to prison. I don't know when the sentence began or how long her term was to be, but she was released on November 22, 1932, at 10:08 a.m.—how painfully precise Bavarian bureaucracy is about such things. Despite all that, she pursued the matter in court until the end of 1934, at which time a pathetic settlement in her favor was reached. Because of her prior declaration of bankruptcy, she could no longer find employment. What impressed me most about her is that she persisted in her litigation even after you had become Bavarian Minister of Justice. It must have been damned embarrassing for you.

In the last analysis, Frau Breitschaft was lucky. She escaped with her life. Uncle Marian did not; Father Number 2, Lasch, did not; nor did all the millions whom you gave orders to hunt down and kill.

A Genius Becomes
Minister of Justice

By 1932 Mother had been married to you for seven years. About that time she must have experienced a split second of clarity, of truth, after giving you a sudden glance out of the corner of her eye and realizing what a weak, vain, characterless little creature you were. Then she saw that those might be just the perfect attributes for the career you were headed for, grabbed a sample of your handwriting, and took it to a graphologist for analysis.

I have the analysis here. The expert begins, altogether erroneously, by saying that your scrawl "reveals a cultivated person, one with self-assurance in the presence of others, strongly aristocratic traits, and a certain ambitiousness, without, however, vitiating the outward impression of a cultured personality." None of that is correct. I think immediately of the awkwardness of your appearance in Austria, where you had gone just before the Anschluss. I saw the event in an old documentary on television. There you stand, surrounded by a few thuggish types in their bourgeois outfits, being filmed as you speak into a battery of microphones held in front of you, making some statement about your visit. Suddenly you start speaking much louder; in fact, you begin to scream, even though you are not saying anything more momentous than what time of day it is. Why was it that all of you yelled so much—even when saying things that needed no emphasis at all? The gentlemen standing around you remain quite unmoved by the spectacle. But I sat there years later watching you, once again dumbfounded by it all.

The lady handwriting expert gushes on: "His character is open, honest, often very candid. He says what he has to say, puts his cards on the table." Whoa! Lies were your daily bread. You were— whenever I take a look at you, your life, your scribblings, your private utterances—a thoroughly fork-tongued human being. You had the quick, clever, double-talking mouth of the average crook in a courtroom.

Unfortunately, the lady analyst inserted a phrase into her evaluation of your handwriting that henceforth separated the Franks and their relatives from the unwashed public, the one that made them all proud of you up to the time of your execution and beyond, the one that permitted them to interpret your death on the gallows as being no more than a temporary disorder of your circulatory system: "His intellectual qualities are excellent—one is obliged to speak here of genius." Genius. You? A genius? Someone who could come out with a statement like this next one? "Whoever attacks the unity of the German People with criminal intent, that person is done for." Yes, I'll admit, that sample was straight from the grab bag. But it's true. You often spoke like that, in that stupid, hard-assed way. If the lady expert can manage to extract the marrow of "genius" from your ridiculous scrawl, I can be just as much of an expert: e.g., whenever the pointy tips of your old German script begin to show signs of proliferating within a narrow space and getting out of hand, what comes out (at the least) are words like "victorious" or "colossal" or "tremendous" or pure crap like "profoundly experienced communality of destiny."

How can a person live his whole life long (or should I say, "his whole *short* life long"—thanks to Hangman Woods) with so many replacement parts in his brain? Was one bit of ganglion left over for thinking? How can that handwriting analyst jabber on about your "rich treasury of thought," about your "logical thinking,' about how you would, as we Germans say, "walk over corpses" if there were "attacks on your honor"? In a terrible sense that last one was true, for you were a superb walker over corpses; you had them stacked up like firewood—but not for the sake of your honor. Whenever your honor was at stake, you just chickened out.

"Though he is, to be sure, impulsive and vehement in the erotic sense, his eros is even more evident when it comes to mental activity." I've been searching and searching in your writings, in your speeches, and in your commentaries for manifestations of your erotic thinking, hoping to find Rabelaisian passages, sensual and inventive metaphors. And what do I find? "As the leader of the German defenders of justice I can say that since the foundation of the National Socialist State is National Socialist law and order, the Supreme Führer is by definition also our supreme judge [*according to the transcript of this speech, this passage was interrupted by "long and thunderous applause"—from an audience consisting of "upholders of the law," needless to say*], that his will must now also be the foundation of our law and order; and that we—we who know how holy the principles of a just and righteous life are to our Führer, above all—can also assure you, German compatriots, that your lives are likewise holy to him. Your existence as citizens of this state is guaranteed in this National Socialist State of order, of freedom, and of justice."

The man who wrote this kind of blather is supposed to be "erotic"?

The eroticism in which you took your delight, in which you bathed, was applause. I have photographs of you standing behind a lectern, always with those foolish boots on—this military getup was terrific for a Minister, but for a genius or someone devoted to refinement? One leg is placed slightly before the other, a slight bend at the knee; the chin on your gross and pudgy face is stretched forward and tilted up; both hands are boldly clutching the edge of the lectern, nails digging in as if you were fiercely squeezing a lovely woman's breast in each hand. And from your lips that filth is pouring forth.

It's incredible that you were still able to utter the word "justice" after what you wrote in 1930 in your congratulatory telegram to Frick, that brand-new Nazi Interior Minister for Thuringia (who, thank God, was executed along with you). Let me refresh your memory with a delicious taste of that missive. (It boggles the mind to think of the level to which you sank even before you began raking in those titles of yours.) "In the name of all German National Socialist members of the bar I extend to you, as our premier minister, the heartiest 'Heil' and our most sincere congratulations. For myself, I am most especially pleased at this, your appointment. From now on it would seem to be eminently advisable to implement as severely as possible the legislation regarding the defense of the Republic, especially for Thuringia. I positively delight in the thought of several Jewish editors being put behind bars forthwith for having slandered the National Socialist Minister of the Interior."

How I would have enjoyed sitting beside you on your cozy bed in your cell at Nuremberg.

By the time you reached thirty you were already without any moral scruples, thirsty for revenge, and full of disdain for your fellow human beings. Do you recall the time you were defending a case in Itzehoe and rejected both judge and jury—those red-headed citizens of Steinburg and Dithmarsch—on the grounds that they were Jews? Do you remember your revolting treatment of Ödön von Horváth at the trial in Weilheim, when you were questioning that great writer, who had been witness to a Nazi-organized brawl in a tavern? Should I recite to you all the complaints lodged against you before the bar on account of your anything-but-professional behavior? How wickedly you must have enjoyed your own rotten insolence; how your thuggish Nazi buddies must have thanked you, congratulated you for repeatedly defending them against charges of manslaughter. You probably never realized, right up to your yammerings about the state of injustice, that your appearances as a Nazi prosecutor helped to corrupt the system of justice whose disappearance you so poignantly lamented.

You and the other Nazi bums just hung around, until you finally took over. Germany greeted you with jubilation. It was March 1933 when you wrote your reassuring words to Frau Breitschaft: "I would be very grateful to you if you might be patient for just a few more days. I must undertake another trip this evening, and it will be a few more days—possibly a few more weeks—before I know to what extent the political situation will affect me." It certainly affected you. How cheerful you were that day you became the Bavarian Minister of Justice. The family still talks about it. I think about it every time I walk past the newly cleaned Palace of Justice in Munich. (Do you suppose they might have exorcised your ghost with an extra bit of sandblasting?)

You were sitting in the bathtub in your Munich apartment. Mother was all upset at the time because the district attorney was on to whatever shady fur dealings she was up to and threatening to bring suit against her. The telephone rings; Mother answers it. It's an adjutant of Hitler on the line, saying the Führer wishes to speak to you. Mother screams, "Hans, the Führer! Quick! Well, come on! It's the Führer, and look at you, naked." You erupt from the tub with a splash. (You are still far from being the Nazi Party fixture you became a few years later, 1937, with Furtwängler and Daddy Number 2, Lasch, in Berlin.) You run bare-assed to the phone, stand stiffly with the receiver in your hand, longing to be with your beloved Führer. Mother stands beside you, smiling now after her initial shock. You bark in your disagreeable voice, "Mein Führer?" and then in a second, "Ja, mein Führer!"—and that's all it takes to make you Bavarian Minister of Justice. What you should have said was "No." What you should have said was "Kiss my ass, mein Führer." But to resist the temptation of becoming Justice

Minister in Bavaria, at the age of thirty-three, that would have taken more character than the two of you put together could possibly have mustered.

From the moment of your "Ja" on, your hands—and mine—were covered with blood. It was at this time that the concentration camp at Dachau was being constructed. It was all still quite new to you, the way people could treat other people in such a place. But you adapted with amazing alacrity. The only resistance you ever put up was the little it took to ensure that no one got his hands on your Horch automobile, so ardent was your love of the Fatherland.

The Bavarians were the last ones to capitulate to you and your ilk. But on March 9 and 10, 1933, the SS and the Storm Troopers finally took over in Munich. Ritter von Epp was installed as Reichsstatthalter in Bavaria "in order to re-establish law and order in the land." And there you are for the first time in a group photograph of the first Nazi Ministerial Council—you, the Minister of Justice for the Land of Bavaria. Out of the bathtub into a job paying 2,580 marks and 44 pfennigs a month. Now *that* was money! Remember, Father? "A thousand a month, that's what we've got to aim for, Brigitte."

How the two of you must have sat around the table holding that first paycheck. What did it matter to you that in the very first night after the Nazi takeover in Bavaria the Minister of the Interior at the time, Dr. Stützel, was forced out of bed by party members and dragged off to Hitler's headquarters, the Brown House, "in his nightshirt, barefoot, and beaten bloody," as the much-admired representative of the Bavarian farmers, Georg Heim, wrote to Reich President Hindenburg?

Now that was a great way to open your show in Munich. Maybe you joked at the time, as you did later with your son, that Dr. Stützel could at least prove to them whether he was a man or not, half-naked as he was.

Two thousand five hundred and eighty reichsmarks and forty-four pfennigs a month—quite a fat paycheck for a grubby little climber like you and for a sleazy fur dealer like Mother. With that kind of loot in your pockets, you can't afford to waste any time on that poor jerk in his nightshirt. For Mother, something else was equally important at the time. How she loved to tell the story (another of her recollections of the grand and glorious time of the Franks) about the public prosecutor, the same one who had initiated a suit against her because of her fishy fur-trading deals. As soon as you became Minister of Justice (she would gleefully recount for me later), this man came creeping obsequiously to your new office to pay his respects and to let you know that, of course, the files regarding Frau Brigitte Frank would be closed at once. She got a wicked laugh out of that story to the day she died.

Mother reveled in her new life from the first day of your appointment. How she loved the letters of solicitation sent her by various businesses: "Honorable Madam, most esteemed Frau Staats-minister. Allow us, if you please, to recommend to you our old and established specialty firm, one with which you are surely familiar, and ask you to bear us in mind as purveyors when your household is preparing to replenish its supply of tea...." Whenever she received such a letter she was out the door in a flash and headed for the shop in question, accepting free samples. It was impossible for her to forget her bitterly impoverished years as a secretary. Furthermore, one never knew with such a jellyfish of a husband how much longer things would go smoothly with your official career, with Hitler, and the free tea at the specialty shops. So Mother was off to an early start in preparation for her mon-umental career of raking in loot in the Government General in Poland.

Meanwhile, you were taking yourself very seriously. You de-manded obsequiousness, "respect." After your elevation to Minister of Justice, the secretaries in the outer offices of the lawyers and politicians you deigned to visit were expected to leap to their feet the moment you entered. Frau Mylo told me about it. She became your secretary in Cracow, but at that time in Munich she was still Lasch's receptionist at the Justice Department, the Reichsrechts-amt. You were paying a visit to your "blond rascal," and at the moment of your appearance in the outer office everyone except one girl sprang to attention. She remained seated. You complained to Lasch and demanded to know what sort of impropriety that was. (Incidentally, what were you doing there in the first place anyhow? Were you bringing Lasch the doctor's dissertation you had written for him? And why didn't you enter anything in your diary about that girl's outrageous disregard for your position?)

You had one opportunity after the other to reverse your course. You could so easily have rejected the whole disgusting mess when you first encountered the reality of Dachau. For example, you could have done it at your meeting of ministers on April 4, 1933. Your words are recorded in the minutes under "Point IX. In re: protective custody." You start out pretty well, but I'm just as glad I don't have to hear that high voice of yours speaking; it always gave me the shivers. The entry reads: "The Minister of Justice-Designate Frank states that there is a compelling need to regulate the whole question of protective custody." Quite true. Himmler had become the Chief of Police for Munich. His standing order was "Send them to Dachau!" The deportations to the concentration camp there were so frequent and steady that a little rhyme quickly sprang up in Bavaria: "Sweet Jesus, keep my lips sealed tight/And spare me Dachau's pain and plight."

You continued: "The prisons and labor camps are overcrowded. The number of detainees was five thousand on April 1 and is estimated to reach six thousand or seven thousand." At this point did you have a brief, portentous, purposely awkward pause recorded in the minutes? Did you pick out Minister of the Interior Wagner and fix him with your pop-eyed gaze? (You did have that touch of the goiter.) Did Ritter von Epp nervously clear his throat and rustle his papers (so much for clichés)? In any case, you spoke even more to the point: "When a sentence of protective custody is imposed, often enough the grounds are not sufficiently convincing." Hear, hear! Such euphemism! The following sentence, too, shows you at your best in formulating evasive yet nonetheless felicitous politico-language: "There is no guarantee that there may not be innocent persons also held at present in protective custody." The whole roundtable of ministers must have been flabbergasted at that statement. Wagner shouts, "But that can't possibly be true, for godsake, for chrissake, for marysake!" Epp, Ritter von, declares: "Herr Dr. Frank, we shall of course all resign as a group if there is but one single instance of an innocent man having been arrested!" Stentorian shouts of assent; the recording secretary is totally flummoxed. Is that the way it was? It isn't? No sense of embarrassment among you? Really not? Not even one teensy-weensy bit of a bad conscience that might have found a voice among the whole lot of you?

No. Nothing. You were permitted to continue uninterrupted: "In the court records we frequently find as substantiating grounds merely an appeal to the public order. A very large number of arrests have taken place in the Palatinate." Now that was a major political mistake on your part, Father, because the Upper Palatinate is way far away over there in the northern part of Bavaria. The gentlemen all breathed a great sigh of relief. The world keeps a sharp eye on Munich but pays next to no attention to the Bavarian Palatinate—and as to the people's problems there, well, that can easily be taken care of with a telegram or something.

Maybe you realized your mistake right away, for you added in a threatening voice, "I, as the leader of the National Socialist legal profession, have not been doing battle these past thirteen years in order to allow a few criminal ruffians to wreck our legal structure. I shall direct the state's attorney to . . . ruthlessly, and without regard to party membership, to . . ." Right? Those were your words, right? You were always full of such windy militant trash in your great days of battle.

Yes, all these hyperbolic, theatrical quotations that I am grouping together here come directly from you. But relax, I'll stick to the secretary's minutes. Here are the "principles to be followed in dealing with protective custody," proposed by you, viz.: "Arrests made pursuant to hearsay, i.e., simple denunciation, and gratuitous arrests made by subordinate branches and divisions of authority are to cease at once!" Very good. "The interrogation of those taken into protective custody, if not already carried out, must be immediately guaranteed." Keep it up, Father! "If sufficient grounds for detention are not established, the prisoner must be released immediately." Three cheers! Don't tell me I wasn't going to be fair to you. Don't let them stop now. "A formal procedure must be arranged to determine the jurisdiction of each case and to guarantee the detainees certain assurances and recourses to appeal." I no sooner begin to praise you than you begin to weaken. What do you mean, "certain"? There's another one of those damned elastic sentences of yours that played right into the hands of Himmler & Co. Am I correct in seeing your fear showing through here, your fear that you do not have the power to assert yourself, you Leader of Justice, you? "The commandant of the police must procure a precise roster of all those in protective custody. For this purpose, forms must be sent to all district offices and police stations to be filled out, at his personal recognizance, by the chief official at each office and station, giving a full and complete list of all prisoners."

Is that all, Father? Why didn't you enact a resolution then and there that would compel Ritter von Epp to go public with a statement like "Protective custody is hereby abolished"? Yes, I know; very naive of me. How do you continue instead? "For the evaluation of appeals and complaints, a commission is to be established to which are to be appointed, with the active cooperation of the SA, senior officials of the police and one or two judges of the Administrative Court"—which, needless to say, the Council of Ministers instantly and gratefully approved. And thus a few

more sections of rail were laid for the trains which were soon
headed for the extermination camps. Thanks to you. Thanks to
your having proposed the formation of this commission.

But let's imagine that at that very moment you realized what
it was you had done; so you opened your fly and with the powerful
stream of which you were so proud you pissed all over your fellow
ministers; then, with dripping tool, you left the room, drove home,
grabbed Mother, and headed off to Italy with the words: "I would
rather work again as a lover-boy on the North Italian lakes than
spend another minute serving this lawless state."

Instead, you were puffed up with pride after your momentous
statements on the subject of preventive custody and lit up a fat
cigar. You had reserved for yourself a few more juicy items on
the docket. One was as antidemocratic as the next. "Expropriation
is the only way to assure ourselves permanently of the confiscation
of the property and assets of Marxist organizations. According to
the law of the Reich, expropriation is legal only when there is
indemnification. The commission that is to determine indemnification shall be mandated to calculate the potential damage to the
general welfare should these properties and assets be used for
Marxist aims and purposes."

You must have known what a filthy rotten decree that was.
How is it possible for someone even to formulate such a thing?
How can you bring yourself to say it aloud? Weren't you as red
as a beet? Or was the only thing ticking in your brain the thought
of how much money you were earning?

It was your show, that council session. At Point XII you were
on again. According to this one, all government officials were to
be compelled to report any memberships they had in Communist
organizations and to leave these organizations within a specified
time. According to Point XIII, all government publications were
to be reconstituted and "above all, those news publications are to
be favored which represent the Reich's policies." At Point XIV

IN THE SHADOW OF THE REICH

you issued a decree forbidding all government officials from "submitting to central offices complaints against their superiors either directly or via nonofficial routes."

Pretty neat, I must say. Such was your debut in the central powerhouse of government. Imagine for a moment life without that neck snap at Nuremberg. How would you have dealt in your memoirs with the minutes of this council session? Would it have turned out that you had been standing in a corner the whole time behind a pillar, and someone else, one of your top officials, without your knowing it, had actually been doing all the talking?

In Point XV you—the Führer's chief law officer—demand "first, that all Jewish lawyers be forbidden from entering any courts of law; second, that Jewish judges and state's attorneys be removed from office and that all Jewish notaries be prevented from exercising any further official duties."

And now—home to Mother. That was a lovely morning's program, Father. Reach just a little farther for your pistol, and blow yourself away.

Another vain hope, I'm afraid. You knew that whoever is credited with having been the guiding hand for an agenda like this one has it made in Germany. You remained in office. Only one year separated you from the Röhm putsch—and that made a murderer of you. How much more loot did you get when you were named Reichskommissar für die Gleichschaltung der Justiz in den Ländern und für die Erneuerung der Rechtsordnung, which is to say, Reich Commissioner for the Equalization of Justice in the German States and for the Restoration of Law and Order? Some crazy title! Reichspräsident Hindenburg himself signed the document of appointment—by this time he must have lost the rest of his marbles (or did he ever have any to begin with?). The two other signatures are those of Hitler and Dr. Gürtner, whom you were more than eager to replace as Minister of Justice for the Reich.

Your "restoration of law" can be detected in these minutes of the meeting of the Council of Ministers. The "equalization of justice" had been achieved by January 1, 1935; the entire legal branch of the government sullied its hands in that effort. Soon afterward the sullied hands became bloody ones.

Come, Father, let us get on with it. Permit me to dissect the great moment of pride in your life, your alleged act of salvation as Bavarian Minister of Justice vis-à-vis the rabid Hitler. In addition to his plan to murder leading members of the SA, he also wanted to dispose of many more Röhm supporters than you thought was appropriate. To the very end of your life you made a fool of yourself with your boastful claim about having rescued so many from Hitler's rampages . . . but then there are those whom you handed over at Stadelheim during the Röhm putsch for on-the-spot execution, as Hitler wished, without any prior trial—and those were your very first murders, Herr Minister of Justice.

So that, then, was the face of your New German Law? You should have resigned well before, when the Munich attorney Strauss was slowly tortured to death at Dachau. To be sure, you did assert your authority in some puny way and summoned the state's attorneys to investigate the situation. But when their access to Dachau was blocked and Himmler and Hitler let it be known that the whole thing was not a matter for Justice, it was settled for you then and there. What do you mean, "matter"? We're talking about the life of a human being!

How did you deal with all of that in your head? Did you fuck away your guilt complex in bed with Mother? Did you drink yourself into oblivion? Did you compose one of your insufferably trite "poems"? Did you gloomily portray yourself as a helpless victim of prevailing circumstances? Yes, you probably did—you had plenty of time in twelve long years to perfect that art.

You had your first look at the concentration camp in Dachau as a member of a guided tour. You saw nothing, of course.

Target Practice
Before the Evening
Murders

Off to the Röhm putsch! Reich Chancellor Hitler had driven to Bad Wiessee in June 1934, and there he had Röhm, the highest-ranking SA leader, arrested, along with his top men. The hooligans were taken completely by surprise. They were delivered to the Stadelheim prison near Munich together with the other SA leaders from all over the Reich. The director of the prison asked you to come there. You complied. You paid Röhm a brief visit in his cell, where you had a little "soldierly" conversation—i.e., you exchanged platitudes. Then, as you note, "came the dreadful hours." Sepp Dietrich and Prince Waldeck, two high-ranking SS men sent by Hitler, "entered my rooms in their SS uniforms and said they had orders to shoot all the SA leaders immediately. The Führer himself, they said, had sent them a list on which approximately one hundred and ten SA leaders had been 'checked off' with little pencil marks. These were the condemned men. I told the two of them that was completely out of the question. . . . They said then, 'The Führer himself gave the order. The responsibility is on your shoulders!' I said, 'Yes, I take full responsibility. You are standing here on territory belonging to Justice!' "

Class act, Father. Both of us are on Justice territory here now—so let's see if you can still keep your balance. Dietrich telephoned Hitler and blew the whistle on you. The Führer was enraged and read you the riot act over the phone. "You hesitate to carry out one of my orders? Are you in sympathy with these treacherous rats by any chance? It is my intention to eradicate them root and branch!"—and more of the same. And then he said something unique and momentous, your Führer did: "The only reason these men are in your prison is because I had no other secure place to put them. They are merely your guests. I and the Reich have full power over them, not Bavaria."

That really is quite a nuisance, wouldn't you say—when the Chancellor of the Reich has to go out on the hunt himself, arrest people, and then have to worry about secure places to put them. Father, didn't the similarity in attitude occur to you between the actions of this man and those of the people responsible for the St. Valentine's Day Massacre in Chicago?

The story goes on. You didn't say so much as "boo" to Hitler on the phone. But then you called up Hess, who was with Hitler at the Brown House, and asked him to intervene with the Führer on your behalf. Hess hung up. At this point in your recollections you introduce a couple of thoughtful remarks about how not very many lives were really at stake, actually only 110 men. "I sat and waited and smoked with the good prison director. There was a frightening tension in the air. [*According to your report, Father, you didn't do anything—all you did was await the outcome.*] Then the telephone finally rang. Hitler had refused to have a personal exchange of words with me. Hess informed me on the line that Hitler, with the express approval of the President of the Reich, had the legal authority [*Ask him to show you this mandate, Father; ask him to show it to you!*] to undertake directly and unreservedly any and all necessary and appropriate steps to prevent the threatened putsch from taking place. [*Insist on proof, Father, proof!*] The chief perpetrators are to be shot at once. I then asked, 'Which ones are they?' [*Father, that's impossible, that cannot be! You are already giving up? You, the Minister of Justice, allow yourself to be told all this—on the telephone—by Hess? But yes, why not? I know that fear in you; I knew it from the beginning—the fear that always made you retreat, the fear that Hitler might ask you to come to the phone and that he would then scream at you again, tell you what a ball-less creature you are. That perverse politician's brain of yours had sent out a signal: Hold fire. No opposition. Too dangerous. A position sufficient for purposes of contemporary history.*]

"With the list in my hand, I heard nineteen names read out and put a red check in front of each. After the last one there was a pause. I asked, 'And all the others whose names had been checked off before?' Hess replied, 'The Führer has gone over the list again and intends to limit himself to these now.' Röhm was not one of the nineteen. Hess told me, 'Wait for further instruction concerning Röhm. Meantime, all are to remain in custody. Now, if you will, hand over these nineteen! Any court in the land would condemn them to death for their crime!' "

So, Father . . . Sepp Dietrich should have put you up against the wall without further ado. You have checked off the names of the candidates for the firing squad, listened without comment to some baloney about a putsch, and smoked an occasional cigar to relieve this "frightening tension in the air"—and as for the rest, you remain inert, passive.

Here's how you continue your reminiscences in Nuremberg: "Even though my first thought was that I had saved the lives of almost one hundred people by hesitating to obey, I asked Hess anyhow, 'On the grounds of what law exactly have all these men been condemned to die?' "

Chew that sentence over again, Father, and let it melt in your mouth. You, the Minister of Justice, the Reich Commissioner of Justice for the Unification of the Law. Did some law slip past you, one you didn't know anything about? Had one of your officials been messing around with the new German code? Or was that only a bit of mockery that escaped your lips? The only thing for you to have replied was "My dear Nazi friend Hess, there is not a single solitary law that justifies the execution of these nineteen men. I shall let these nineteen men go free, just as the others. Heil Hitler, you pig-brain."

Or words to that effect. But, please, do not put it in the form of a question. Hitler's reaction was a logical one, for he was capable of thinking at least as far as I can; Hitler knew, one more bit of grousing and you and your whole legal conscience would be lined up against the wall with the other nineteen. Do you recall your words? "There was a brief pause. The Führer was back on the phone and spoke to me loudly: 'What are you asking Hess? I'll tell you that the legal grounds for everything that happens is the very existence of the Reich! Do you understand?' [*At these words you should have burst out in laughter and scorn.*] His voice was like a hammer. And I, fearful that he might fall back to his initial position, said merely, 'Yes, your command will be carried out!' [*With that little sentence you turned yourself once and for all into a murderer.*] Then I handed the nineteen over to the SS and calmed down the others."

What follows after your account of this telephone conversation is the typical bullshit between two men after their crime: "Then I sank down in the desk chair and the director said to me, 'Herr Minister, you have saved the lives of one hundred men.' But I replied, 'And I have killed nineteen.' He wanted to console me and spoke of revolution, a putsch, extraordinary and extenuating circumstances, etc."

You knew the law. You stepped all over it. All the more disgraceful for you, twelve years later at Nuremberg, still to be able to write, "And yet I bore the traces of some terrible wound within me."

Not "some," Father—a very definite one, one that you could have defined exactly. From that point on, you were co-opted, you had blood in your throat, on your hands, in your soul, on your conscience. You sat there with your good director like some bloody afterbirth of yourself.

"He said to me, 'If you had refused to cooperate with regard to these nineteen, there might have been a terrible backlash and all the others would have been taken from you and shot as well. You clearly acted under the most frightful compulsion and in utter powerlessness.' [*The director cannot possibly have said those words—they are unmistakably typical of your unique pompous style.*] However, I retorted vehemently, 'It is precisely this compulsion which is the dread threat!' "

Curtain. Applause. Now come on out front, the audience wants to see you—not only as the actor, but also as the author of this profoundly crude scene. You don't think I would have misread it, do you? This closing scene is built up dramatically in such a way as to relieve you of the responsibility of having to articulate your cowardice yourself by putting it in someone else's mouth. Even if this "good director" of yours had said something of the sort, one simply does not put it down in such a sniveling, groveling way, not in a Nuremberg cell in 1946, not with the gallows right around the corner. One would have seen it for the miserable drivel it is.

Here is one of the scenes I particularly loathe, because of one detail. "The firing squad was pushing me, drawing my attention to the fact that twilight was fast approaching, that it was rapidly 'making the execution very difficult.' "

Why didn't you work up that part of the scene more effectively? You could have been sitting there in "frightening tension." You are smoking; there is a knock; the director calls out, "Come in"— with a muffled voice, of course, because the terrifying fate of the other Germans down there in their cells oppresses him. A sergeant says that Sturmbannführer X of the SS would like to speak with the Herr Minister. You give permission for him to enter; the SS man does so, stands before you, and clicks his heels. You remain seated, for after all you are the minister. "What is it?" you say. The SS man replies, "Herr Minister, we must have the condemned men now—the light we need to aim straight is getting very dim. We will soon have no guarantee of accuracy and will end up with a bunch of seriously wounded men instead of corpses. So please hand over at least four of them immediately, so that we can do some target practice and get used to the fading light." You spring to your feet, no longer in control of your anger, go directly up to the man, grab him by the shoulder, bellow for the provincial police who are under your command here at Stadelheim, and have all the SS goons arrested. Something like that? No? Why won't you answer? Is it because the only answer you would have given him was "Herr Sturmbannführer, you must be patient; I am waiting for another call from the Führer." That must have been what the tried and true Herr Justice Minister replied.

Oh, and just one final note. The fact that Röhm was brutally slaughtered in his cell one day later—no trial, no sentence—was not worth a single syllable in your reminiscences.

Buddha and the
Goralen Dirndl

What else were you up to between 1933 and 1939? Well, you had the Forestry Service nursery plant a spruce hedge about four or five feet tall around the Schoberhof, your country place in Bavaria—"very strong, bushy, and well-rooted plants," at forty-eight marks apiece. They thrived—but today are the usual brown, withered, acid-rain trees of Germany. You built your Justice Academy on the principles of that splendid legal text of February 28, 1933, which, with slight variations, is the same for us today as it was then, thanks to your efforts. At that time the text was known as an "Ordinance of the President of the Reich for the Protection of the People and the State," and was brilliantly formulated: "The articles of the Constitution of the German Reich are forthwith and until further notice declared null and void. Therefore, limitations on civil rights, freedom of expression, including freedom of the press, on freedom of assembly, protection against invasion of privacy (with regard to postal, telegraphic, telephonic communication), protection against searches of house and home and against expropriation, as well as limitations on ownership, even beyond the jurisdiction formerly stipulated by law, are herewith legally permitted." Now, that is lucid prose. On March 3 you gave an evening musicale, at which the guests were requested to appear in either uniform or white tie and tails, in order to have the honor

of hearing, among others, the great German singer Heinrich Schlus-
nus. For the official opening of your Berlin home you asked once
again (and once again in vain) for a signed photo-portrait of Hitler.
It wasn't until after much further boot-licking and bowing and
scraping that Lammers, Hitler's chief administrative officer, had
the pleasure of informing you on October 16, 1935 (well, what do
you know! exactly eleven years before your date with the noose):
"In response to my petition today, the Führer has declared himself
prepared, somewhat belatedly, to provide Herr Reichsminister Dr.
Frank with the requested portrait." On July 12, 1938, you were
delighted to discover on your desk in Berlin two letters written
in his very own hand by the great Bavarian popular writer Ludwig
Thoma, which your friend Luxenberg had acquired for you. I
wonder where they came from—and where they eventually got
to. Then, you declared yourself most pleased with a bronze figure
of the Buddha which a certain Herr Hobelsberger (otherwise unknown to me) gave you as a talisman. The man was evidently
suffering from a jagged swastika caught in his spleen; anyhow,
Grandpa wrote you, "Herr Hobelsberger has been a patient in the
Nymphenburg hospital for over six weeks, with terrible pains. He
is a man of much character and quite replete with the spirit of
nationalism." (No wonder he had such pains.) You had the further
honor of receiving a letter written to you, in German script, by
the great composer Richard Strauss: "I should be enormously
grateful to you, Herr Minister, if you could issue the order to . . ."
and so forth, all very Strauss-like. Then you paid an official visit
to Poland on the occasion of a treaty of friendship, and brought
Mother back a dirndl from the Goralen region. It was presumably
hand-made by the family that later during the GG period always
appears in photos with you, to symbolize the radiant population's
joyful appreciation of your wise and beneficent rule. You rejoiced
when the membership badge designed for your front-line law-and-
order organization was officially accepted and registered as one of
the party devices. And you took shorthand notes to give to Hitler

on a conversation you had with Mussolini, your alleged friend, during which event you had the opportunity once again of seeing what a gang of idiots was at the head of the Axis.

Mussolini on France: "A stomach culture! A state that has raised the culinary art to a matter of principle! That country must be expunged!"

On England: "I would bomb the English to bits with my planes if they so much as made a single move!"

On Hitler: "From the beginning, the concept of a Führer was an ideal I always had in my mind."

And an especially significant insight which you found worth passing on to the Führer: "Before the Suez Canal was built, even the English had to sail around the Cape."

Another item: Mother and you were attending an official dinner hosted by the Führer; that was on January 17, 1939, and the guests of honor were the royal Yugoslavian Minister-President and Minister of State Dr. Milan Stojadinovich. Naturally, you were not to be found at the head table with Hitler, but instead in a remote corner next to Frau Meissner, a lady from Neuhaus whom you knew very well indeed. Opposite you was Frau Lutze, the wife of the new chief of the SA—"new" thanks to you for having permitted the slaughterhouse execution of his predecessor, Röhm. (Did she drink a toast to you for that?) And next to her, Reichsminister Kerrl. Mother, at least, had the honor of being seated above the salt and, wouldn't you know it, right next to the Reichsminister of Justice, Gürtner, the man who still held the position that was the object of your dreams. Opposite them were Frau Frick [wife of the Nazi Minister of the Interior], Goebbels, and Frau Kerrl. At the head of Mother's table, just around the corner from where she was sitting, was Ley, the same Ley who had more success with his suicide attempt in 1945 than you did and thus escaped the agony of the gymnasium at Nuremberg.

All right, perhaps I've gone a little too far with my anger at your messed-up life; and I must admit that, yes, Himmler—your

The official Nazi photograph of Hans Frank (taken shortly
after the war began), intended for gifts and presentations.

LEFT: My father (left) in 1904, at the age of four, with his mother and my uncle Karl, who was killed in France during the First World War.

BELOW: Hans and Brigitte Frank, 1926.

Prior to 1933, my father (here in black robe) was Hitler's defense attorney at more than one hundred trials. The passionate young Nazi with arm extended makes this, for me, an especially haunting image.

ABOVE: The top Nazis at a ceremony commemorating Hitler's 1923 attempted putsch in Munich. This picture was probably taken on the occasion of the tenth anniversary in 1933.

RIGHT: Dr. Hans Frank (left) in SA uniform, shortly after Hitler became Chancellor of Germany in 1933.

The "folksy" Bavarian in his native costume: My father in 1936, Minister of the Reich without Portfolio.

Brigitte and Hans Frank at a prewar state reception in Berlin.

During a state visit to
Rome in 1938. My
father—a personal
friend of Il Duce—
looks on (with hands
crossed) as Mussolini
performs an official
function.

In the fall of 1939, the
Nazi battle flag is raised
over Cracow Castle,
the Governor General's
seat of power.

After the occupation of Poland, Polish civilians were arbitrarily selected to be hanged. Photographs of the executions were favorite mementos of German soldiers and civil servants, who took their film to be developed at a particular camera store in Cracow which secretly provided the Polish underground with prints of each photograph.

MUZEUM HISTORII FOTOGRAFII (CRACOW)

Cracow Castle, where the kings of Poland, as well as Marshal Pilsudski, are buried.

MUZEUM HISTORII FOTOGRAFII (CRACOW)

Map of the Government General, 1942. Occupied Poland was
divided into five districts, each headed by a Governor.
Officially, Governor General Frank reported directly to Hitler.

LEFT: My mother in 1942 at the castle in Cracow, photographed as "the Queen of Poland." RIGHT: Governor Karl Lasch, my father's personal friend, my mother's lover, and my "suspected" father. Lasch was executed by the SS on June 3, 1942.

My father standing behind his desk in Cracow Castle, distributing letters of appointment. (The others are unidentified.)

MUSEUM HISTORII FOTOGRAFII (CRACOW)

mortal enemy, as you so often boasted—was not at the head table, either. He was someone who was already very powerful indeed on that January evening. It was a mere eight months before the outbreak of the war was to relieve you of your aggravating job of trying to establish the new German State of Law and Order. Once again, as part of this valiant struggle of yours, you typically found the perfect opportunity to send the Führer your candid opinion. This time it was in the form of a tough-as-nails telegram: "Heartfelt thanks for your thoughtful wishes on the occasion of my birthday. My life is and will remain devoted to serving your cause. Heil to you, mein Führer. Your Dr. Frank."

But even this feeble message went awry, for someone at the post office—or was it you yourself?—messed it up. Anyhow, at the bottom of the glued-down strips of text there is a fragment that says, "and good your Dr. Frank." It was crossed out with pencil but must have been easily legible to the eyes of recipient Hitler. So now the poor man—scarcely had he sent you his gracious birthday message—was obliged yet again to receive a bit of nonsense from you. How did your message actually read? "Heil and good your Dr. Frank to you my Führer your Dr. Frank [sic]." Somehow or other the truth must have slipped out—you and Mother always did have a weather eye out for those "goods"— possessions and properties—and you eventually managed to scrape together quite an estate before it was all over.

The titles that went along with it were frequently the source of much pleasure for you two. How she liked being addressed as "Honorable Frau Justice Minister Dr. Frank" (did the two of you hold the same job?). It was a credit line Mother was only too willing to keep using after the war in order to get hold of some ham or bacon or good Cracow crackers. (". . . May I, together with my family, hope always to be the ever grateful and devoted servant of the gracious Frau Justice Minister. Your Franz Unterholzer.") It didn't take long before Mother was capable of concocting the most wonderful testimonials and letters of recommendation. In 1934 she wrote one for an Anna Fichtner: "I was most satisfied in every regard with her accomplishments, not only with the way she was capable of preparing formal dinners but also, when the situation called for it, with her culinary expertise in good upper-middle-class cuisine." Note, please, the typical nouveau-riche formulation. When was it, Father, that "situations" began to arise in your entertainment schedule that called for solid bourgeois cuisine? Or was the letter of reference for Fräulein Fichtner so enthusiastic because she always addressed Mother as Frau Minister? That's my suspicion, because after her signature Mother has added, "Wife of the Bavarian Minister of State." That's what I'd call dining high off the hog.

Thus did the two of you spend your days, humbly and obediently served by a people who did not wish things to be any different. Even in your Nuremberg prison cell, you still persisted in embellishing your recollections with unctuous descriptions of magnificent state visits between Hitler and Mussolini. Idiotic naval exercises put on by the Italians were something you found terrific; you refer to Mussolini's screwball harangues as being "impressive."

Yes, you were a real golden peacock in your Nazi costumes, but someone who didn't give a shit for law or order or for your persecuted fellow human beings—or for the artists and writers among them, for that matter. You who claimed to love Bavarian literature so dearly did not give a shit whether they burned those books in Bavaria or anywhere else in Germany—the works of Oskar Maria Graf, or Thomas Mann, or Lion Feuchtwanger, all those good people who would have had the right to roast you alive if they could ever have got hold of you. You and your ilk drove the spirit out of Germany; and you, you pathetic scarecrows, were all that was left. I can see you now in the Schliersee in the weeks before Christmas, striding up to the peasants who with their horses and sleighs are bringing down the great tree trunks felled in the mountains the summer before. There you are in your big felt hat pulled down over your eyes, wrapped in your beautiful tent of an overcoat, with its Mafia collar turned up. The snow is falling and you are handing out hundred-mark bills to the good folk. They still solemnly speak of it today. I don't believe a word of it. And even if it were true, your patronizing, popularity-mongering way with "the people" would have fit the situation to a tee. On the other hand, come to think of it, the picture is not complete without Mother, who surely would have been following closely behind you, sneaking up on each of the astonished peasants in turn and grabbing back the bills you had just given them.

Once, Mother did experience a brief moment of enlightenment. You will surely recall it: November 1938. You had just alighted from your private railway car at the main station in Munich, and Mother was picking you up. The Reichskristallnacht, the Crystal Night, had just taken place. She barked at you, in the presence of the chauffeur, "Hans, what is going on with the synagogues, the Jewish shops? Do you have anything to do with that?" You answered her, frightened like some innocent but suspect schoolboy, "No, Brigitte, really not. I give you my word!"

Mother was satisfied. And you, too, the President of the Academy of German Justice, the institution you had managed to establish quick as a wink in 1933, at the very beginning of things. Even then you knew the Bavarian Justice Minister's job was nothing more than a temporary expedient.

By January 4, 1935, you were again standing, with your left knee slightly bent, behind another lectern, your ring fingers cupped again as if to suffocate two breasts, your nails dug into the edge of the lectern, and bellowing one of your official harangues, this time handing the Bavarian justice system over to the Reich and into the capable hands of Dr. Gürtner. Your guest performance at the Munich Palace of Justice had lasted only twenty-one ineffectual months. After the war, whenever Mother and I would walk past that monumental structure, she would always remind me of who used to be there. It was almost as if she were about to enter and have the porter announce the arrival of the Frau Minister to Herr Minister Frank.

That "Academy" of yours was formally recognized by a proclamation of the Reich. Hitler had it established officially and issued a ceremonial document: ". . . and I hereby name you to the honorary post of President of the Academy of German Justice." Mother thereupon breathed a sigh of relief, for, honorary post or not, there was always an expense account attached to something like that.

Unfortunately, it turned out to be not much of an allowance. But to compensate for that, there soon arrived by government mail, just before Christmas 1934, at your newly rented villa on the Widenmayerstrasse, yet another billet-doux: a document naming you Minister of the Reich without Portfolio. Smiles of relief all around. The new status symbols were safe. What you had called your "battle for the Führer" had finally paid off.

What was it Nazi Minister-President Siebert telegraphed you on the occasion of your elevation to Justice Minister? It must have sounded as if he were mocking you: "May your success in establishing German justice, a universal awareness for it, and its meting out reflect the loftiest values of our new Reich!" That wish—in itself nothing more than Siebert's typical Nazi drivel—was something you managed to turn inside out. The name of your "Academy for German Justice" was naturally twisted by the citizenry quite soon into an Academy for German Injustice. And you established its home right next to the University of Munich.

"The construction of the House of German Justice was initiated today. Beginning with the very first hour of work on the edifice, the guardians of German justice, standing alongside German construction workers, send you their most sincere words of greeting and a Heil Hitler! This noble structure shall be a symbol of the ascent of our National Socialist Reich under your leadership. Heil to you, mein Führer!" That was your slimy message to Hitler,

March 1, 1937. You were thirty-six years old. It was three years after your role in the Röhm putsch, which had demonstrated your "general awareness for justice."

You wormed your way into the Führer's attention again on October 26, still concerned with that damned building. For God's sake, Father, didn't you know that Hitler had other things on his mind, like getting ready for the war, getting rid of the Jews, arranging for the return of Austria to the Reich with the help of his underhanded party comrades there—the ones who proved themselves later so perfectly equipped to be concentration camp torturers and executioners? And there you were, begging for his attention and his presence: "Mein Führer! I should once again like to send you an appeal from my heart, this time to request your presence at the consecration festivities for the Academy of German Justice in Munich. [*And it was really from the heart. Incredibly, you and all your cronies had almost a sexual feeling for Hitler. You wanted only to bathe in his glow, to be near him, to touch him, to have intimacy at any cost. It is something that has always fascinated me.*] I know very well indeed what an enormous burden of responsibility lies in your unrelenting labors for the Fatherland. [*Hey, come to your senses; you're talking about the laziest chancellor any German government ever had; you must have known that. Still, it was not in you to write, "Since you never have anything better to do, mein Führer, why don't you just heave that lard-ass of yours out of the easy chair and get yourself down here."*] If, however, there should be even the slightest possibility of your coming, then I would, in view of the fact that well over one hundred of the world's leaders in jurisprudence will be coming [*liar—very few countries were represented*] to this year's meeting of the Academy of German Justice [*the more "German" justice is, the more inhuman, no matter how you slice it*], and in view, too, of the appropriateness of this great edifice of the Academy of German Justice [*again, Father? Repetition is the soul of witlessness—Gerhart Hauptmann, your beloved writer, thought so, too: he called it suspect. But you keep on parading the name of that stupid building for the simple reason that you have nothing more to show*] to the realization of the great principles of our movement, to which it is dedicated. . . . I would deem my request justified that you, mein Führer, be present at this consecration ceremony, which will be kept as brief as possible. Heil, mein Führer! Your ever faithful and devoted Dr. Hans Frank."

The reply to your letter was brief and sullen. "Dear Herr Minister, I acknowledge the receipt of your memo of 10/26/37 to the Führer. Unfortunately, because of the many official claims on his time here in Berlin, it is not possible for the Führer to appear at the inaugural ceremony." That is all there was to it. It was signed by Widemann, Hitler's adjutant. Once again you stood empty-handed, without the Führer, in front of your construction workers in Munich. For them, your fat face wasn't enough to make up for the absence of their great leader's little moustache. In truth, you were actually never much more than a fairly tepid brew—of both the good and the evil.

Did you ever receive the blessing, the one you requested of the Führer in the telegram you sent at the start of the project? "For this new edifice to be built in solemn declaration of the justice of your Reich, I ask of you, mein Führer, your blessing."

With the nineteen murders of the Röhm putsch on your conscience, with countless others committed under your aegis at Dachau, you were still presumptuous enough to preside at the opening ceremonies of an institute ostensibly dedicated to justice. And then to have it turn out to be such a flop! On the mimeographed program for the laying of the cornerstone the full schedule appeared: "Noon: entry of the Führer. The Führer reviews the Honor Guard and the Storm Troopers . . ." and so on, then, "Fanfares to continue until the Führer and his party have arrived at the rostrum," blah blah blah—and then (especially impressive): "Minister of the Reich Dr. Frank presents the hammer to the Führer." Instead of laying down the first brick, he should have whacked your fat head. But you weren't worth even that much energy.

A Really Super
Battle for Justice

In your posthumous memoirs of 1946 you see the whole picture somewhat differently, of course. You portray yourself as a clever politician, write about how many telegrams and other communications it took to get Hitler to come to your first congress of legal experts and have him address the multitudes. And you recall your conversation just before he flew back to Berlin, thus: "As he was about to leave, he said to me, emphasizing his words by tapping his forefinger on my chest [*yes, Father, you were really so very close to him, right?*], 'Ah, yes, my dear Frank, what you have to say about law and order is all very well and good, but first we must have a strong Reich.' I said, 'Mein Führer, all great empires of the world have been strong for the very reason that they were also just.' And he looked at me earnestly, thought it over, and as he was getting into the plane, he said to me, 'Do not ever forget that in order to establish justice for sixty million people, circumstances may oblige us to be unjust to a few thousand.'" All told, your Führer miscalculated to the tune of about fifty million, the total of those who perished before 1945 was over.

Back in 1936 you already knew that your academy was a preposterous front (which fooled no one, by the way) for a state of injustice, with its Gestapo and persecution of the Jews. Well, you know what I'm talking about, don't you? Nevertheless, you still had the gall to write such hypocritical garbage as this ten years later in Nuremberg: "Work in the justice organization went on with increasingly determined energy. In opposition to our efforts, Himmler was building up his SS with the more than tacit approval of the Führer and was obtaining a greater and greater share of the power. On my side, the progressively more demanding work was forced to keep pace with no additional support. After 1933 Hitler no longer showed interest or sympathy with the work of the legal branch. He reeled himself in, jurisprudentially speaking. [*Now there is one of your really birdbrained sentences.*] At the same time, Bormann was gaining too much favor with him, and it was he who was determined to undermine my efforts. If I were to summarize my general and specific political activity in the years following 1933, the end result would be that, to the extent it was important at all, it found its source exclusively in my own initiative, was emphatically dedicated to the service of justice, and consequently, since it was in no sense a part of Hitler's overall plan, led an ephemeral existence."

Now, let me translate that for you, the way it should have been phrased, if one had been aware during its composition of one's impending death sentence and had been capable of articulating an honest confession of guilt: "After 1933, by which time Hitler no longer had to concern himself with due process and such trivia, I and my services were no longer needed. As Bavarian Minister of Justice and Reich Commissioner, I was permitted, on a short-term basis, to carry on with the insignificant job of unifying the legal code for the Reich, but to tell the truth, even that escaped my clutches. I was in my thirties and did not wish to be written off as a poor bet. For it was so wonderful to have and to enjoy those titles and status symbols. For that, I sacrificed my sense of justice."

But how do you put it? "Although they [*i.e., your initiatives*] did not lead successfully to a position of official power asserted within the Reich, the prolonged attempts to assert them despite my failures amounted to a perpetual and debilitating demand on my energies and nerves." Those are lies and nothing but lies. Without the slightest protest from your side, the Ermächtigungsgesetz—the 1933 Enabling Act of the Nazis—was easily slipped over on the nation; then the decrees bearing upon the Aryanization of the German People (in plain language, the racial—i.e., anti-Jewish—laws promulgated at Nuremberg), the expropriation decrees, and finally those exclusionary laws regarding employment in the professions and the civil service: all that went through, and without one word of protest from you. So what is all that about stress on your nerves?

Now you really begin to pour it on about how everyone was ready to cut your throat—even before the bell tolled for you at the Nuremberg gym. "The fact that I was able to persevere in those years from 1933 to 1939, I owe to my conviction that if I had given up in my battle for justice there would have been absolutely no one else there to stem the rising tide of the police state threatening our land."

So what did you do in 1939, you stemmer-of-the-tide-of-injustice? You went as Governor General into a raped country and helped like a good German to pave the way for the mass extermination of human beings. Six years later you take off the mask: "Whenever I think back to this time [1933–39], then I know that before God [*hi, you old crook up there, are you in on it, too?*] and my people [*where do you get off talking about "my people," when you did your damnedest to decimate them?*] I stand exonerated. The documentation of all that I did proves it."

All right, I'll bite. Name me a couple of documents; give me a few examples of how you put the brakes on—anything that would show that you tried to keep Hitler, Himmler, Bormann, the Gestapo, the police, the entire German nation from indulging in their ancient, inbred, eternally recurring pleasure in imprisoning, torturing, and killing people. You have nothing to say? Your ugly face is twitching down there in hellfire, is it? How about it: one little document! I shall find it wherever it may lie concealed! . . . Still

silent? No indication whatsoever that all your sentences are anything more than self-serving? Nothing, zero? Well, what more
should I have expected? For if there actually had been anything
at all to help exonerate you, you would have mentioned it; you
would have written, for example, "The documentation of all that
I did—e.g., the law against the persecution of members of non-
Aryan races, the law guaranteeing the security of those under
arrest, or the law forbidding the addition to village signposts of
such messages as 'Jews Not Welcome'—proves my innocence."
Right, or not? Yes, I am right again, aren't I? Even at Nuremberg
in 1946 you went on babbling your set speeches from the years
before, oblivious to your situation, forgetting your prison cell. You
forgot reality. You kept on lying to us as you went on writing—
even in your Latin quotations (as today's politicos like to do) you
lied to us. "As for the rest, it remains true: *Si quis tota die percurrens
venit ad vesperam satis est!** And still I am faced with my guilt."
 Stuff that guilt of yours up your ass, if the only way for you
to verbalize it is in Latin. What you did, *in reality*, during those
years was to give one speech after another, talking, talking. And
here I am, poring over this indigestible, shapeless mass of hair
balls. Here is one: "The respect for the inner laws of reality had
been lost to the epochs immediately preceding ours, and thus we
experienced the destruction of the foundation for a genuine way
of conceiving of justice as well as the foundation for a truly secure
legal system." And another one for the road: "The pervasive humanistic ideology during the Enlightenment and the nineteenth
century, invented by Jews and exploited for Jewish purposes, had
dimmed our perception of the true racial substructure of humanity
and of nations. In every respect, it had expunged the concept of
race from public, political, and legal discourse."
 Those who listened to that sort of thing did not drive you and
your bullshit from the podium; for the most part they reacted

* If he who struggles the whole day through comes at last to the evening, it is enough!

with "deafening applause." You had all the time and repose you needed to prepare yourself for those "mincemeat" and "lice" statements you were getting ready for Poland. Here, for example, is a 1934 adumbration, a sentence belted out in your best Hitlerian oratorical style: "Through the strength of our actions against the criminal element in the broadest interpretation of that word [*who is that, Father?*], above all through the ruthless carrying-out of the death sentence, the establishment of special courts, the introduction of the People's Court for the protection of Nation and State, we have achieved a disciplined control of all the inferior movements and types in our midst, and have guaranteed the security of the decent part of German society in all its breadth and depth."

That was 1934. You had another dozen years to live.

For years you and Roland Freisler edited the *Deutsche juristische Wochenschrift*, a German legal weekly. That publication was one of my first real confrontations with you—after an innocuous and unenlightened youth, during which you were not around much. As a student after the war, I used to sit in the law school seminar room in Munich and occasionally would read the forewords you allowed yourself to write for each of those fat red volumes. The more I read, the more nervous I became that other students might catch on to the fact that I was reading your stuff and that I was, in fact, your son. But I kept on, overwhelmed and appalled by your fulminations on the new and potent law for the Germanic Race, for the Germans themselves in particular, and against the Jew-infested, libertarian and libertine Roman Law.

You already had a full tank of that poisonous bile, which for me, in my days of the Third Reich, was turned into chocolate and lollipops.

My ears burned with shame whenever I read in the secret reports of the forbidden Social Democratic Party about one of your public appearances; then as before you acted the role of prosecuting attorney. One account reads: "During a speech given to young students of the law by their leader, Reichsminister Dr. Frank, the following event occurred: Frank seemed suddenly offended by the behavior of a young member of the audience and interrupted his talk with the words 'You there in the fifth row—wipe that eternal grin off your face, it makes me nervous.' And when it was clear that no one realized he had been singled out as the target of the attack, Frank came down from the podium and identified precisely who it was he meant. The student was conducted out of the hall. The audience reacted with loud shuffling of their feet"—the traditional way for students to indicate strong disapproval.

I daresay that was the last and most outspoken manifestation of disapproval in our times on the part of the German legal profession. For after that, when the students became our judges, they judged just as you wanted them to: they judged as murderers. Where is that fellow who was grinning now? Is he still alive? He must have seen through your hollow bathos; and you—admit it— you realized that he saw through you. After the event, you surely recommended that he be dealt with appropriately. Was he sent to a concentration camp?

Sometimes when I am in a somber mood I put myself in your shoes and am standing there behind a lectern and mouthing some sort of shit about racial purity, and then I see that grinning face in front of me, interrupt my talk, go from the podium down into the audience. My question to you: *How, what did you feel while you were doing that?* Imagining that I am you just before your execution is something else I have been doing ever since I was a young boy, especially during the nights up to the sixteenth of October each year. It is not hard to do; the only thing I cannot manage is kneeling in the cell; it goes against the grain. Try as I might, it will not fit the script.

And what of Mother in those years from 1933 to 1939? I picture her now: greedily bustling about, out buying dresses, having tea at the Carlton, riding with her friends in the big Mercedes, none of them dressed with quite so much ostentation as Mother. Aunt Margot told me that it was always the better part of wisdom not to try to outdo Mother in any way. I picture her as some enraged figure in a George Grosz caricature. I hear her in my mind's ear talking about you to some woman friend or other, her head tossed back with a stupid and haughty gesture, her lips pursed, saying perhaps, "Actually my husband is one of the few human beings one can say is truly overendowed by nature." She takes a sip of tea. The friend nods obediently. She might continue, "In our circle of friends and acquaintances there are only people of true substance, people who all exist on the same *niveau*, intellectually and spiritually." Mother's hand describes a plateau somewhere above her head, suggesting the lofty, Olympian level where she and her kind thrive. The friend nods again and bats her eyelashes, despite her vague discomfort foreshadowing the onset of a major stomach upset. Be that as it may, I love Mother for her hopeless, her ungodly limitations in social intercourse. Permit me to spin out the scene a bit further. She continues, "As far as my husband is concerned, nothing is too good for me. Anyone who desires a closer acquaintance with us is naturally first tested to see what sort of character and mind he has." Now her friend has begun to choke a bit on her tea and cake; it simply cannot be possible for this woman to go on talking in such an idiotic way much longer— or can it? The scene might be further embroidered. The friend takes out her fine batiste handkerchief and dabs at her lips. Mother notices everything. (You know I do not exaggerate: in matters of tact and consideration of others, Mother was an absolute clod-hopper.) "My husband," she blathers on, "is truly, in every respect, such a paragon that he is altogether justified in placing the greatest possible demand on others. Everyone who knows him idolizes him. But it is not only his—" Now Mother must stop for a moment: her friend obviously has to go to the bathroom at once, and does so. There she bathes her temples with cool water and takes a few deep breaths. She totters back to the table, pale and exhausted, says she is sorry for having had to leave so suddenly, and sits down again. Mother, oblivious to her friend's true state, continues her sentence at the very syllable where she broke off, "—his excellent character and his whole demeanor that are so outstanding in the minds of others; his intellectual qualities in general, and his legal capacities in particular, are so fantastic that everyone who knows him predicts the greatest future for him."

Mother sips her tea, leans back in her chaise longue. Her friend's legs are trembling from the rage within her—it is as if she were having an attack of gout. But she knows she is dependent on Mother's favor, that her limousine is purring out there by the curb, that the loge at the opera is in the name of Frank; so she endures. "Let me tell you that I drew the winning ticket when it came to my marriage. [*Brief, telling pause. Heart of monologue. Mother looks deep into friend's eyes. Friend twists napkin in lap nervously.*] What still most delights me is the fact that I am, truly, the right woman for my Hans. We understand each other perfectly, and he loves and honors me with such a depth of feeling that I am the object of envy everywhere." Mother has had to shout these last words after her friend, who has dashed back to the bathroom. The morsels on which she had been strangling have erupted into her mouth and are about to burst forth from her nostrils. She must escape, or die of asphyxiation. Mother stops speaking, then mutters, more to herself than to the empty seat opposite her, "And from that you will perhaps realize that my husband and I, by our very nature, are above and beyond harm from any possible gossip. We have our own world here, and within it we are immune to all such filth."

With a long and contented sigh she concludes her monologue, while back there in the bathroom, leaning over the toilet, Traude is vomiting and vomiting—vomiting up all that I have just recorded here. For, despite the pretense, I have not invented a single word of this monologue. Word for word, syllable for syllable, she wrote this to her friend Traude.

What a couple you were. Go on paddling around in that bubbling cauldron down there. The sound of the water, the sound coming from your anguished chest, pierces my brain. This evening I stretch out in my bed, comfortable as usual, ever since I let you out of me. Contentedly I contemplate my day and think, "I dealt my father some very severe blows again today."

If I had only done that twenty years earlier, I would not have become so obsessed about the date on which I finally became a day older than you were on the day you died. Stop your grumbling now, and your rage down there in Hell—naturally I understand that you, the epitome of talent, are embittered about what you did with all that talent and what you made of your life.

Remember Ines? Was she our housekeeper in the thirties, before you began your work in the Government General on decimating Poland? You know her, don't you?

Mother needed a housekeeper. And they were a dime a dozen in those days. But not just anyone would do for Mother. Being the nouveaux riches you were, there had to be a sense of personal power attached to your selection; you had to satisfy an urge to torment and to get even. And so the housekeeper had to be someone one knew from those earlier days when one still belonged to the People, when one was a secretary.

Mother cannot have been searching for long before she dug up Ines, one of her earlier girlfriends, someone who had been unlucky in marriage, gotten hold of the wrong husband. Mother must have written Ines a really insane letter, but unfortunately I do not have it; all I have is Ines's answer. Let me read you a few passages from it: "As to my continuing to use *du* [the familiar, informal mode of address] with you—it goes without saying that it is out of the question and needs no further discussion. If I did not have the proper feeling for that, as for other matters of tact and discretion, then I should hardly be the right person for the position. For this one last time, I permit myself the use of *du* in this letter."

So Mother must have written something like this to her: "And naturally, my dear Ines, it is out of the question for you to use the informal mode when addressing me from now on."

Poor Ines continues, "I shall be as tough as iron with myself and see to it that I succeed in making you satisfied with my efforts. In every instance I shall keep the interests of your household foremost in my mind. I shall aspire to guarantee your confidence in me through hard work, conscientiousness, and meticulousness. . . . I shall acquire and maintain the air of authority appropriate to my position. . . . I shall supervise the laundry well and see to it that there are no problems or difficulties with the proper care of your personal possessions and those of your husband [*at this point it must have occurred to Ines that her tone could be construed as lacking in the proper respect and being awkwardly intimate, for she quickly rephrases*]—I mean, of course, of the Herr Minister. . . . I feel more comfortable myself with simple food and shall train the household personnel to do the same, emphasizing its benefits on grounds of good health. . . . Your wardrobe shall look as if it came from Schulz or Hinzelmann, so that everywhere you go, you will always be the loveliest."

And here is the hardest sentence of all to take, Father: "I shall not be dragged down to the level of the personnel, since you have raised me up by virtue of your offer and your confidence." You'll note that I have abandoned the attempt to reconstruct what Mother must have written Ines to evoke these lines. It is more pleasant to sense the presence of a river nearby than to see it. In the same way, it is more macabre to get the general feeling of what must have been an appallingly arrogant and stupid letter than to reinvent it.

There are letters of hers, like the unknown one to Ines, that make me hate Mother the way I hate you. But Mother was better than you—she wasn't as effeminate. And you never did catch up with those five years she had on you. Is she, by any chance, in the cauldron next to yours, and are you still afraid of her frigid personality—or has she already left the fires of Purgatory and started her lift-off to Heaven? Is it even possible that you have, too? Maybe I underestimate the power of the Catholic Church.

Those priests in Koblenz, for example: together, they can pray a strong enough uppercut to lay the old Lord God out on the canvas—especially when you take into account the fact that they have been praying nonstop since 1946. Not only have they presented you with a complete indulgence, they are also good for six thousand masses celebrated and launched heavenward annually in your name. Perhaps you are already seated at the right hand of God the Father Almighty and helping to direct the new anti-Semitism, the act of German forgetfulness.

Run, Run,
You Poles and Jews—
the Franks Are Coming

Y ou have probably noticed how I have been avoiding the hardest
chapter: Poland. Well, let's get to it. No more delay.

Let me set the scene: Rivers and forests, native Polish costumes
and wooden houses, roadways deep in mud, and peasant carts,
and women in babushkas. I group them all together and evoke a
wondrous and beautiful country with its lively cities and shtetls,
great marketplaces, horse-traders, squealing pigs, buckets filled
with freshly picked cucumbers, gigantic sausages, tobacco-chewing
tradesmen, Orthodox Jews with their beards and flowing black
coats, churches filled to the rafters, and little villages in whose
midst Jewish laborers and shopkeepers live in beautiful houses
adorned with elaborate carving. In my next background projection
are the remarkably pretty walls of the Cracow ghetto, quite like
the great Arabian harem walls; Auschwitz with its endless rows of
barracks and smoking crematoria, the ramp where the sorting out
was done. (What's that? Oh, right—you kept repeating that at
Nuremberg: Auschwitz did not lie within the boundaries of the
Government General. But how pedestrian, how academic of you—
as if all those trains with all those people did not go right through
"your" GG to get there. But all right; I'll trade you fact for fact
and let you keep Maidanek, Treblinka, and Sobibor.) I project all

the images I have in my head: of the two old Jews compelled to
run through the streets of Cracow, the woman clutching her one
last suitcase in her hand; I follow that up with the two professors—
or were they rabbis?—forced to sweep the sidewalks of Cracow,
and the image of the uprooted section of streetcar track stretched
like a beam between two posts, from which, gazed upon by frightened, bewildered children and immortalized in German soldiers'
photographs for home consumption by their loved ones, there
dangles a row of freshly hanged Poles, hands tied behind them,
caps still jammed down over their ears, and among them a woman
in a skirt, plump bare arms, a young girl. . . . It's something one
shouldn't even write down, because our perverse brains twist that
into: if only it were some poor old hag, that wouldn't be so bad;
she would already have lived her life anyhow.

And then I give you the Franks and all their relatives who rode
into this land, lived there, made themselves rich, without so much
as a glance to the right or left, and above all without a glance
down to where the blood was running; who put their hands over
their ears so as not to hear the screams of pain we pressed from
the lungs of the people of this land.

"Brigitte, you are going to be the Queen of Poland!" you said
to Mother in Berlin—you were kneeling in imitation of some
imagined Shakespearean scene. How Mother loved those long silk
dressing gowns; she had one on at the time. In reply to your
fervent promise of queenship, she should have shattered your larynx
with a karate chop as you knelt there. Oh, why did we have to
wait for Hangman Woods! But there were those seven years yet
to go before he managed to put an end to your grisly work. I
would have given anything for the opportunity of talking with that
hangman. He could have told me every last little detail about your
end. Hangman Woods, he was the one I used to beg in my
childhood fantasies to put your noose around my neck, just to see
what it might feel like.

While the Germans were busily invading Poland, you approached your tasks filled with poetic ardor. You were in Potsdam
with your company at the time, a volunteer.

You had put on quite a few pounds by then. I have the "farewell
photo" in which all of you are staring into the camera, stiff as
ramrods and like a bunch of idiots—you seated in the middle, a
thirty-nine-year-old face without the trace of a wrinkle, plump
and healthy, as if your orderly had taken your head between his
thighs every morning and like the Alsatians thrust a funnel down
your throat and force-fed you with roast crown of pork, roulades
of beef in mayonnaise, rare lamb kidneys, and the fattest mutton
imaginable.

I believe it was even before the clarion call of Hitler reached
your ears that you had already composed your "Song of the Germans at the Lowering of the Polish Flag in the Land of the Vistula,
1939":

> *So holen wir die Flagge nieder*
> *Wie stolz und hoch sie auch geweht—*
> *Und Freiheit zeigt sich fröhlich wieder,*
> *Denn alle Tyrannei vergeht—*
>
> *Vergeht wie trüber Stürme Brausen—*
> *Verklingt wie heulend Ungestüm,*
> *Verbrennt wie zehrend Flammen Sausen,*
> *Verweht wie raubend Ungetüm:*
>
> *Doch richtet sich empor zum Licht*
> *Was stumm getreten freudlos war,*
> *Denn aller Schmerz sich nun verbricht*
> *Und herrlich Hoffen wird jetzt klar:*
>
> *Nie wieder wollen wir zu Sklaven werden—*
> *Nie wieder beugen uns dem trügend Gaukeltreiben,*

Nie wieder dulden, Daβ auf deutscher Erden
*Die deutschen Herzen sollen Opfer bleiben!**

Did you plan on reciting these immortal lines to Hitler on the occasion of your appointment as Governor General? Was Himmler standing there next to him, impressed with your literary talent? Did Hitler nervously motion for you to stop—seeing that you rhymed about as well as he painted? Did Himmler, every inch the German humanist, counter with a quick six-liner:

> *Eins, Zwei, drei, die Polenlümmel*
> *Schick ich alle in den Himmel,*
> *Auch die Juden und Ukrainer,*
> *Nein, da überlebt mir keiner.*
> *Und wer hilft mir, Gott sei dank?*
> *Unser Reichsminister Frank.†*

Then in your mutually infectious hilarity you all slapped your leather breeches. It must have gone something like that, right? Or was the setting different? Were you maybe sitting in your automobile on the way to Cracow, deeply worried about how you were going to summon the firm technocratic fist you needed in order to rule these Poles? And for a bit of relaxation you composed your song about the land of the Vistula?

---

* "Behold, we lower the flag now, no matter how proud and high above it may once have waved. And Freedom shows its happy face again, for all tyranny comes to an end. It disappears like the roar of sullen storms, echoes away like violent howls, burns away like the crackle of consuming flames, blows away like the husk of the ravening monster. For everything that was once downtrodden in joyless bondage is now resurrected in the light. The chain of woe is broken, and glorious hope comes clear: Never again shall we endure slavery, never again bow down to deceitful trickery, never again suffer German hearts to be victims on German soil!"

† "One, two, three, the Polack rabble / I shall send straight to Heaven, / And also the Jews and Ukrainians, / Not a one shall outlive me. / And who's the one to help me out in this? Thank God, / Our Reichsminister Frank."

Or was it more likely that instead of being worried, your heart was singing for joy? For what Hitler had announced on October 12, 1939, made a powerful man of you (at least on paper): "In order to restore and maintain public order in the occupied Polish territories, I issue the following decrees: §1. All Polish territories occupied by German troops, to the extent that they have not been absorbed into the German Reich proper, are to be placed under the command of the Governor General for the Occupied Polish Territories. §2. I appoint Minister of the Reich Dr. Frank to the post of Governor General for Occupied Polish Territories. [*Run, you Poles—run for your lives! And you Jews, too! The Franks are coming, the Himmlers, the Wehrmacht, an army of murderers, greedy people, greedy for lives, greedy for loot. Run! . . . But no, Father, they wouldn't run; they stayed. It was not long after this that Mother could shout with glee: "I declare, no one makes more beautiful camisoles than the Jews in the ghetto!"*] . . . §3. The Governor General reports directly to me. All branches of administration are under the direct command of the Governor General."

Despite this unequivocal language, Hitler permitted all sorts of other governing and administrative offices of the Reich to have a finger in this pie. Here, too, he made a total chaos of the chain of command and the system of jurisprudence. But even with all those loopholes open to you, you never took the opportunity to get out from under the whole mess.

It is not exactly known what prompted Hitler to appoint you Governor General. I believe he did it because he knew what a sycophantic character you were. He knew that you were drooling for recognition and that consequently you would go along with anything that came out of Berlin in the form of an order.

After making Mother the new Queen of Poland, you must have ridden off to the East in high dudgeon. In your mind's eye you saw dreadful deeds being committed in your new territory. You saw your little Polacks peppering your game animals with buckshot from dawn to dusk. You saw them pursuing beavers and marmots in endless drives and shouting at the top of their lungs. You saw them criminally ignoring the sanctity of the border at the Danzig Corridor. No wonder, Father, that Warsaw's army had been neglecting its real job and was thus incapable of putting up much resistance against the German Army.

Nor was it any wonder that as early as December 1939 you put your signature to this beautiful new law: "§1. With regard to the regulation of hunting in this territory, we proclaim the validity of German rules as practiced within the Reich. The goal is to be the maintenance and cultivation of a rich and healthy variety of game to accord with the demands of responsible agriculture and forestry. §2. It is forbidden (1) to shoot at hoofed game with buckshot or with coarse lead shot, (2) to use steel traps, self-firing devices, or nighttime lures of any kind or sort whatsoever, (3) to poison game. §3. In the interest of maintaining the present population of game animals, the hunting of the following is to cease immediately and entirely: (1) hoofed game of all sorts (with the exception of the black deer), (2) beavers, (3) marmots."

Since Hitler did not want to have Warsaw as the Government General's capital, you took a look around Cracow and its Wawel fortress to see how they might do. Then you said, inverting the meaning of the first words of the Polish national anthem ("Poland is not yet lost") by deleting the modifiers of the verb: "Gentlemen, Poland is lost!" Whereupon, as always when you used such grandiloquent and gutsy language, loud applause was to be heard.

Someone else was also on his way to the eastern territories at this same time: Friedrich-Wilhelm Krüger, a man from Himmler's SS staff. He was supposed to become your upper-echelon Chief of Police, East. Krüger, slender and with a far more Nordic look about him, was infinitely superior to you. Yes, I know, he did have the SS behind him as his source of power. And if you were to look at him very closely—aside from any problem about morals—it could not have escaped your notice that Krüger was just as much of a weasely little Nazi as you were. His eyes, too, were filled with that passion for murder that comes from cowardice. Himmler once said about Krüger, after getting rid of him on the telephone by simply hanging up in the middle of a conversation: "If I am forever going to be bleated at by these office-manager and division-leader types with all that pathetic old crap of theirs, I'll never get any proper work done!" Isn't that wonderfully put, Father? The "proper work" had to do with the extermination of human beings—and you, as you loved to let everyone know, supported this "proper work" with heartfelt fervor.

In order for Krüger to get even a general idea of where you were to be found, you sent a map to Berlin on which you sketched for him the precise outlines of the newly annexed territory, where it all was located, and so on—otherwise the poor boy probably would have begun making mistakes with his first efforts at murder and started shooting in Brandenburg or somewhere like that.

In the letter of appointment to him that you enclosed with the map (where, by the way, I count eighteen instances within forty lines of "I," "me," "my," "mine") you are at pains to establish a decisive and forceful tone designed to show who's boss. It corresponds perfectly to your idiotically overblown letterhead, which reads, "The Executive Head of Administration," and below that and somewhat smaller, but still in letters more appropriate to a billboard, "For the Civil Government of All Occupied and Formerly Polish Territories Under the Supreme Commander, East."

You write Krüger: "Any absence from your post likely to last more than three times twenty-four hours is to be reported immediately and directly to me." And then there is a fine sentence that asserts your instantaneous and gratifying metamorphosis into "King Stanislaus of Poland." (That's what Göring called you on some later occasion, to Mother's immense and lasting delight.) "To facilitate our continuing personal contact, I am at your disposal at any time." There would be nothing unusual in that if that were the way the sentence had been left. But you carefully inserted a few words so that it then read, "at any time convenient to me." In other words, you made sure he knew that you were someone to be reckoned with.

And so you took possession of the Cracow Castle on the Wawel. From there you wrote Mother ecstatically, "The castle is fabulous. You should see all the gold leaf around the windows, in all the rooms, the treasures here—magnificent."

You were the King.

You arrived in somewhat tattered condition, to be sure, sartorially speaking, so that in December 1939 you felt obliged to spruce up your wardrobe at the expense of the government, which is to say, of the Polish people. Dress shirts, half a dozen each, in white, silver, gray, and brown, at 7.80 marks each, were soon delivered, together with 156 meters of dress-shirt material and (your passion for raw action broke through here) 42 meters of pajama material at 42 marks.

I can still see you in your castle bathroom. You had them install a tub for you there big enough for short walks. It had—the height of luxury to my childish mind—a side door in it. Its dimensions could have accommodated any given threesome, to say the least: e.g., Krüger, Himmler, and you. And you could have had a really crazy time there with all that space. I see you entering the bathroom, taking off your pajama top. It's one of the pictures of you I shall carry with me until I die. And yet the image did not begin to fascinate me until quite recently, when I suddenly realized that it is the sole recollection of the one normal, daily routine I experienced with you.

You would be standing there in silence. I would be standing there, too. You would be shaving. And I would pretend that you cheerfully plopped a little gob of shaving cream on my nose.

"Fifty bars of chocolate @ 0.50 pfennigs." That shows you were acutely aware of being in a land populated by inferior human beings. I see you ambling down from the castle hill and, like the colonial masters of old, bending over to offer your little Polish subjects a piece of chocolate in your outstretched hand and beckoning them enticingly with your "chick chick chick chick."

That's the way it was, correct? If so, then your success in requisitioning the chocolate, the great bolts of pajama and shirt fabric, must have been your first attempts to see just how easy it might be to enrich yourself as a "Reichsnebenlandstaatsoberhaupt"—i.e., the big boss-man of a state bordering on the Reich. It was also part of a test to see how easy it might be for you to get a substantial part of the loot to your family in Bavaria.

That makes you splash around in your cauldron, doesn't it? But never you mind. I must continue.

I can see you as a human sausage: several brand-new dress shirts pulled on over a few layers of pajamas, lumbering down the castle corridors, chewing on a mouthful of chocolate. Some picture, eh? Anyhow, I like it. As you lumber along, it's increasingly evident to you that the castle is lacking in art treasures, at least compared with the masses of them you dream about in your connoisseur's greedy imagination. Since you have recently learned that Göring has begun to send his Dr. Mühlmann on a treasure hunt through occupied Poland and has already confiscated one piece of art after another, your challenged greed knows no bounds. You devise an amazing political trick and, presto-change-o, you have turned Dr. Mühlmann into your art procurer, too, so that henceforth the man has two gaping maws to fill at the same time. Mühlmann was one of those elite gents who seemed to us Germans and Austrians suspiciously, and too frequently, successful in his career: Ph.D., sometimes museum director, super-educated, hypersensitized to the fine things of the world, with the perfect knack for sniffing out the choicest. This connoisseur of Western art set out as rapist in a raped land. Soon he filled your rooms and halls with the best of the best.

Your favorite piece of booty was the so-called Beautiful Madonna of the sixteenth century, a masterfully carved wooden statue. There you were, face to face with the Virgin Mary, at the Wawel Castle in Cracow, in the music room, in a place of honor behind the grand piano. What can Mary have thought? Shortly before her rape she was probably looking into the eyes of devout Poles, people desperately beseeching her for protection against the German invaders, praying for their very survival. Now she was looking into your full-moon face, where not a feature, not a wrinkle, indicated that a life had been lived. Didn't the Beautiful Madonna have to vomit at the sight of you? Didn't a morning arrive soon enough when you had to begin the secret routine of wiping away the traces of her disgust? When the German program of human extermination had become a horror to every soul in Heaven, you furtively had to begin wiping away little traces of nausea and revulsion gathered at her tiny feet.

There was another triumph to make you proud right up to the day you were hanged, the fact that you had put under your personal protection the famous Black Madonna of Czestochowa. Yes, you were one of those for whom human existence was nothing compared to the ecstasy you found in religion—even in the contemplation of art. That is a facet of your inner life I can never begin to fathom.

As Herr Frank did, so also did his noble retinue. The Government General became a borderland polluted with swindlers and black marketeers, of bloodsuckers and also, naturally, of murderers and executioners—for that is what happens wherever we Germans go. And that, Father, is all documented; you can't wriggle out of that. Or were your intentions quite opposed to all that? Were you, yet again, under pressure and stress? Did it come from Mother? Did it work something like this: How was Mother supposed to tell a Jew from someone else? Not all of them were Orthodox, right? And so how was she to find out which ones made the camisoles? To help out, you issued a decree that beginning on December 1, 1939, all Jews ten years old and up were to wear on the right sleeve of both their indoor and outdoor clothing a white stripe at least ten centimeters wide with the Star of David on it. And because Mother wanted a demonstration of their sartorial talents, each Jew had to produce his or her own stripe with a star.

Mother was now satisfied—except for the fact that the Jews were still running around wild in the Polish territories, and so walls had to be erected to keep them in. Ghettos had to be created so that Mother could have all her tailors in one place. In spite of your valiant efforts, you still weren't happy to have Mother with you in Poland. To tell the truth, what you really wanted to create up there in your Wawel Castle, with its lofty ceilings and its spooky royal tombs, was a fabulous love nest. So you got hold of a whole bevy of female "artists," and then it was grab-ass everywhere. Too tasteless? Yes, too tasteless. Believe me, I horrify myself with some of the sentences I'm writing—but where are the tasteful ones of yours to emulate?

We had a dog named Tommy. You loved animals, with that special German type of love that prefers to slaughter humans rather than sheep. With the righteous indignation of the stolid burgher, you issued this statement: "In any territory under German rule all acts whose purpose is to torment animals of any kind is an impossibility." What peculiar sort of legal text is that, this decree of October 26, 1939? It continues: "And therefore I forbid immediately all so-called *schächten*, i.e., the torturing-to-death through bloodletting of animals, whose purpose is the consumption of so-called kosher meat." That royal "I" is something you borrowed directly from Hitler's decrees, by the way.

As soon as you installed yourself in the castle at Cracow you must have gone to the parapet and gazed far down into the land below; you must have taken a deep breath and inspired yourself with your new role as lord over all the Poles and Jews. You knew what was going on. Though you claimed to have first learned with amazement certain facts at the Nuremberg trials, you betrayed yourself in paragraph 5 of this *schächten* ordinance with unequivocal language and with your very own signature appended to it: "Sen-

tencing [for infringement of this statute] may stipulate imprisonment in concentration camps."

On the other hand, your sentence concerning how the Germans
were to deal with the Poles themselves is so full of empathy. It is
couched in informal, almost cozy German, reflecting the informal,
cozy session where you administrators gathered to hear your formulation: "The very fact that we have taken every possible step
toward assuring the positive development of the Polish people
obliged us to take them under our wing. We must feed them,
clothe them, secure their personal property, and reassure them
with the prospect that if they behave well they will have nothing
to fear."

Oh, those incorrigibly naughty Polish boys and girls—right,
Father? Even your Executive Chief of Police, Krüger, must have
seen the situation in the same light when he issued his document
setting forth the conditions for exportation of Jews for forced
labor. It seems that at first he was all for the cautious civilizing
of those mischievous rascals: "The length of term for compulsory
labor will average two years; it will be extended, however, if within
that period its pedagogical aims have not been fulfilled." Later on,
when it was obvious that the Jews simply would not learn and
were so terribly rebellious, you had to send them to the gas
chambers; that was all there was to it. According to the little
saying you devised for the occasion, whoever refuses to listen must
take a deep breath.

Now that you had saved Tommy from the Jewish butchers, you
were left with an insidious and creeping problem. To satisfy your
new role as monarch you could not allow yourself to lose too
many of your subjects—for what would be the point of your
standing up there at the parapets of your castle, chest swelling
with pride, propping yourself up against the railing, another con-
quest, gazing out in every direction over the roofs of St. Mary's
Cathedral and the clothiers' guildhalls, if there were nobody down
below to gaze up in awe at you? Why else bother to do that, if

all you could hear were firing squads, if all you could see were piles of corpses? It is true that your least favorite view was to the south. You had, oh, such sensitive eyes, so maybe they were unable to bear the sight of the concentration camp at Plaszow in the far distance, or of the Cracow ghetto much nearer.

Unfortunately your conjunctivitis (remember how dramatic you were about it?) obliged you to wear dark glasses while you were sitting in the dock at the Nuremberg trial. But isn't it time to admit that all you were really up to was trying to be incognito, like some Mafia killer? For at the start of the trial you were actually counting on acquittal. Himmler was dead, Krüger presumably dead—you still thought you could wriggle out of it.

Your first legal texts composed for the GG show that experience had taught you something. Ever since your first murders, of Röhm and the SA boys, there was something constantly tucked in the back of your head that the SS had wised you up to: be sure to arrange it so there is enough daylight left for accurate shooting. So you introduced daylight saving time in the GG. That way there was good hunting well into the evening hours. That must have been your reason? Naturally I'm not talking about the hunting of animals; with the full weight of your office behind your decrees, you had already seen to their protection. I'm talking about human game. Those you left alive for whatever reason were nothing more than vermin, as far as you were concerned. At an administrative session in January 1940 you were quoted as saying, "My relationship to the Poles is that of the ant to the aphid. Whenever I seem to be furthering the cause of a Pole, giving him a friendly tickle, so to speak, it is done solely with the expectation that the fruits of his labor will be of benefit to me."

Understandably you were embittered when you heard a saying, put in the form of an elliptical question, that was soon making the rounds of the GG: "Frank, or free?" people would ask each other, and then answer with a long drawn-out groan filled with both profound longing and the fear of death: "Freeee."

You really did deserve a congratulatory telegram from the beavers and marmots, too. After all, you saw to it that no one was allowed to touch a hair of their hides. Bravo for the great German victory of wildlife protection in the Occupied Territories.

The animals came down on the side of "Frank"; for them that was the same as "free." The judges at Nuremberg should have appreciated that more than they seemed to, right? Decree Number 9, signed in your hand, placed the entire realm that comprised the GG (96,559 square kilometers) at the animals' disposal. The rigorously protected critters multiplied like crazy. Hitler, still ecstatic about your Vistula song, found it in his heart to attack Russia in order to enlarge your zoo for the benefit of the marmots by adding Soviet-occupied Galicia to it. Now your, and the little animals', Reich embraced 142,114 square kilometers. What a triumphal entry that was when you entered Lvov, or Lemberg, as we still called it then.

And whom did you appoint as Governor there? None other, of course, than the blond rascal, your bosom friend, my Daddy Number 2, Lasch, who had been Governor until then in the district of Radom. It was Lasch's principal task in Galicia to guarantee more unrestricted room for the wildlife; and thus, in order to remove all obstacles to their fruitful multiplication, it was up to his office to pack and send off to the West whatever might stand in their way, such as: Oriental carpets, Gobelins, choice pieces of furniture, clocks, vitrines, jewelry. (Yes, you were quite right—what Polish beaver has ever been seen swimming around wearing a necklace, anyhow?) Some few trinkets must have fallen by the wayside for us. Right after eastern Galicia was added to your beloved Reichsnebenland, a splendiferous new glitter emanated from Mother. Besides that, her behavior also took on a restless character. No, not because of Lilly—not yet. It was more like a sort of heightened avarice, and it imparted to her a new and lively jauntiness. She was lusting after furs.

It was harder for me to read emotions in your face than in

Mother's because yours was so plump and characterless. But one thing that does stick in my memory about you is the total absurdity of your poses. Once, when I arrived at Kressendorf, you were standing at the top of the outside staircase. I felt as if I were climbing up toward some famous portrait of Louis XIV. Mother was next to me. I could feel her anger. You did not descend to meet her—that's not what royalty is in the habit of doing. Instead, you greeted her at the top of the stairs; me too. All around us we heard the clomping and patter of your retinue, the feet of the "Ladies and Gentlemen of the Entourage," as they were known.

They all stuck around—until your arrest, that is. Then they vanished for good.

Breathing
Good German Air

Seventeen million subjects in your inventory, most of them still alive, at least when you first took over. But the exact number of souls was hard to keep track of, because the transport of Jews from all over Europe was cause for statistical confusion, though it was true that most of them were bound for Auschwitz. Auschwitz—yes, yes, I hear your whimpering, Waldheim-like objections—was not part of the Government General.

In any case, you thought of the GG as your land of milk and honey. Little did you realize that a storm was beginning to brew over your pomaded head.

Himmler wrote a letter of complaint to his lethargic friend and ex-colleague Krüger in which he "quite candidly wish[es] to express the serious reservations [he has] about your behavior." He takes him fairly bitterly to task about his failure to perform, and adds: "In personal terms I have a high regard for you. But in the interest of the Schutzstaffel [the SS] and of the whole enterprise, I shall not stand idly by as a witness to any further deterioration of the situation. Instead I shall intervene with an iron fist."

That must have scared the shit out of Krüger. For the first time he took a good look around the GG and, with your backing, he— the Höhere Polizeiführer Ost—and his SS men commenced their extermination of the "subhuman creatures," whether Jew or Pole.

They did not need to worry about further deliveries of matériel to the Reich. On the contrary, the GG was overflowing with victims sent in on the Jewish transport trains. Thanks to our victories on all fronts, we Aryans could slaughter without pause. You wanted to put a stop to it. The rifle barrels were too hot, and waiting for the victims to starve to death took much too long. You succeeded. Without your express permission no further transports were permitted to enter the GG. For a moment it seems that I might actually be defending you.

But what did you do then? Your mouth stuffed full of chocolate, you mounted to the lofty Wawel ramparts, and behold!—down below was a sight degrading to the German soul. The countryside is still swarming with Jews. The noble Wehrmacht generals pointed that out to you and then gave you a piece of their mind. Result: at a meeting of division chiefs on April 12, 1940, you announced, "It can no longer be endured for our generals to have to live in houses where the only other lodgers, besides the generals themselves, are human vermin, i.e., Jews." And how right you were, Father. Such a mixed household could only cause a terrible upset in the daily slaughtering schedule of a busy German general. Just imagine his feelings if on his way to work in the morning he should happen to meet up with a Jew in the hallway—and especially if the Jew wouldn't stand aside and let him out the door first. Nor should any of your officials, you added, have to put up with such a situation. "In the long run, this state of affairs is insufferable!" With no trouble at all, you were able to add the final and telling touch to my scenario in the hallway: "If the authority of the National Socialist Reich is to be upheld, then it is out of the question for its representatives to be compelled to encounter Jews while entering or leaving buildings, for them to run the risk of contracting some disease!" On your knees in the evening, reciting the Lord's Prayer, you surely wished to make that clear to the Beautiful Madonna, too. She must have understood the problem— how could she possibly imagine our carrying out a successful attack on the Russians under the command of a pack of generals covered with pus and open sores and with slimy snot running constantly out of their noses? But what was her answer? She vomited, that good Jewish woman.

"Therefore it is my intention that the city of Cracow, if possible by November 1 at the latest, be emptied of Jews." You went on babbling more of the same, but it must suddenly have occurred to you that you would be needing workers for the installation of your new bathroom, and so you swiftly added: "To be quite precise, there should remain in Cracow no more than the five to ten thousand Jews necessary for the labor force."

As for the rest, you concluded decisively, employing another of your dishonest superlatives—as for the rest, the city of Cracow "must become the most *judenrein* city, the city cleanest of Jews, in all the Government General."

Then you studied your clean and polished fingernails, as the gentlemen of your administration hung on your every word. Surely you had some swift and cleansing final remark to add, namely, what was to happen to the ghettos once they were "cleaned" of Jews. "The ghetto will then be disinfected and it will prove feasible to erect healthy German housing there where one can breathe good German air."

Technically that would have proved to be very difficult, Father. Did you intend to set up pumping stations over the border into the pre-1937 Old Reich and send genuine German air through mile-long pipes into the GG? Or is air automatically "German" when it is inhaled and exhaled by German lungs, no matter where? But what about the Polish air surrounding the Germanized ghetto? That problem is something you must have been considering, for quick as a wink you added to your sentence about German air: "What we are going to do about the Polish population is a question to be addressed at a later time. For the present they are to remain here." Whereupon you took a deep breath—unfortunately of polluted Polish air.

These quotations are all straight from the record. They were taken down, at your express orders, by two stenographers who, like Rosencrantz and Guildenstern, were expected to immortalize your appearances on the stage of history. But they must have been overcome by the Great Yawn caused by your endless sermonizing; in any case, your Nuremberg lawyer, Seidl, was at pains to prove that these stenographers were hardly ever present at your administrative sessions, that they made most of it up out of whole cloth based on secondhand testimony, and that what actually was said was completely different from their faulty record.

So I'll try to go along with that, Father. As your son, it must be my sacred obligation to search out the truth about you, whatever it might be. Let me take one of your most pregnant sentences, allegedly uttered at a cabinet session: "Once we have won the war, then for all I care you can make mincemeat out of the Poles and the Ukrainians and anything else hanging around here." For the sake of the Beautiful Madonna, for the sake of your son, you can never have said such a thing. Not you, not the Chopin idolizer, not the friend of Richard Strauss.

All right, let us suppose that once again the stenographers were not there and that this sentence was actually never uttered, not in so many words. Instead, one of your officials had just been speaking of the physical condition of the Poles and Ukrainians. Your mind was wandering, and so you asked him, "What are you having for lunch today?" That confused the official, so he asked in return, "Do you mean, Herr Governor General, what sort of food rations are we giving the Ukrainians and Poles?" You realized your mistake and said, "Yes, yes, of course, that's what I meant to ask. How very fond I am of them, my ethnic groups. How concerned I am that we get them through this war. Once we have won it, then everything will be better." Then your mind wandered off again, because you had put yourself on a strict diet, and you asked the official, "You aren't having mincemeat for lunch, by any chance?" Now he was slightly miffed at you; and because he happened to be going through a crisis in his marriage at the time, he retorted with an unseemly lack of respect for your person, "I don't give a damn if she has made mincemeat for lunch or not—in fact, I don't even know where she is or what she's up to!"

That got you confused all over again, but you dropped the subject. You did notice, however, that neither of the two stenographers, Gnauk and Mohr, was present at the meeting, and so you said, "I couldn't care less what happens professionally to Gnauk and Mohr after the war!" and went petulantly up to your ramparts to eat chocolate. The two stenographers, it turns out, had been playing a terrific game of pinochle with two SS guards all the while; afterwards they happened to ask one of the gentlemen present at your meeting what had gone on. He hadn't been paying any attention and all he could report was, "Well, I think they were talking about how to grind mincemeat for meatballs and what the Ukrainians and Poles were going to do after the war and what Dr. Bierkamp's wife was up to." That was enough material for Gnauk and Mohr, and by adding a little bit of ill will to the brew, they quickly concocted this terrible sentence, leaving out the business about Frau Bierkamp because they felt sorry for her husband. Yes, that must have been how it came about.

Or possibly, Father, just between the two of us, didn't the two of them, even if they weren't present at the time, know your crude way of talking so well that they didn't even have to be there to get your thoughts and words down verbatim?

You see, nothing can make us deviate from the truth. You said the sentence about the mincemeat, and that is that. You were fully conscious and aware. No brain tumor was clouding your thought processes. Seidl's theory about the absence of the stenographers was not enough to save you from having your third cervical vertebra snapped, so that more sentences like this one were left dangling on that rope with you; one, for example, that so touchingly reflects your eternal battle on behalf of the human rights of all peoples: "As for the rest, we are not in the least concerned with the welfare of this land. Our sole concern is the establishment of German authority in this area. We are thinking here in imperial terms and in the grandest style known to the history of mankind. The Polish people must be made to feel that we are not here to establish a system of justice for them." In that, Father, you truly lived up to your word and most gratifyingly turned your thoughts into action. So stop being so ungracious and putting the blame on those two stenographers.

The following sentence, too, is now part of your life—as it is of mine. "We must not be squeamish when we hear of seventeen thousand Poles executed. I have not been afraid to declare that for every German killed, up to one hundred Poles will be taken out and shot."

Another quotation of yours about the starving Poles (it was recorded at the time of one of the many diets you underwent in order not to get too fat for your uniforms) is nothing less than a stroke of genius. You work a marvelous contrapuntal element into this sentence. For one daring moment the listener is made to think you are leading him in an unexpectedly pro-Polish direction, until all at once its refined element of destruction becomes clear: "The majority of Poles consume only about six hundred calories per day. The population is by now so debilitated that it becomes an easy prey for typhus. [*Here it comes:*] We may further decrease the diet of the Polish peasant only to the point just short of where he is no longer fit for manual labor!"

There are people in Germany today who do not object to these sentences of yours, who claim that you said them only when Krüger or someone else from the SS was in the room at the time—someone you thought might have spilled the beans to Himmler, that mortal enemy of yours, as you loved to boast. And there are also people today in this country of ours who are still gushing about what a good-natured, charming man you were, full of wit and bon mots, whose very "personality" was proof enough that he could never have uttered such terrible things. You are not going to get away with that, not with me. I compare such sycophantic bleating over you with the exoneration of a certain type of brutal child rapist on the grounds that while the perpetrator was committing the act, he was smiling. And incidentally, such justifications of your behavior are not totally without an element of self-interest: the gentlemen of your retinue who managed to have survived past 1945 could hardly be expected to admit now that they had been associated with a murderer—you, the murderer who begged the tribunal for mercy on the grounds that he had been a "head of state."

Why didn't you pull your rank on January 2, 1943, after the attack on the police station in Zarnowiec? Seven Polish policemen were on duty at the time when the precinct was attacked by twenty members of the Polish Underground. The police surrendered after the first grenade was tossed. The insurgents didn't bother their countrymen, but for you and your accomplices they left behind the following outrageous receipt: "We acknowledge receipt of the requisitioned sum of 213 zlotys from the precinct station in Zarnowiec, 6 carbines, 3 revolvers, 3 rubber truncheons. The money will be put to good use in the battle against our enemy-occupiers." It was signed, "The Leadership of the Partisan Group." Such incredible insolence, eh?

That must have sent Krüger into a terrific rage; he put the policemen through an intensive interrogation and organized a manhunt for the insurgents. After all, such appalling mockery cannot go unpunished, especially if it is Germans who are its target.

But the perpetrators escaped. Five days later, a murderer in German uniform named Hochwald sent this telegram to Himmler: "In pursuance of our orders, the police officers at the Zarnowiec precinct were summarily court-martialed and executed on 1/7/43. All members of their families have been deported to a concentration camp."

That's the way things were done.

At the same time you were yakking about the spirit of unity in your administration, you were also going along with the mass executions of Poles and Jews under Himmler's boys. Krüger and Globocnic [Himmler's deputy in charge of the extermination of the Jews of Poland] carried out their task as if they were in training for some great German sports competition and wanted all the blue ribbons. The Tribunal at Nuremberg determined that you had been a willing accomplice, and a cowardly one at that. Surely, somewhere in the primal nucleus of your being (I use your own language so that you can understand what I am trying to say) there must have flickered now and then some residual sense of justice which you were desperately trying to extinguish. And how did you do that? By eating great masses of chocolate?

You suppressed, or tried to, the fact that Krüger ordered one hundred Poles shot to death in reprisal for the killing of an ethnic German family in Lublin. Thanks to your having introduced day-light saving time to the GG, the light must have been just perfect for picking off all the women and children with a single shot apiece—at least the records indicate that no cries of pain were heard afterward.

You, however, had not been previously informed of the action. That pissed you off, and so you launched a furious verbal attack on Krüger for his arranging this act of "atonement" for the victims. He, that old tattletale, informed Himmler of your reaction, and Himmler decided to give you a real chewing-out. He was unable, however, to reach you by telephone at your castle in Cracow. Instead, he got hold of Seyss-Inquart, who was still your staff representative there. (He was another one who had the ultimate privilege of looking into Hangman Woods's eyes in 1946.) But he was not to be at your disposal much longer—he had so little to do in the GG that Hitler was obliged to take over the Netherlands to give him something to keep himself busy with. In any event, Seyss-Inquart didn't know anything about anything; he had prob- ably confused the rifle shots with popping champagne corks, per- suaded that the Poles were still celebrating the German takeover.

He told Himmler the entire thing was your responsibility, then managed to get hold of you in Berlin by phone, and afterwards wrote the Führer a most obsequious letter in which he detailed verbatim your comments during that telephone conversation.

What you were doing all this while was fucking your ex-fiancée, Gertrude, at the Kaiserhof Hotel in Berlin. Yes, Father, writhe around down there . . . just as I am up here, recounting all this garbage. Try to recall that phone conversation. I found this transcript of it in the archives. (And at the same time, try to remember how you shouted that sensitive statement of yours into Mother's face, telling her that Gertrude and Lilly sufficed now for your "physical needs," that there was therefore no longer any reason for you to lust after her when it came to sex.)

Seyss-Inquart said to you on the phone: "An ethnic German family was murdered in Lublin. In reprisal, appropriate measures were taken. Krüger informed the Führer that you took him bitterly to task for having done that."

Now it was your turn for a quick reply. It must have dawned on you that those Cracow-to-Berlin phone calls were expensive, and besides, you shouldn't tie up the lines: some war or other was in progress. So you managed to sit half-upright in bed, removed your thigh from Gertrude's thigh, scratched your head through your pomaded hair, and came to the rapid conclusion that a face-to-face meeting with Himmler was in the cards, no matter how you cut the deck. (To this day, people are awed by your lightning-fast and prodigious gift for assessing the facts.) You took the position once again of not having been aware of any of this—you, the great "head of state." And so you said: "I haven't even discussed this matter with Krüger! . . . Gertrude, cut that out! [*Seyss must have deleted these words from the transcript; that at least is my contention.*] . . . Krüger and Zörner [Nazi governor of the Lublin region of Poland] weren't with me until yesterday, and that was the first time Krüger even reported on the matter. Of course, Globocnic has already given you his report on it."

Now it was Seyss's turn again, and he used the occasion to refer also to his leaving his post with you and going to the Netherlands. Naturally, you construed his irony as sincerity: "I'm going to Holland to take up a mere *job*. You, Herr Governor General, have a *mission* to fulfill here!" Such flattery went down your fat throat as easy as one, two, three. True, he had called you "*Sie*" on the phone after you had used the "*du*." But all of you Nazis always said "*Sie*" in public anyhow (just as Mother's former friends were expected to address her)—if you hadn't, it would have made it obvious to anyone listening that the whole crooked bunch of you were thick as thieves. After a word from you, Seyss resumed: "*Jawohl*, that was in Radom. I gave Globocnic the order to apply the strictest possible disciplinary measures, following the precedent of Kamiena." I don't know exactly what was implied by the term "Kamiena," but at a rough guess I would bet it was equivalent to two hundred dead Poles.

Seyss waited for a reply. You kept silent, presumably in anticipation of the very next moment, when you could finally have said, "Now listen to me, Seyss! Tell that shit Himmler that I'm going to kick Krüger's ass out of here and put an end to this whole murderous regime!" But the moment passed you by. Nothing, it seemed—and especially not Himmler—was going to spoil your fun with Gertrude's hot little body on that May afternoon in 1940 at 4:15 in the afternoon. So you said: "I am in complete agreement. It's all fine with me; just deal with the matter." I must reproach you once again for your imprecision, Father. To be truthful about it, you should have said "bodies," not "matter." You meant, "Just deal with the bodies," didn't you?

Aside from these minor annoyances, 1940 was a splendid year for you.

"You Can Get the Prettiest Camisoles in the World in the Ghetto"

You had even better luck that year with the deposits you were able to make to your private account at the Merck and Finck Bank in Munich: 5,200 marks on September 12, 1940, for example. And why not? Obviously it was easier for you to put a little extra aside now. You didn't even have to pay for your breakfasts at the castle—or for anything else, in fact. A week later your bosom buddy the Bavarian Minister-President Siebert, under whom you had been Minister of Justice, sent you a present in gratitude (gratitude for what, I wonder) of twenty-five bottles each of 1937 vintage Dürkheimer Schenkelöl Spätlese, Dürkheimer Nonnengarten, and Dürkheimer Michelsberg Auslese. They were obviously most welcome. That inferior race of Poles never had been able to develop a decent viniculture—in fact, none at all. Siebert closed his accompanying note with a superbly ambiguous sentence: "My wife and I are still living off those wonderful days in the GG." (I guess they must have been guests of yours. What did you give them to take along—a ton of goose schmaltz?)

How happy that made you, to be able to invite all your friends from the Reich to your Polish castle. Now you had a lot more to offer them than only your Bavarian country place, the Schoberhof, or the villa in Berlin, or the House of German Justice in Munich. And your savings account flourished. That same month, you were able to deposit 7,000 marks, and then another 7,000, and then another 5,200. Hitler must have owed you back pay for vacations you didn't take or a holiday bonus at harvest time, or whatever. All that money couldn't possibly have been profit from some shady deal that His Honor the Minister of the Reich and Governor General Hans Frank pulled off right at the source in Cracow, could it?

I'll have to grant you that your relatives kept pouring into the GG in droves, and that they were willing witness to the sight of your strict diets coming to a crashing halt, one after the other. And no wonder, with all the delicacies available in your monarchy that were yours for the taking.

While your brother-in-law Marian was obliged to pay for his greed with his life (thanks to Himmler's alertness—although he probably wasn't aware of your private conviction that the fertility rate of the Frank family had gotten out of hand and that its ranks needed a bit of thinning out), your cousin Richard persisted in his intention of establishing himself in the GG and had already outlined a plan for the "Renaissance of Film in the Government General." He wrote: "I am aware that this personal letter does not belong in your official files. Nevertheless I should like to express the conviction that my guidelines for the reorganization of the film industry in the GG are an absolute guarantee of success. Of course, they could be put into practice by some other specialist in the field [*meaning, I suppose, someone not related to you, Father? And of course he couldn't stop there*], but I should regard it as a great honor to be permitted myself to direct this aspect of the restructuring process under the aegis of your constant personal supervision."

That's what I call great ass-kissing style. You must have received letters like that by the carload. Maybe they were the source of inspiration for your own obsequious prose.

Cousin Richard's full proposal must have gotten lost in the shuffle. No cinéast today, at least, knows anything about any guidelines for an independent GG cinema program. Too bad, be-

cause Cousin Richard's ideas as outlined in his letter are wonderfully thought out. Here is the central statement of his
featherbrained "guidelines": "In order to be in conformity with
all political realities and requirements, a taut and concentrated
realization of filmic demands is necessary. In direct connection
with that is my total rejection of any and all private or special
interests [*whom was he thinking of in particular—Aunt Else, Aunt Martel,
Uncle Otto, Uncle Heini, Uncle Walter, maybe even Mother?*] and the
assurance that film production shall be under the direct authority
of the Governor General, who will name his own general deputy
director." Now whom might you have had in mind for that post,
dear dead Cousin Richard? I can't imagine.

All those goings-on soon became something of a burden for
you. You were obviously very concerned about your savings account at the Finck Bank, too. Around this time you received a bill
for medication purchased for your wife and your sister. You decided
to put a stop to that and had a junior assistant of yours, yet another
brother-in-law (what a tight-knit little community that was becoming), tell the pharmacy that enough was enough and "that the
Herr Governor General has given orders that under no circumstances will anything be paid for until a complete bill, itemized
down to the last mark and pfennig, is submitted." It came to the
not exactly negligible amount of 250 marks.

And right you were. Just as the money you received from those
you were about to murder was recorded down to the last zloty,
careful order also had to reign in accounting for expenditures.
Take care of the pfennigs and the marks will take care of themselves,
as we are fond of saying. Whoever does not keep careful track of
even the tiniest transaction has not fairly earned his share of the
Jewish gold fillings.

Many a tasty crumb also fell in my direction. Never shall I
forget the heavenly bouillon with tiny dumplings that Netty from
Vienna, your cook for formal affairs, would make for me. I can
still see a bowl of it before me, and see myself bent over it, protected

by the obligatory linen bib—the broth a golden yellow, glistening with little eyes of fat swimming lazily amongst the bits of chive that hadn't yet reached the bowl's edge and were about to cling to it. I would enjoy it in the solarium at Castle Kressendorf. Or I would go into Netty's gigantic kitchen, where I remember once seeing vast mountains of egg on the table (I could draw a picture of it even now). Heaven knows for how many people she was preparing omelettes on that day, an image branded forever in my childhood memory.

Mother must have been eternally grateful to Hitler and Himmler for the ghettos, those first supermarkets with discount prices—especially for the Frank family. With what consuming greed she would set out on a shopping spree in her Mercedes, accompanied by an SS escort. I was also permitted to accompany her there, hand in hand with Nursemaid Hilde. On the way, I would stand, not sit, on the backseat of the Mercedes and press my nose to the window. With black uniforms of the SS surrounding the car, I would ride in stately progress through the narrow streets, past trembling grownups, with other children staring at me. It must have been on Sundays, for I remember wearing my charming little "Pepita" trousers and jacket with their pattern of tiny checks.

Mother, I thought, why aren't they laughing, why do they look so cross? It's Sunday, Mother, and they have such nice stars on their sleeves. And look at the men there with the whips.

Oh, never mind, child, she would have said. You wouldn't understand. Just enjoy the ride, we're going bargain hunting. Stop at that corner there, driver. That's where they have those beautiful camisoles! Oh, and just look at those furs, will you!

I remained in the car and stuck my tongue out at another kid. He went away, and so I won. I laughed, but my nursemaid, the beloved Hilde, pulled me over to her side, where she was sitting quietly. The chauffeur also waited in silence for Mother's return.

Once I was permitted to get out of the car, my reward for all that patient waiting. A house with barred windows, a half-lit corridor; someone picks me up when we come to a door, and I am supposed to look through the peephole. The man says to me, "See the wicked, wicked witch sitting in there?" I see a woman seated near a wall. She doesn't look our way, but only stares at the floor. I begin to cry. "She won't hurt you," the man consoles me. "She'll be dead soon anyway."

Yes, those ghettos of yours, Father, they certainly did have something to offer. But I had more fun once on an excursion out to a camp with barracks and masses of barbed wire all around everything. I know now that it was some sort of outlying camp for internment before the concentration camp proper. But at the time, all it meant to me was the presence of a cheerful, friendly man in a uniform who had a wild donkey, and he would keep putting skinny men on the donkey's back, lifting them up with his massive arms—how I laughed!—and the donkey would buck and the men would fall off and had a terrible time trying to pick themselves up off the ground. They didn't find it as comical as I did. Over and over again they would be put on the donkey's back, each of them trying to help the others, and the donkey would get a terrific whack on his flank. It was a glorious afternoon, and afterwards we went inside, where I got a cup of cocoa from the head soldier.

I carry these unspeakable images around in my head, Father; and you had them in your head, too, filed away in your brain. As your secretary testified at Nuremberg, you had a remarkable memory, and so it must have been good for remembering pictures and scenes like these.

I always wanted to get to be at least one day older than you got to be, and now I have passed that day, and I know now what awful shit can get into people's heads, what images. And I also know that one can never get rid of them; one can't forget the soup, the Jews, the Poles, the faces. And I know I can never get rid of that image of you standing before me, your hands clasped over your genitals, the same way Hitler always stood. You imitated him in everything you did. I have heard recorded speeches of yours, speeches in which you were trying so pathetically to copy that horrible strangled voice of Hitler's. There really should have been a law against you, against all of it.

Another wonderful thing in the Cracow castle was the big play car I was presented with. I remember pedaling down endless corridors, swerving around corners, always hoping to run into someone's legs and hurt them. I would lurk at corners, evilly calculating the moment when the steps I heard coming would give me a good target. Then my feet sticking out from the bottom of my little checked trousers would slam down on the pedals, off I would go and bang into someone, scratching their legs, scuffing their ankles, making my victims utter muffled cries of pain—as I would gaze innocently up from behind the steering wheel into the forced smiles on angry faces. After all, I was the son of the Governor General, the Lord of the Castle.

You never much liked to have me come into your office suite, where that ugly painting hung—the one with the woman wearing what looked like a bandage around her head. Her hair was smooth and perfectly combed, the part so straight that you used it as an example to me for how I should comb my own hair. She had a string of black pearls around her neck, and, ugliest of all, she was carrying a little white animal in her arms that looked like a rat and was petting it with one hand. The woman did not look at the animal, though, but out into space. The picture gave me the creeps. Only much later did I learn it was a work of Leonardo da Vinci, a portrait of Cecilia Galleroni and called *Lady with the Ermine*.

You certainly had settled yourself into elegant surroundings; and yet—there was that oh-so-appealing quality in you: you truly loved the simple life, home cooking. At least according to your secretary. You felt most at ease among "the simple folk." (Damn it, how familiar that somehow still sounds.) You also loved to read for hours, uninterrupted, she said. And she was right. In my search I have found book orders and bills en masse, and they are quite astonishing—Max Weber and Nietzsche, all the authoritative books on chess. You would think the soul of intellect and spirit was at home up there in the castle, gazing down on the ghetto.

Did you ever *see* the ghetto? Or did you look away every time you passed the windows with that view? Too modest, were you? Or simply too depressed?

The ghetto was always one of the most important sights for visiting dignitaries from the Reich. On one occasion, Professor Mikorey, the sculptor from Munich, was taken on an outing there in the big Mercedes by your chief architect, Rattinger, and your chauffeur. Rattinger had the driver stop in front of a certain house in the ghetto, and according to the story, a pretty young Jewish woman came out and Rattinger said to her, "Hi there, sweetheart. We've already got your husband out—just be patient and you'll be out in no time, too." Mikorey was puzzled and Rattinger explained, "Oh, Frank and me, we're having our own little battle with the SS."

Just another one of those touching stories the family tells to justify your past as they gaze piously upward with dachshund eyes. The sustenance of my youth, poisoned manna.

So, was "sweetheart" saved or not? You always fell for pretty women. Remember the Polish countess (anyhow, she was supposed to have been a countess), the one you and Lasch shared? She suddenly appeared one day at the castle, and after some months of sex à trois she just as suddenly disappeared. Was she shipped off to Treblinka because it turned out she was Jewish? Or was it that sex without love becomes very boring—was that what was going through your head? Or did she disappear into life, having finally gotten hold of the necessary documents?

Another time, when you were confronted with the reality you tried to ignore, you looked away in embarrassment and then said with paternal severity, "I never want to hear anything more about that again!" It was one of your pedagogical attacks, so like the millions of others that German children heard from their German fathers somewhat later, after the war. The occasion was a soccer game being played in a field by children of the German Army of Occupation in Cracow. Suddenly they heard singing coming from behind a building, at first nervous and tentative, then stronger and louder: the Polish national anthem. One of the boys says, "Wow, now they're shooting the Poles again!" They're curious, of course, to see what's going on, and as they're running they hear the machine guns. When they round the corner, there they see them, already dead, lying contorted in a pile, covered with blood, young men, old men. They had simply been lined up against the wall and murdered. And you, the man of justice, said, "I never want to hear anything more about that again!" and turned back to your delicately herbed and spiced salad that you enjoyed along with your steak. In her testimony, your secretary did not neglect to give us that nice little detail about your dietary preferences.

She also let the world in on the fact that you knew how to appreciate a fine wine, though of course you never drank to excess, and above all that you were the best of chess players. "None of the gentlemen could hold a candle to him in that regard; but if he had had to deal sternly with one of them during the day, he would invite the man over that evening for a game of chess and would let him win for a change." What a royal gesture, what tact and intelligence in dealing with others. Is that what you're thinking? It's what you doubtless thought at the time, too.

But that macabre, twisted order of events: the fact that after hearing the men sing the national anthem, that young boy knew enough to say, "Now they're shooting the Poles again." Did the horror of that strike you when you heard the story?

In this connection, let me quote a couple of your sentences right back at you. "The Government General is today the most brilliantly administered and the most securely governed of territories [*those shitty superlatives of yours. How could you, lover of Shakespeare, allow yourself?*], and from it has arisen and still arises, for the German Reich in its difficult wartime tasks, unending aid and support. . . . The populace is at peace [*because it's dead, Father—is that what you mean?*]. Its industry proceeds apace with the greatest possible energy. The Government General will someday be one of the most flourishing lands of our great German community of states."

Aren't you a little bit off base there, Father? Especially if you take a good look at the map of Europe today. But you knew all along that one day you would get stuck in that cesspool. Remember when you heard the news of the defeat at Stalingrad on the radio? You were standing in your immense office at the castle. Your Minister of the Interior, Dr. Losacker (he had only recently been appointed), burst into the room. "I was probably being a bit tempestuous in my new position," he said, years later. You were standing near the window. "I shall never forget the intense blue of his uniform," Dr. Losacker went on. At first you placed your finger on your lips in an effort to calm him down. And then, with arms outspread and an air of terror in your voice, you cried out, "The angel of death has just flown through this room and touched me with his wings. Stalingrad has fallen. We shall lose the war."

What an intense scene. Is that the first time you felt a little ominous snap at the top of your neck? When the angel's wing brushed you?

Or was that not perhaps a bit later, when Himmler, slowly but surely, got you onto the hot seat?

By then (you know what I'm leading up to now, don't you?) there were reports making the rounds about you, about Mother, about all of us. The most elaborate report was made by SS Untersturmbannführer the Honorable Justice Dr. Reinecke—with complete judicial independence, of course. (Surely he was one of those adaptable judges who fit effortlessly into the seamless web of defense woven by the Federal Republic's legal mafia after the war.) His report went to Reichsführer of the SS Himmler: "In the matter of the litigation against Untersturmbannführer Lorenz Löv, head of the chief administrative office of the GG in Warsaw, I was the one to preside at the principal trial and pass the sentence of life imprisonment."

Poor Löv. Just to think that the only nests he helped to feather were yours and Mother's. Do you recall Dr. Reinecke? Surely you must have had occasion to shake his hand and he to make a little bow before you, as is the custom of German judges. But behind your back, Father, oh God, oh God, the things he said about you to that paragon of virtue Himmler. He wrote to him that Löv was only a little fish in a big pond, that's what he wrote; and he also wrote that during the course of the trial a lot more dirt about a lot more fish had come to light—on the staff of the Governor General, he wrote—and he wrote that even members of the Governor General's family were implicated, even you yourself, that's what he wrote. Isn't that just awful! And to think that at Nuremberg you swore over and over again that never never never did you enrich yourself illegally. Imagine that putrid German judge, that rotten tattletale, saying that you had been made extremely uncomfortable from the moment of Löv's arrest on, because of "the [Governor General's] cognizance of the incrimination of himself and his staff." That's what he wrote in that German style you used to be able to outdo and with ten times the eloquence, once you put your mind to it.

Anyhow, you were successful—only temporarily, thank God—in putting the blame on a man who was favorably disposed toward you, Meidinger, your chief office manager. "Yes, yes, good old Meidinger," I can hear you sigh. Nevertheless, Löv stuck firmly to his testimony against us. Such obstinacy would never do, of course; so you tried to have his incriminating testimony removed from the records forthwith. In a word, you saw yourself faced with a "campaign of libel and slander," as it is called now. The concept may be new to you. It's what your successors in political office call it these days whenever one is caught red-handed, laboriously dragging one's crimes and misdemeanors behind, weighed down by all the filth clinging to them.

With the newly cleansed and purified records in hand, you lobbied the upper echelons of the SS, presumably speaking that charming Bavarian dialect of yours: "Come on, be a pal, why not put the brakes on the whole trivial Löv case? Easiest thing would be to call it just a negligible offense, right?" However—and this is something that does you honor and also helps my search for everything I can find out about you—Himmler really wasn't a friend of yours at all. You were actually so afraid of him that you were shitting in your pants—so much so that it must have been running down over your castle ramparts; you couldn't even get the side door to your bathtub open for all the shit jammed in there. And Himmler (I can see his big mouthful of teeth shining in glee) had the case against you continued.

And so Reinecke could carry on with his report: "Three main incidents stand at the center of the case being investigated by the police and the SS, viz., the misappropriation and theft by the accused from the fur vault and warehouse. [*Father, whenever I hear the word "fur" I see Mother pawing through gigantic heaps of fur coats stolen from Jewish women before they were taken off to be gassed—I see her twirling and dancing among them like some mechanical doll.*] Secondly, his punishable business dealings with Jews. [*Here I see Mother again, and maybe also your sister, beloved Aunt Lilly.*] And finally, his dealings in connection with the Textile Salvage Company [*an obvious reference to Aunt Else and your brother-in-law Uncle Marian*]. In all three cases, highly placed members of the staff of the Governor General are involved; furthermore, his wife [*I told you so!*] and sister [*didn't I tell you?*] and to a certain extent he himself are guilty of punishable offenses."

You were getting pretty deep in doodoo there, Father, weren't you? I can see you now, having heard about this report, racing berserk around the four walls of your courtyard, as if trying to escape the clutches of Polanski's young vampire hunting down the professor's assistant. The fat was really in the fire now, I'll bet. Wouldn't you say so, you great Father of the GG? Mother told me after the war that as soon as you arrived in that plundered land you started getting paranoid about attempts on your life. It all fits in. And then to have the SS on your tail because of your cheap little robberies. Cheap? Little? Well, they found out that you (or was it more likely Mother?) had assembled a small warehouse of furs worth at least 75,000 marks. In this connection, Reinecke composed one of those glorious sentences which your generation has bequeathed to the tradition of life-styles of the rich and famous. "To be sure, only about half [of the collection of furs] had been paid for out of public funds; the other half had been requisitioned at no cost."

Well then, Father, they had sniffed out your furs. At least now I know why all the ladies in your and Mother's retinue were reduced in my memory to a cageful of animals: Frau Ocelot and Aunt Persian; the funny Frau Mink parlayvooing with Fräulein Silver Fox. Your women had become a pretty furry lot on the surface, if still featherbrained within, as they went tottering along in their finery like a flock of stupid egrets.

Meidinger must have been the first to let you in on the news about Löv. How might he have broken the news to you there in your castle office? Did it go something like this: "Herr Governor General, I must call your attention to the fact that we have something of a problem with the Löv case." Or was his language a little more hip when you were speaking among yourselves? Maybe he came in, perched on the corner of your desk, tossed the transcript of the trial at you, and said, "Hey, Hans, your fur caper is down the tubes if you don't get a quick brainstorm. No other way out of this squeeze: You have to goose that old girl of yours out of the GG—or else that greedy gullet of hers will blow the whole scam." Whereupon your superior taste for the cultivated rebelled and you countered with some Latin phrase, like "*Pacta sunt ser-*

vanda," which of course meant nothing to you. Or, because you were more nervous than I've been describing you, "*Navigare necesse est*," pure nonsense. You got up from your desk, thoroughly rattled by the news, went behind the great refectory table in the center of the room, the one that you had moved in from the museum because you thought it so appropriate to your office, and the light bulb in your head flashed on with the phrase "Appropriate to your office"! "Send for Bühler!" you yelled. Or "I want to have a word with Bühler."

Bühler, Chief of Administration, came in. The two or the three of you cooked up the perfect scheme. You could slip into Löv's file a forged statement to the effect that this collection of furs had been assembled to make an impression "appropriate to your office," and that the same was true for all the other objects (value: five thousand reichsmarks). All of them were "for official daily use." Now, you thought, I'm out of the frying pan. Especially since Judge Reinecke made quite a point of the fact that when you had learned that Löv had requisitioned the stuff, you had said, "It must all be paid for."

Paid for?

Mother stood on the Wawel's ramparts. No sooner did she spy with her vulture's eye a lovely fur coat than Löv and his SS myrmidon fur-snatchers were off and running to see who could tear it off the Polish woman's back. That was the approved method, right?

This eternal fumbling about with women's clothing in public didn't look good, nor did the sight of the SS invading homes while Mother sat outside in her car and waited. Those dashing SS boys, quite contrary to their normal duty, did not emerge from the homes poking guns into people with hands over their heads. Nor was any shooting heard, even though Germans generally loved to shoot up the enemy's homes. No, they came out laden down with furs. Now that did not make a good impression, either, so they forced a few zlotys into their victims' hands, muttering something about contributions to the winter relief charity fund, while Mother lounged in the backseat of the car, clapping her hands with joy as they buried her in more and more furs. Was that the approved method?

The question still remains, however: how were I or you or Mother or anyone expected to make an impression "appropriate to your office" with furs? Did you give formal parties and print invitations saying "Furs Compulsory"? Or was it hard to heat the Wawel Castle? I, for one, was never cold there. Or did you like to "do it" with Mother on furs?—something it would be difficult to call "making an appropriate impression," unless of course you instituted it as a daily public event, something perhaps to replace the eleven o'clock trumpet blast from St. Mary's Church, a daily regal fornication on furs for the benefit of the good folk assembled below: both of you naked, screwing up a storm on Persian lambs and silver foxes, after which, hand in hand, you would take a few deep bows.

No matter how these furs were intended to be used, that damned fool Reinecke was thoroughly envious, as is quite evident from his report. "Both of the quarters where the Governor General was billeted gave the impression of excessive luxury; official funds should never have been expended for such purposes." Father, do you know what else it is about Reinecke that infuriates me? It's that he was one of those people who no matter how they love to suck up to their superiors by squealing on others, are also so damned eager to please and obey their orders. No doubt about it, he sentenced every offender either to death or to life in prison, just as he was ordered to.

Back to Löv. Finally, nothing came of your underhanded plan to appeal on the grounds of having to make the impression "appropriate to your office." Löv testified that the Herr Governor General requisitioned from the warehouse, "at the very least, several silver fox and three blue fox furs."

I would give a year of my life to have witnessed the following
scene when Löv is handing them over to you.

There is a knock. You say, "Come in." Löv enters, but you
can't recognize him at first. Startled, you look up and think a great
bear is coming at you, or some colossal marmot grown to such
vast proportions thanks to your wildlife protection legislation. You
soon come to your senses and take a deep breath—but then you
are upset that someone has seen your altogether unstatesmanlike
lack of composure. You bark at the walking pile of furs, "Who
are you?," and it answers, "Got these for you, Gov'nor," and he
puts them down and it is Löv, the lovely old Löv, and you get all
warm and sentimental inside. You walk out from behind your desk
toward him, caress his shoulder, and say, "My dear Löv, my good
Löv, how positively charming of you." Then you say, "My, what
pretty furs those are in your arms!" and "Where on earth did you
get them?" And Löv answers—at least he claims he told you—
"They were requisitioned at no cost." Well, isn't that just wonderful. Now, of course, you want to pay for them and reach for
your wallet. But you quickly remember that you do not have one,
that you gave up such habits when you became lord and master
of the great Reichsnebenland, Germany's colonized neighbor. Quite
rightly you reminded yourself: would Charles V have carried a
money purse about with him, or Frederick the Great?

You gazed around the enormous room, looking for some object
with which to compensate Löv for his largesse. You did not want
to give up the Beautiful Madonna, or the *Lady with the Ermine*. But,
ah yes, quite right: Raphael's portrait of the young man—that
might be just the thing for Löv. Could that decision account for
the fact that since the days of your sovereignty this painting has
never resurfaced? But maybe the good Prussian Löv didn't have a
feeling for the old Raphael's oil colors. After all, there was no
regal Germanic stag in the picture, and the handsome lad with his
un-Aryan black locks did not have his hands folded in Düreresque

prayer, nor were his arms holding any of that German master's rabbits. So the upshot was that the gov'nor said he would just receive the furs without remuneration—for the time being, mind you—"and when the opportunity presents itself I shall contribute something to a good cause." Those, at least, were your words according to Löv.

Fine, all you got were a few furs. "But to make up for that, the Governor's wife, his sister, and other members of the staff were all the more favored with gifts of fur," said Löv, your chief procurement officer.

Mother, now it's your turn to lend an ear. Löv was a precise record-keeper of all that transpired: "The Governor General's wife removed from the warehouse a variety of fur coats: broadtail and Persian lamb, at least ten silver fox coats, and other fur pieces in great number, all of which exceeded by far what she could possibly have needed for her own personal use." Now, don't start screaming, Mother. I was just about to mention that naturally you paid something for them, in zlotys, and, to be sure, based on the assessment of an appraiser who had been bribed by Löv to give a very low estimate. Calm down, Mother, for heaven's sake! Wherever you may now be orbiting in the universe, no matter how hard you try to put spiral nebulae between yourself and me, Löv's continuing testimony cannot be escaped: "That is not all—the requirements of the Governor General's wife insofar as furs are concerned were far from satisfied with those. For instance, she procured from the firm of Apfelbaum in Warsaw a moleskin jacket [*how the little Polacks must have had to scurry through the mole runs to get enough skins together for you*], a beaver coat, a muskrat coat, an ermine coat, a silver fox cape, a blue fox cape, and other furs."

Mother, don't try to hide from me in one of those black holes— you won't be able to avoid hearing this. Whoever might think that Apfelbaum & Co. was doing a terrific business with you as its customer is quite mistaken. What you did was to go to Apfelbaum, look at their beautiful furs, have them put what you liked aside, bid Apfelbaum a friendly *"auf Wiedersehen"*—and Apfelbaum & Co. was overjoyed.

Too soon for that. Their door is flung open, uniforms, threats, intimidation, rifles; the director of the firm is summoned. He comes and is confronted by people telling him they represent the interests of the Frau Governor General. The director sighs in relief. Too soon for that. He is requested to produce the pieces put aside for her. He is told to name prices. "And, if you please, be quite precise; we can check up on anything you say, mein Herr." Fear returns. The glint of sunlight on the rifles outside is seen through the glass door. Standing alongside the curb opposite, German automobiles bearing the personal standard of the Governor. The director names prices, and one of the "representatives" writes them down. Suddenly, there is a relaxed smile on his face: "Shall we then say fifty percent of the retail price?" And he pays out the money to the pale, frightened, despairing, and enraged man and gives orders that the furs be taken out to the waiting vehicles. That, or something like that, must have been the way it was. It's all in Löv's testimony.

Goodbye, Mother.

Evidently, Father, we must have lived either (a) in Alaska or (b) in an extremely moth-ridden area; otherwise one cannot explain this extraordinary consumption of furs. In her moth frenzy your sister had them confiscate a valuable Persian lamb coat without plunking down a single zloty. And what does Dr. Reinecke say? "With that act she incriminated herself and became guilty of the theft of state property and of receiving stolen goods." My God, Father, something was really beginning to brew there. And don't forget, either, that Löv was after you too, claiming that you had requisitioned food and alcohol to the amount of six thousand marks for your private household and your railroad car and that you hadn't paid a penny for any of it—although (somebody like Dr. Reinecke will always know that) according to the law you were supposed to pay for all private household expenses yourself.

One day the Jewish Council in Warsaw received a letter, return address "Castle, Cracow." One of the council members opens it, reads the ostentatiously printed letterhead "The Governor General," and for a millisecond cherishes the totally insane hope that the letter contains the news that the ghettos are going to be dissolved, that everybody will be requested to return to their homeland or wherever they may want to go; and also that at the same moment all concentration camps will be dismantled and that the law concerning the protection of marmots will immediately and henceforth also apply to Jews; and finally that there would be a personal sentence from you, such as "By the time you receive this letter I shall have shot myself out of profound shame, or shall have thrown myself from the ramparts, or shall have choked myself to death on the sleeve of a Persian lamb coat." (Please check off your preferred method, Father.) But no, none of that. What the letter contained was approximately this: "To the Jewish Council of Warsaw, present address, the Ghetto. In the name of the Herr Governor General, I order you to procure from somewhere within the Jewish population a Turkish coffee machine, and for Governor Fischer's wife, two picnic baskets. Signed Brigitte Frank, Wife of the Herr Governor General."

Yes, yes, Father, that's the way reality really looked. That's the way you created it. Löv said that this order had been obeyed and also added, "This document was discovered in the possession of the Jewish Council and requisitioned as evidence." I can easily believe how eager you were to get hold of that piece of paper when you heard what Mother had done. She goes into your office, pockets a couple of pieces of your stationery—Heaven knows what other tricks she'll be up to. Maybe you had to threaten the Jewish Council that you would send them all to the concentration camp to make them hand over the letter. And how sweet too must have been Mother's and Fischer's mental image of the Jews with their picnic baskets, drunk on their freedom, sunburned, sitting by the roadside and on the town squares, stretching out in the sunshine unpacking their picnic food with pleasure—something that Mother must have observed on her trips through the ghetto when she was out looking for new camisoles. Then she must have reported it all enthusiastically to the Governor of Warsaw, Herr Fischer. On the other hand, one must consider that Himmler was taking such pains to accommodate the Germans' wish for the removal of Jews in the neatest possible way. But flying right in the face of that, he sees intensive mercantile transactions developing between the pragmatic Governor General's family and the Polish ghettos. The inexorable Reinecke writes on, "The Jews were active even in providing for the daily needs of the Governor General. They delivered to him the finest gourmet delicacies and once even sent him a gold fountain pen." Reinecke gives full rein to his resentment toward the German economy in the GG when he appends to his fountain-pen sentence this bitter remark: "It must have been known to the Governor General that in Warsaw such things could be obtained only through the Jews." Now things get really first-class—I ask you, who can claim that we Franks harbored any animosity toward the Jews? "It was a topic for daily discussion within the German circles in the GG that the family of the Governor General did its shopping in the ghetto."

Meticulously (you always thought you were so meticulous) you raised questions concerning the development of the facts of this third charge. Listen to what your Judge Reinecke had to say: "We have just been dealing with such transactions on the part of the wife of the Governor General and her retinue concerning their exploitation of the office of the Governor General in connection with their dealings with the Textile Salvage Company. There they bought, without any proper permit, enormous quantities of goods and demanded that in spite of the already low prices they should also receive an additional fifty percent reduction, which after some initial hesitation was also granted to them."

Did Mother say something like "I believe you are not properly informed that you are speaking here with the wife of the Governor General. Nor do you seem to realize that we are dealing here with purchases necessary for our role as representatives of the German Reich"? Or did she lodge her complaints with you, and then you gave the orders? (In matters like these you had a great opportunity to show how powerful you were.) "For all my wife's future purchases I demand that she be granted an additional fifty percent reduction. I shall assume the responsibility for that." Is that how it went?

How much hope the two of you must have awakened. What kind of hearts did you have to be so totally indifferent to the fact that one day your close business partners in the ghetto are simply taken away in transports? Or to the additional fact that more and more of the famished and dying are lying underfoot and making it difficult and smelly to go shopping? How appallingly greedy you must have been to transact such business deals with human beings who were suffering so terribly from the fear of death, and to compel them repeatedly—as Löv testified—to hand over their wares at cheaper and cheaper prices and to provide little incidental favors free of charge, such as a diamond ring for your sister.

And on top of that, to dare even to utter the word "God." And to set up the Beautiful Madonna in your room. And to pay the local priest from Castle Kressendorf a "considerable fee" for the renovation of the chapel designed by a superb architect like Schinkel.

The rings were taken away from the Jews, the picnic baskets, the camisoles—business deals concluded with hollow-eyed people. And then one day the Franks didn't want to go shopping anymore. They had their fill. They belched. They had everything—and besides that, it stank too much in the ghettos by this time. We already had our storehouses filled with treasures, anyway. And there were the Jews, probably still thinking that Frau Frank would not permit them to be transported. But then no one named Frank came around anymore. They were driven from their houses into the streets. No longer did Mother's car, heavily guarded by the SS, round the corner into the ghetto. Finis. We were stuffed.

Through the burning land filled with screams of pain, your private railroad car glided like a warehouse on wheels from Cracow via Vienna, Freilassing, and Rosenheim to Munich. By the time the private car had arrived in Munich it was empty—generally everything had been unloaded at Rosenheim. It's obvious, of course, why. It wouldn't have looked so good, the endless unloading of geese, furs, and canned goods at the main station in Munich. Even I can understand that.

So much for the testimony given before Reinecke by Löv, whom you naturally did not support in any way. Later they tried at least to get Löv out of jail and stationed at the front. I have no idea what became of him. There's only one thing I know: I am sorry for him. He was the little fish, and they had to let you off the hook. But what else could they do? The ones who could have hooked you were all big fish too. Above a certain rank, the trail of official corruption grows cold and is no longer traceable. The identical arrangement has been established here in Germany again since the war.

Dr. Reinecke must really have been an upstanding German. He hadn't even gotten to the end of his report when he simply swept the table clean for you, put in the records that our Castle Kressendorf had not yet been inventoried. That was in 1941; you were living in the third year of your artful regime, and Mother was sending, as Dr. Reinecke wrote, "state-owned objects like bed linens, down comforters, furnishings, etc., to the private home of the Governor General in the Reich, the Schoberhof. When the final audit came down, all these objects were listed as having been borrowed."

So there was an inventory after all, Herr Dr. Reinecke. If you please, no unjust accusations against my Mother and Father.

And as for you, Father, I can only whisper my congratulations; the two of you got away with it again. That business with "borrowed" was an inspiration. The auditors must have assumed that our house in the Reich had been terribly bombed out.

Geese, Cupids,
and Marble Slabs

You must have been angry that day when you tried to climb
aboard your private railroad car in Cracow but couldn't even
find it because a convoy of big trucks was blocking the view. When
you looked closer, you discovered your Polish slave laborers from
your Kressendorf Castle and estate and saw them as they were
singing Polish chain-gang songs while loading one jar of fruit
preserves after the other from the trucks into the train car and
stowing them there. What's happened? you asked yourself, ap-
prehensively rubbing the inner sides of your two feminine thighs,
encased as always in those jodhpurs I hated. Then you found out.
Mother had ordered her personnel to boil up and preserve the
entire harvest of fruit from Castle Kressendorf so that she could
send it home to the Reich on board your beloved status symbol,
the private railroad car. Alas, if only the assassins who were after
Heydrich had exploded a gigantic bomb under your ass as you
were riding through the Protectorate. The look on their faces
would have been worthy of preserving too. Your car bounces up
from the tracks, bursts apart in a huge flash of fire and noise;
Antek and Jurek, or whatever their names are, stare at it, hear it
crack asunder—and then, an unbelievable tinkling sound (a sound
like the one a piano makes when carousing Baltic folk toss it out
the second story of a manor house onto the terrace to crown their

little festival), and then your and Mother's squished bodies come oozing out of the ruined car on a colorful and sticky stream of jam and fruit compote. It's a perfect image in its sliminess; it would seem as if the two assassins had also managed to reveal your true characters with their bomb.

Since the private car had been commandeered by Mother as a multi-fruit express and was gliding through the landscape fully loaded, the desperately needed provisions for my healthy childhood at the Schoberhof had to be transported by truck as "military provisions" in November 1940 across the GG border into Bavaria: 150 pounds of beef, 45 pounds of pork, 20 geese, 50 chickens, 22 pounds of salami, and 27 pounds of ham sausage. Loaded into a second truck, along with additional "military provisions," were things for my breakfast table for that month: 170 pounds of butter, 105 pounds of cooking oil, 1,440 eggs (I always loved two eggs in my egg cup), 42 pounds of coffee beans, 120 pounds of sugar, and, to cap it all off, 25 pounds of cheese. Jesus, Dr. Reinecke, you fussy list-maker, if you only knew how soon I got sick of eating those geese.

The greatest puzzle I'm left with is this one: what the hell prompted you to have two hundred thousand (yes, yes, it's a fact— two hundred thousand) eggs preserved in lime. Either we must have had so gigantic a herd of chickens that we could count on a stampede every day, or (as in your commercial dealings in the ghetto) you personally put the chickens under such terrific pressure that in their fear of living or dying they shot out eggs like an attack of the runs. The totally unnerved Dr. Reinecke said, "The question as to the whereabouts of the two hundred thousand eggs has yet to be resolved."

Were they all actually sent to you, despite the fact that Reinecke's official itemized list reveals that one thousand eggs per month were personally reserved for you anyhow? Just imagine one of the prosecutors at Nuremberg shouting at you in the witness stand, "Sire, hand over your eggs!"

One thousand eggs just for you. Did you practice egg-pecking with your subordinates? Did you take a bath every day in whipped egg whites? Were you worried about your potency? Did you open up a little private egg business on the side with a Pole? Or perhaps sneak down every evening from the Wawel with a basket full of eggs on your arm and earn a few zlotys on the side in some hidden corner of Cracow?

At some hour on the first day when you arrived at the Wawel you must have stood on the ramparts of the royal castle and promised yourself that you would never want for anything again. Suddenly the recollection of a certain period in your former life must have steeled your battle-ready limbs, the time when the still democratic Bavarian state was benevolently paying you a subsistence allowance (as in fact it was still doing so when you had already become a legal trainee).

Father, if you think that Dr. Reinecke, that flower of enlightened jurisprudence in the Third Reich, has also come to the end of his brief against you, you're quite wrong. He saved his best for his conclusion: "According to the testimony of the witness Fräsdorf, a doctor in attendance at the Cracow hospital, the Governor General gave orders that certain objects removed from churches, such as statuary, Madonnas, fat little cupids, Russian candelabra, etc., be sent by special train and brought to his private chapel in the Schoberhof."

And he ends with a really wonderful sentence, you good, pious Father you, you who claim, according to your replies at the cross-examination at Nuremberg, never to have had the intention of feathering your own nest: "The objects were acquired at no expense."

At this moment, you and Mother, like the Furies of ages past, are hunting me down. In my imagination, you press forward and start slavering and ranting: "You know very well that there was never a private chapel at the Schoberhof." Hey, you're right. But when I close my eyes and banish the piles of furs from my inner image, other pictures appear: putti and Madonnas, everything gleaming gold. Right before my eyes I can see the plump leg of a little angel, yellow, cold to the touch; I see the intense blue of a Madonna's robe, I see her head tilted to the side, much too small for her garments. Where were they standing; where were they hanging? How long had they been there? All I know is that it was not in Poland. It was at the Schoberhof.

Dr. Reinecke's conclusion: "Senior civil servant Keil, who had done two audits at the administrative offices of the Governor General and was an expert witness during the principal hearing, describes the entire situation at the castle in Cracow and in the Cracow administration as corruption."

That was your life: corruption. And that puts me in the horrible position of having to believe an SS judge more than I believe you. Since we would both like to change the subject now, let me figure out with you how this same Fräsdorf, that sleazy assistant doctor at a hospital in Cracow, could have claimed to be witness to all the things the master of his land was plundering. Were you personally the thief? Did you meet one night in a Cracow church; did you introduce yourselves to each other; and did he say, "I'm a physician," and you, "I'm the Governor General and an art thief. I have also black-marketed two hundred thousand preserved eggs. Come on, help me. Here, take this putto, and here, this crucifix. Psst, not so loud—we'll wake up the priests. Any more sacramental wine there? Quick, take a swallow. Hold it—let's get this sack up on my shoulder. God, is this stuff heavy! Jeezus, church art sure weighs a lot"? And then the two of you enjoyed a wicked little chuckle?

As art connoisseur you were in your element. And by this time you had already furnished your quarters. The first meager months (when the Herr Governor General was still picking up his official and private mail in person at the Cracow post office, when you didn't even know where your bedroom was going to be) had been quite forgotten. But now, by September 30, 1941, your deliveries home to the Reich were well underway. One could already hear them complaining at the Academy for German Justice in Munich about what to do with all the crates arriving (some of them partially damaged), packed full of bureaus, Louis XVI Gobelins (seven of them), and one from the sixteenth century. I'm not going to say that you stole all of that personally; you earned a good salary. But if things had taken an honest course, you really could never have afforded such things. With the best will in the world, I can trace no genealogical connections between us and the house of Louis XVI. The Franks were not regulars at the court of Versailles.

You certainly can confuse me. What, for example, am I supposed to make of the notation "608 marble slabs"? What did you want with them? Where did they come from? Was that meadow around the Schoberhof in Bavaria supposed to be paved in the Nazi style? You also must have had a bureau fetish; in every one of those many crates there were four of them. Did you plan on placing a Madonna on top of each? Were they supposed to ward off evil, like putting garlic all over to keep vampires away? Yes, bureaus would make good platforms for such an arrangement.

I am also still trying to puzzle out a message from the transport firm Schenker & Co. to the Herr Reichsminister that says twelve evidently colossal crates had arrived from Paris for him. That was after Germany had knocked off France, and Hitler had already performed his St. Vitus victory dance by the railroad car where the surrender was signed in 1918. So could the bill from Schenker & Co. explain the wonderful Renaissance *cassone* and also the beautiful folk-art cupboard, certainly not Bavarian? And doesn't it also explain the many putti and the Madonnas, the spacious armchairs, the pictures, carpets, candelabra—all those things I see everywhere in the family photographs, behind, next to, over, and under you, Mother, and your guests?

There was indeed something called a trust depository (what a euphemism, Father) from which the Nazi bosses could borrow what they liked. Is that where the huge sword with the diamonds came from, the one I used to chop down the nettles with? But maybe I'm drawing the wrong conclusions, and all of those things were household goods paid for by you on the installment plan from your meager salaries as Minister, President, and Governor General. I agree with you that it was nice living with all those furnishings; I particularly liked the furniture at the Schoberhof in the so-called Great Hall, formerly the stable of the Schober peasants and now fitted out with a grand fireplace. You'll have to admit that radio and phonograph console of yours was a little ostentatious. One of the few times in my life you were a father to me was when we would lie next to it in the darkness on the carpeted floor listening to the *Fra Diavolo* overture and you would tell me the story about Tony Huber shitting all over the place.

Here's another bill from Schenker that bewilders me: "Nine boxes as well as five crates and two cartons of art objects from Berlin"—all of which had probably come rolling in from France. You knew that Göring had already taken the best of everything. What we could manage to get our hands on until 1945 is all still in my memory. I can see myself as a little squirt, steadying myself up against that precious Renaissance chest, so richly painted and carved. There were wonderful scenes on it that I imagined were teaching me how to walk. I thank the French people for their help in my childhood training.

Tell me, Father, do the Capuchins still have our bureaus and those 608 marble slabs? You always had religious plans at the back of your mind, and it has earned you the gratitude of the Seraphic Order of the Mass at the Capuchin monastery in Koblenz-Ehrenbreitstein. As you perfectly well know, and as has been drummed into me more than once, you are "for eternity to participate in the fruits of mercy and grace through the six thousand high masses per year and six hundred masses per day which the Capuchin Fathers celebrate for the benefactors of their heathen mission, and in all prayers and good works of the entire Order." Did you perhaps in the full awareness of your impotence insure yourself for eternity, you fruit of mercy and grace?

In the earthly realm, thanks to Himmler and Krüger, you did not shine so lustrously through your acts as you might have imagined. On the other hand, it did give you time to cultivate your contacts with the homeland: "It is an urgent desire on my part," you wrote to a certain Herr Baumgartner, "to voice my appreciation for the magnificent *gamsbart* you have sent!" Something like that must really overjoy a hat decorator specializing in mountain goat beards. The *gamsbart* had obviously been a Christmas present, because for New Year's gifts you big-shot Nazis used to give each other photographs of yourselves, either autographed in an overelaborate hand or embroidered with hearty reciprocal dedications. You didn't know if 1942 was going to be another titanic year for you or what else might be in store. It's just as well, because, first, Lilly was about to enter the picture once again in your erotic life; second, it was all over with those heavenly adoring gazes between you and Mother, despite being surrounded by so many earthly goods; and third, Hitler and his mob were finally going to teach you and your family some lessons.

During the time that the Frank clan was enriching itself at Poland's expense, more and more informers' reports were winging their way to Himmler in Berlin. The little saying *"Im Westen liegt Frankreich; im Osten wird Frank reich"* had now been switched from the present tense into the past: *"im Osten ist Frank reich geworden"*— in the East Frank really became rich. You had far more than a thousand marks per month, and the fur mania of Mother and those other relatives of mine had accelerated to such an extent that the German officials began to fear for the very survival of the Jews. A certain honorable Hans Peter Krämer reported, with the intent of denouncing you, "In accordance with regulations, every Jew who leaves the Warsaw ghetto without permission will be shot to death. But if the Jew surrenders a fur, he will no longer be shot to death." In any case, the Berlin bigwigs could see no other way out of the situation than to invite you to participate in a so-called "comradely interrogation."

That took place on March 5, 1942, in Lammers's private railroad car. Lammers's private car might well have been one class better than ours, and certainly it was not such a mess as ours had become, what with all its jam and jelly shipments, the transport of rapidly decomposing geese, unwieldy Madonnas, and bulky pieces of furniture. Maybe you even used it to send those two hundred thousand preserved eggs home to the eggless Reich.

How it must really have griped you up there in your castle when you received the friendly but stern invitation, presumably in a note from Lammers, to go to the special train of your arch-enemy Heinrich Himmler, to which Lammers's private car was attached. "Krüger is behind everything again," you probably said to yourself, and then gathered around you all your faithful cronies. You were in deep trouble. Dr. Weh, for example, was hardly in a position to say (after he had sworn eternal fidelity to you at Christmastime and had served so fervently and obsequiously in your benevolent reconstruction activities in the GG): "Minister Frank, I'll wager that they got information from some informer that two hundred thousand preserved eggs are missing, not to mention all the furs, the fruit preserves, the tobacco monopoly for the Warsaw ghetto which your sister wanted to procure for the Jew Henlein because he had got hold of a gentleman's ring for her at no cost—that is to say, in a word, your corrupt style of living and your corrupt relatives are going to be the main topic of conversation." You would naturally have flown into a wild rage and would have shouted Dr. Weh down with such vehemence that he would have dropped dead on the spot (instead of a mere three years later when you arranged for him to join the troops at the eastern front). Generally speaking, that was a terrific educa-tional device one had in those days: "proving yourself at the front." Seen in that light, Stalingrad was actually one big educational experience for the German killer-boys—lots of good air, lots of exercise and character-building outdoor sports before they headed for the big exit. Even Dr. Bühler, your permanent representative, your state secretary, even he couldn't tell you that he considered your conduct in office to be nothing less than utterly disgraceful, the conduct of a pathetic and crooked puppet. But since they didn't dare talk, you must have just sat there telling fat lies to one another at the big table in your office. You, naturally, interpreted the letter telling you to meet with Lammers, Bormann, and Himmler completely differently: "I've got nerves of iron and steel," you must have said at that moment. It was a favorite statement of yours. "I always have my enemies just where I want them." Whenever you wanted to arouse sympathy for yourself in a big group, and at the same time felt like sucking your thumb in utter fear, you always resorted to speaking in your home dialect. That makes everything so comfy, doesn't it? "I'll rub their noses in it. I'm not taking anything like that from those guys, gentlemen, that's what I'm gonna tell 'em."

And those blockheads sitting around you up on the Wawel, that scuzzy bunch, doubtless nodded their approval like the good old boys they were. "The Führer gave me full authority. I am subordinate to him only. The unity of my administration means that the police and the SS must play second fiddle in the Government General—will you please finally realize that, Party Comrade Himmler?" "Bravo, bravo!" your sycophants must have shouted. "The Herr Governor General is really building up a head of steam—he'll knock them for a loop"; "Magnificently spoken, Herr Governor General, truly splendid"; "Ach, if only the Führer could hear you talk like that once, he'd sweep Himmler right out of office."

While your yes-men were babbling all this flattery, you probably threw your head back proudly, took a look at the Beautiful Madonna or the portrait of the young man by that Sunday-painter Raphael, or some other valuable piece, and desperately tried to suppress the truth and your whimpering cowardice by pushing them to some remote recess at the back of your brain.

You probably intoxicated yourself with thoughts of how you were going to let Bormann and Himmler really have it, and so you took off in the direction of Himmler's special train. A slight fluttering of the eyes and twitch of the hands was already a trait of yours; so perhaps it was then, during your automobile trip to the train, that you first covered up your shaking with the obscene gesture of sticking your thumb between your two middle fingers, this big fuck-you. It was the same gesture you later had to make with your damaged left hand in the dock at Nuremberg after your ridiculous attempt at suicide—you did that in order to stop yourself from trembling, too. What you were experiencing on your trip to the three other Nazi big shots was the most profound sense of fear. That, you see, is the other side of assholes like you: they have a terrific anxiety about falling out of favor. You most likely had your adjutant with you, and he must have dealt with the demeaning job of getting you through all the checkpoints, until you were able to get out of your car. Then the two of you were escorted through the woods to Himmler's train by some SS murderer, who finally said, "Herr Governor General, the gentlemen are expecting you." And when you didn't catch on right away, he added, "Alone." Your adjutant had to hand you your briefcase with all your notes and other junk in it, while your heart was sliding down into the seat of your foolish jodhpurs. Taking the high step up to the bottom rung of the railroad car, you let loose with a modest fart out of sheer fright, which you excused with a bleating laugh. At the sound, your adjutant turned quickly to Lammers's adjutant, who was climbing aboard after you, and (just to set the scene right) gave a sour but knowing smile at the fart of the Herr Governor General. You were received by Lammers in his private car. He asked you in a friendly fashion to remove your coat and then led you into the salon. Himmler and Bormann were already seated and they let you stand there for one decisive second longer than necessary, so that you, the accused, would take note of it before they rose to greet you. It was five minutes to noon, and for some stupid reason the old saw "Five minutes early, don't you see, / Is royal punctuality" came to mind; but because of Göring's rhymes about King Stanislaus and Frank-Reich, you swallowed your clever words.

A Comradely
Interrogation

And now, Father, I am going to leave you. I have brought you here to Lammers's private railroad car; I have been sitting next to you in the car all the way from Cracow. Here you are, forty-one years old—judging by your titles, a powerful super–big shot, but in reality a mini–hot dog of a murderer. I've been listening in on your thoughts; for somehow or other, there was probably still the tiny modicum of a sense of justice in you, something that may have occupied your thoughts again on that very journey through your slaughtered Government General, on your journey to the mass murderer Himmler, thoughts about the Reich and about justice and about what a terrifying world all of you together had created. Good, you helped the German people to attain their true nature: war, murder, and slaughter, just as it used to be in long-ago times in the dark forests on this side of the Limes.* But you nevertheless could not have completely forgotten the enthusiasm of your youthful diary. Thoughts of Lilly arose again in your mind; you saw yourself as a boy standing at the fence of the Weiderts, the rich banker's family: a little girl, as young as you were, came up to you, to the fence, you spoke with one another,

* Limes Germanicus was a part of the Roman defense system built c. 74 A.D. east of the Rhine.

you liked each other as children, and that liking turned to love. The love lasted until you were both twenty, and that love was forbidden because you were a poor beggar (according to family lore). But I don't believe that was the reason; it was probably that fawning way you had of putting your head down while looking at someone which Lilly's father couldn't stand, that ingratiating look of subservience he knew so well from his employees at the bank and which he didn't need in his own household.

Now, next to me on the journey to the interrogation, twenty-two years later, you were fat from having stuffed yourself so full; the upholstery on the backseat of the Mercedes (license plate EAST 4) was squashed down under your ass; your adjutant sat in front next to Schamper, your chauffeur. You were musing; it was a cloudy March day; and the two up front knew just as well as you did that your potent words up there at the castle . . . You're grinning in your cauldron? You weren't even coming from the castle, were you? I know it; so I'll take back what I said about the Mercedes. You were coming from some other direction. You had fled from your own little empire after Lasch had been arrested, Lasch, your friend, my Father Number 2, the blond rascal. The first thing you did was to clear out; right in the middle of the war, you were flitting from Vienna to Munich to Berlin. You wanted to take a break from your murderous regime, even though the problem with Lasch and the enterprises involving your own clan had really been keeping you on edge and fully occupied there. What happens if Lasch spills the beans? And that stupid Brigitte, you can't even trust her anymore. And what am I really going to do with those 608 marble slabs? Fear kept pumping through your veins.

In Lammers's private car I quickly steal over to the enemy's corner, for starting at five minutes to noon on this March day, Himmler and Bormann and Lammers begin to have more of my sympathy. And yet I still allow you this teeny-weeny final chance to prove yourself to be the only true one of my three fathers.

Well, let's start the scene. "The journey from Berlin was very pleasant," I can hear you answer to Lammers's perfunctory first question. You cross your legs, but you don't succeed in doing it very elegantly, because the table is too close to the chair for that, or the other way around. Well, anyhow, perhaps I'll remove those damned jodhpurs of yours and have you enter in civvies. Let's say that Chief Sergeant Nickl selected a smashing suit from your wardrobe that morning in Berlin. Or maybe it was Gertrude, at whose house and with whom you slept the night before the "comradely interrogation." In the morning, after endless difficulties, you finally got through to Bühler in Cracow, questioned him once again about any news you might make use of in your "important conversation"; surely you were preparing everything you intended to say and supplying it with all kinds of impressive adjectives. On the other hand, the two of you did not dare to speak openly on the phone; you knew it was bugged. What you really wanted to say probably was "God, Bühler, I am so frightened. Let's talk to each other, buddy to buddy." Instead of that you just babbled on and said that you were hoping to be back at the castle by tomorrow evening; and you shouted at Gertrude that you, "God damn it, can't stand even looking at another egg," which startled poor Gertrude at breakfast as she was taking the treasured eggs from the egg warmer and putting them in the egg cups. She knew nothing about the thousand eggs you got each month, not to mention the other two hundred thousand.

And then you got going, perhaps even in your own private railroad car, so that you could have a contest to determine which private car was the most prestigious; maybe you even had yours cleaned and polished in Berlin, and Himmler and Lammers heard about it, and they, no lazy bums themselves, fitted out their private cars with ruffles and garlands, here another photo of Hitler with personal dedication, there another bureau from France, here an icon from Russia, and there (particularly perfidious of Bormann to have beaten you to it) a framed page from the famous Cracow

Guild Book painted by Beheim in the sixteenth century, while Himmler had a great big horn attached to his car, and he tooted like mad at your arrival, so that poor little Hitler got all mixed up and finally decided on another location for his headquarters, which in turn cost the lives of several hundred thousand German soldiers in the area of Oberkursk, because Keitel confused the departure time of Hitler's special train with the time of attack for one of his blitzkrieg offensives, and so one tooting caused another one, and your private car rushes alongside those of Himmler and Lammers and Bormann (or maybe Bormann didn't have one—oh, that's not right, none of you would have deprived yourself of something like that).

Anyhow, now you sat there and I'm sitting opposite you, between Bormann, the top secretary-stud of the Reich, they called him the typist-fucker, but no matter, Bormann at one side, Himmler at the other side, and he really had himself specially tarted up for the occasion, in the very same uniform that he had on a year later when he came to visit you in Cracow so that you could pay homage to him there.

Off to one side, more in the role of a moderator, sat Lammers, the one you really left dangling at Nuremberg during the pretrial hearings. Himmler stank of perfume. You were sitting opposite us. Here we are facing you, the representatives of cleanliness, godliness, and mass murder with a German flair. And you, what do you stand for? Good Lord, Father, I can be fair, you'll get your chance. But I ask, beginning at what time in one's life is one responsible for his own face? At the latest by thirty-five. But evidently not you—not until your face was dangling in the noose.

Okay, okay, I'll take it back. . . . And so Lammers begins, after the four of you have quickly gone over the state of the war, discussing how the Volga is being fought for, how some Norwegian fjord or other has been taken, how the white cliffs of Birmingham (all of you were far too weak in geography for a war of that size) were beginning to show signs of cracking, and how Field Marshal

Kesselring together with General Guderian of the tank corps, supported by the air armada under the command of Rear Admiral Milch, was pursuing a Dutch midwife and, following her fierce counterattack, had heroically overcome her defenses.

On all sides you showed yourselves very satisfied with the course of the war; but finally Lammers had to get down to the real subject, the way it had been prearranged with Bormann and Himmler.

Their intent was clear: the limb Frank was now out on should be sawn off, and Krüger should become Governor General. But Hitler had simply said no to that; Himmler could go around blowing his horn as much as he wanted, but Hitler insisted on letting Frank twist slowly in the wind a little longer. Maybe it was because of that beautiful twuzzie of yours—remember, back then when you were marching up to the Feldherrnhalle? The plan was therefore altered to make you so entrap yourself, to wring such terrible confessions from you, that you would find yourself compelled to toss in the bloody towel. I was skeptical right away, told the gentlemen that they should never underestimate the honor lacking in your character. I said you were the typical arriviste who had surrendered all his morals long ago with Grandpa's chickens in the kitchen—but the three gentlemen didn't understand that reference, of course. They showed me a variety of power plays they were holding in their hands, and I thought if they played their cards cleverly maybe they could still be successful, but that they should take precautions not to turn Father into a charity case, they should allow him to retain the attributes of a gentleman. "At least he won't need any more eggs"—Bormann was again getting you where it hurts. But all in all, the gentlemen did not wish to be small-minded at your abdication. You were still vainly hoping that it was again simply a matter of Krüger and the last squabble the two of you had: you had begun to appreciate that a true father of his country had to have a couple of battle forces to keep things in line, above all ones that were not under the thumb of Krüger or Himmler; and so, quick as a wink, you had an announcement published in your Cracow newspaper that a law-and-order contingent answerable only to you (which is to say, a police troop) would be set up. All that did was make Krüger send more telegrams of complaint to Himmler.

In those first moments of this meeting you hardly projected the image of an upstanding man in his best years, one whose own private railway car was parked on the next track. Reichsleiter Lammers picked up a fat pile of paper and said: "Herr Governor General, this pile consists of nothing but complaints lodged against you. They are reports about conditions in your sphere of control, about corruption. There are trial transcripts in here—permit me to mention only the cases of Löv and your friend Lasch. . . ."

"He is not my friend—he was one of my governors," you rapidly interjected. At that moment, for the first time in my life, my little heart skipped a beat, and I wanted to point out to you that sudden disjunctions like that don't go down very well with gentlemen such as these, gentlemen who today between noon and two o'clock were the representatives of the true, the genuinely German, the fundamentally upright, *comradely* world of men.

Lammers continued, saying that an additional hang-up to be noted was the hopelessly ruined relationship between you and Krüger, that is to say, the SS. "We should like to discuss these complications at length with you, Herr Governor General, in a thoroughly comradely way; find out how these difficulties can be settled, just so we don't have to bother the Führer with such things."

Why can't you keep your head steady? Why can't you calmly look Lammers in the eye? At least pretend to have an attitude of cool superiority? But you keep crossing and uncrossing your legs, keep turning your head first to Bormann, then to Himmler; you're even making the stupidest of all signs of embarrassment: you're staring at the notes you brought along. And as you're doing so, I can see fear pounding in your temples. Again your eyes are tending to roll back in their sockets. Christ, Father, there are only four and a half years from the date of this comradely interrogation to your lovely and violent death. In a word, you are no longer making the strong impression on us that you once made on me back at the Schoberhof, the time you shouted out "Then hit him back" after I had been bawling that Farmer Langer's son had hit me.

Lammers stopped and looked at you. Now get on with it, Father. And you actually did—you got going, a fact that Himmler noted in his minutes on this momentous (at least for me) meeting, with the sentences: "Frank replied in a very theatrical way and spoke about his work and about corruption." May I give my version of what you said? "Gentlemen, I believe you have no inkling of what tremendous work I must accomplish in the GG. As you know, the Führer has personally appointed me to that task in order that I, as part of the *most* colossal struggle of our epoch, will be able to ensure that the German Reich can not only be furnished with the *most* abundant supplies from any territory, but also that, in the *most* unassailable sense, peace may reign behind our *most* valiantly battling front." You have gotten rather off the subject with all this verbiage, but you can't help babbling along in your beloved superlative-laden style and trying to keep yourself under control with the junk you are spouting. You have indeed regained your self-assurance and are now looking around at the others a bit insolently and growing more expansive. "Unfortunately, in this *most* violent struggle in the world's history, something arises every now and again, something that surely cannot be reconciled with the glorious German concept of morals, and may I here articulate just what that something is, speaking with full assurance, in a very clear and forthright way. It is corruption."

Then you burst out with a shrill laugh that made us all jump. Meanwhile, Himmler, that dog, was leaning over the papers on the table and beginning to take notes. Your laughter continued as you said, "I am alleged to be the *most* corrupt one of all." And then you really got bold. You rapped on the table with the knuckles of your right hand, but quickly had to shift the point of impact because you were striking the pile of papers you'd brought along, so that no authoritative knocking could be heard. You shifted your hand over to the highly polished, dark mahogany tabletop, repeated the word "corruption" once again, then added with a burst of laughter, "Ha, ha, *most* corrupt one of all," and then said, knocking with the knuckle of your middle finger, "I am solely and *most* uniquely responsible to the Führer alone. Please take note of that. I also add, and in doing so I give expression to my *most* deeply felt astonishment, that I consider it outrageous, I consider it impossible"—every syllable got its own knuckle rap—"that any one of you would conceivably believe of me that the reproach of corruption could apply to me. You cannot think of me in those terms."

Bormann placed his broad hand on my little paw, for I had begun applauding and was now awaiting your ultimate gesture of rejection—waiting for you to pull your revolver out of your jodhpur pocket with your left hand, while you kept drumming on the tabletop with your right hand, and waiting for you to shoot under the table (you certainly had practiced it long enough at Cracow under the Renaissance tables, and ruined a lot of them in doing so), waiting for you to shoot Himmler and, after him, Bormann, and finally Lammers, in the crotch, and then doing it once more, getting them this time somewhat higher, in the stomach. Meanwhile I was beating it out the rear door of the railroad car with Bormann's cocked pistol in my hand, and you were up in a flash and out of the forward door; we secured our position while the three crooks were slowly biting the dust in the *most* gruesome agony (Father, here your superlatives are appropriate—it's wicked to die from bullets in the balls and stomach); my God, what a beautiful bronze tablet we (or at least I) would have today at the Schoberhof! Mother would be getting her (that is to say, your) ex-minister's pension checks, maybe even with an annual increment, like so many Nazi widows. The bronze relief would show us hand in hand, me little, you big. Your crude features would be somewhat idealized, and each of us would have a pistol in his hand, and beneath would be the inscription: "They died with their boots on, while killing for the honor of Germany." For naturally we would never have gotten away, forever, not even with a lucky last shot over the shoulder. You would have ended up on a meat hook and I with a syringe stuck in me; but Mother, after handing over the 608 marble slabs, the eggs, her warehouse full of furs, and the letters with which she could verify the collapse of your marriage, would have barely escaped with her life and endured to the end of the war.

But no. You always wanted to weasel out of things. After your finger-knuckle speech the three gentlemen were silent for a moment, and then Himmler began to speak. Can you imagine my disappointment? Not a shot was heard. You sat there like Sarah Bernhardt with fluttering eyelids. Himmler didn't even react to your words but began to speak in a hard voice, putting steel into every word: "Since you have just been mentioning the front, Comrade Frank, you will permit me to add a bit to your image by informing you that those on the front lines have a very negative impression of your leadership. The atmosphere in the zone behind the lines was like the old Wild West. The news of the Löv trial and the case against your friend Lasch, with his two doctor's degrees, has spread by word of mouth and has produced a most dangerously defeatist attitude.

"Now let me come to the principal reproaches against you and those around you. Those concerned were unable to distinguish between private and official confiscation; and—may I be as serious about this as possible, Frank—it is totally out of the question for private individuals to go shopping in the ghetto. The fact that your wife and your sister have been personally dealing with Jews—yes, the fact that someone even wanted to establish a tobacco monopoly for the Jew Henlein—those things are just as insufferable as the word of your so-called 'appraisers' "—I can see you senselessly scribbling down the word "appraisers," Father—"who cook up

fanciful figures and sums—furs for three zlotys, for example—
and say that the castle in Cracow desperately needs this and that."

You interrupted Himmler before he could continue, got your
tonsils back in gear again—although I could already tell that
Himmler was holding a letter written in Mother's hand. With
your unpleasant voice you shouted, "The representatives of the
Reich—" but Himmler was put off the track only to the extent
that he lowered his hand with her letter in it and continued what
he had to say: "What I also neglected to tell you, Comrade Frank,
is that not only the soldiers at the front but also our German
comrades in both the Reich and the GG are at one in reproaching
you and your government with accusations of gluttony and of
inappropriate behavior in wartime with those theater and opera
performances of yours, your black-marketeering, and your grandiose banquets."

Now your turn again. You shake your head, lean forward, and
fix Himmler with a stare. "The representatives of the Reich"—
too bad you had to repeat yourself like that; it doesn't make a
very good impression, even though I'm not sure if those three
criminal morons opposite you were capable of appreciating rhetorical refinements—"the representatives of the Reich, confronted
as they are by the murderous animosity of a population of more
than sixteen million people, are in such a minority that only"—
and you straightened up your plump torso slightly; you evidently
had the impression that an escape hatch was coming for you—
"that only a ruthlessly determined corps of representatives worthy
of the Reich can maintain administrative authority."

Father, that is brilliant. Clearly that sentence must have circulated widely after the war, because today its message is strictly
adhered to by our political parties here in Germany. You added
one more thing: "Only true representatives of the master race are
capable of leadership in the East." And now, without your realizing
it, you duplicated precisely the gesture that Hitler always used
during his speeches when he wanted to deny something: a hectic

shaking of his fingers, his hand, his whole arm, accompanied by louder and louder screeching. Even for me your voice was too loud, as you continued, "I cannot permit the development of these authentic master-race personalities to be measured according to the yardstick of small-minded, bourgeois convention; rather, I must assure them an open and generous atmosphere in which to develop."

So that's it—feasting and corruption as the means of maintaining the State. Congratulations, dear Father; your ideas were signposts for the future. There and then, in that railroad car (which, you'll have to admit, was better furnished than ours), you couldn't be held back any longer. You screamed, "For the entire future expansion of our great World Reich these conditions will have to prevail!" And then, with a scornful grimace directed at Lammers, you added, "It is high time, my dear Comrade Lammers, to clarify this point of view for the central departments in the administration of the Reich in particular"—you took in enough air for the following relative clause—"this point of view which, with full justification, is constantly emphasized by comrades such as Rosenberg, Koch, and Lohse as well as by me."

Did you have them in the palm of your hand now? Unfortunately, no. Himmler delicately raised that letter from Mother, and said merely, "This is a letter from your wife." At that you turned pale. In fact it prompted you to write Mother somewhat later: "So now you have gone over to the camp of my mortal enemies." In all of this, the two of you—I mean Himmler and you—knew more than I did. I still don't know whether Mother's letter had been directed to Himmler or Lammers or Bormann or Hitler, whether it concerned the picnic-basket letter that Himmler's SS had confiscated from the Jewish Council, whether it was nothing more than Mother's usual shopping list ("Absolutely must have another rat fur coat from the ghetto; have heard that rats are now on all the dinner menus there, so what are the Jews doing with the fur? Leave for ghetto at 8:30 a.m."), or whether she was literally dangling you like a victim in front of Himmler, maybe because your two hundred thousand eggs had slipped through her fingers. Was it a letter phrased already in that tearjerker style she later developed and used to promote the sale of your "gallows" book? "Dear Reichsführer SS Himmler, May I take just a bit of your precious time? My dire economic situation compels me to inform you that my husband, the Reichsminister and Governor General of Poland, has diverted two hundred thousand eggs. . . ."

What was in the letter I shall never know. In any case, you suddenly appeared to grow pale just when your puffed-up face had taken on such a beautiful red color during your excited speech. Himmler took careful note of the expression on that face and then continued his litany by adding (1) that Löv had testified that he was requested to purchase a gold fountain pen for you in the ghetto, one which, however, was not to cost more than one hundred zlotys; (2) that (and here Himmler wandered a bit from the subject) your brother-in-law Heinrich had renounced his German citizenship in 1934 in favor of a Swedish one and had done big business with the GG; (3) that brother-in-law Otto was your private secretary; and (4) that brother-in-law Marian Bayer had been appointed head trustee for the textile industry in the GG and had set about making a real killing from that. After listening to all this, you not only must have uttered a heartfelt curse against your wife's whole family but also must have noticed that the cards you were holding in your hand were suddenly pretty poor.

Himmler stopped speaking. Now it was Bormann's turn, though he spoke only one sentence: "The Führer, by the way, maintains the view that relatives are not to be employed by other relatives." That sentence—it came to you like a flash of lightning—could be your salvation. Now you could hold your head up at the moment of defeat; now you could commit treason by thinning out your family a little; now you could retain your position on the Wawel. Your filthy brain began to function; you leaned back in your chair, relaxed; you nodded; you put that faithful-to-the-Führer look on your face, the one with the solemn, down-turned mouth, the one we Germans always have when we're cooking up murder plans at our desks; and you said to Bormann: "I must express my pleasure at hearing you state this viewpoint as that of the Führer. That's new to me. That is completely new to me. Well, then, gentlemen, I shall try to convince my one brother-in-law to volunteer for the Wehrmacht, preferably the infantry. As to my brother-in-law Marian, I shall replace him on the first of August this year."

Bravo, Father—that cost Marian his life. Anyhow, why did he really want to persist in knocking back his schnapps with garlic cloves every evening as a company trustee in Poland, of all places? Still, that was his own business.

Himmler took notes on what you were saying and continued mercilessly. Now they had softened you up, and everything went very smoothly for them. As always, whenever you were face to face in a battle of personalities, you lost. Himmler mentioned several more instances of bribery and the Lasch trial. You immediately gave your okay for Lasch to be delivered up to the court in Breslau, and your okay to every other corruption case waiting in the wings. "Frank was in complete agreement with that," Himmler noted smugly. Yes, Father, even I liked him for sticking to the subject under discussion and for his complete victory over you, you political hack. Himmler said: "For my part, I no longer have any reservations about you, now that you have given us these reassurances. How do things look from your point of view?" He was directing this last sentence, of course, to Lammers and Bormann, both of whom shook their heads, which must have made your face flush once again. There you sit, letting them throw all that crap in your face, and yet still grateful to them for graciously permitting you to retain your cozy job. Himmler the victor began to wrap things up: "Do you know, Frank, if we hadn't had hopes of an understanding with you, we wouldn't even be sitting here talking. Instead we would have brought all these things directly to the attention of the Führer." With horror, you suddenly saw that you were holding in your hand the gold fountain pen ("not to cost more than one hundred zlotys"). No one had noticed it; you slowly tucked it away out of sight while Himmler went on taking advantage of the lowest point you had thus far reached in your moral and political career. Your battle with Krüger was now decided. Up to now, you had cleverly arranged for Krüger to report to your deputy Bühler in your absence, and even while you were in residence, because Bühler, in order to give you some relief from your tasks (what tasks, Father?), was supposed to concern himself more with matters of governing. When Krüger heard that, his brain practically exploded; he loaded the telex lines with one complaint after another. Himmler was also angry, but by now (you were shoving the golden fountain pen deeper and deeper into the recesses of your uniform jacket) he had such a hold on you that he was later able to report: "Frank agreed without hesitation that henceforth and immediately a state secretariat would be established for SS Obergruppenführer Krüger for all questions relating to the police and to the strengthening of German culture."

I can see you now, fawning, fluttering your eyelids, sitting opposite us, nodding with your head, now and then uttering an "Of course," and accommodating yourself to the new turn of events—for example, when you, eagerly panting, agreed that Krüger's appointment will "most powerfully augment" security in the GG, and other similar shit. You had to sweat blood in order to get into the grace and favor of the mighty ones. The business with the fountain pen was also too stupid, and Brigitte is going to have to listen to a thing or two. You were thinking about what you were going to write her later: that she is a menace to you in your position in the GG. With perfect composure, Himmler accepts one more surrender from you; he writes: "We were in perfect agreement that Reichsminister Dr. Lammers will arrange for a decree from the Führer, which will establish that Reichsführer Himmler will have the authority to issue directives to the administration of the Government General, and more precisely to the State Secretary for Security and Consolidation." So that's the end of it, your grandiose idea of a unified administration—i.e., the idea of your unrestricted power. Now they were even taking away from you the last remnant of authority with which you were hoping to retain a modicum of local power, your Sonderdienst, your own police corps, for it, too, was awarded to Krüger. (Again you said, "Of course.") Can you still feel my spit on your face, the spit I sprayed on you when, after all this slaughter, you issued that invitation to Himmler? You asked him, "now that all questions have been clarified," to visit you sometime in Cracow. Himmler noted with evident enjoyment in his minutes: "I accepted the invitation, after the issuing of these decrees, to come to Cracow sometime in order to discuss our future common enterprise, in particular the German settlement of the districts of Lublin and Galicia."

"I very much look forward to your visit, Reichsführer," you said, marking the sleazy conclusion to your part in the affair. Then you were obliged to take your leave, as at the end of an examination. We remained seated and watched you disappear, you silly fool. But no, you came back again, careful to knock before entering, and when you opened the door to the salon you could still see the ironic, triumphant smile on all their faces. Once again you addressed Himmler: "Reichsführer, there is something else I would like to mention. I would be most eager to have an SS captain of police as my new adjutant. I believe that would re-establish my connection with Krüger—the damage to which, incidentally, I deeply regret." You stood there; Himmler nodded and agreed to your request. "Heil Hitler" were your last words as you closed the door again.

"In One Hour
I Shall Be No More"

My God, Father, I wonder how you must have felt; how can one possibly go along with stuff like that? Had your corruption, your obsession for titles, good food, and lofty ramparts dehumanized you to the point that you were actually incapable of going to your communications center and announcing your definite resignation? In fact, during the interrogation you had already announced you would do that very thing. "It is not at all certain," you had said, "whether I shall even return to my post as Governor General." Well, then, that would have been the time to go through with it, and then afterwards rush back to Lammers's private car, shoot all of them dead—and maybe shoot yourself. But again, nothing like that. Instead, you just stalked away with Lammers's adjutant, who was waiting for you outside, walked past the barrier to your automobile, flung your briefcase into a corner of the backseat, and sat yourself down next to it. Or did you get into your own private railroad car on the next siding? Or maybe one of Himmler's drivers drove you to Cracow. Whatever, no matter where you were headed for after this comradely interrogation, you couldn't show your face anywhere, not even to yourself.

But still, you had made it through. Your sinecure was more important. So you wrote one more letter to Lammers, in which you hoped to settle once and for all the business with the gold fountain pen and the furs: "Should you ever again hear the assertion that Löv bought a gold fountain pen in the ghetto under the pretext that it was for the Governor General and that it was to cost no more than one hundred zlotys, please be assured that the following are the simple facts of the case [*I can see you now—pant, pant, sweat, sweat—cooking up this fable with the gentlemen of your administration, and at the same time shitting in your jodhpurs from fear*]. The officials and employees of the Governor General's office wished to present me with a fountain pen for Christmas, 1940, a pen that could be used every day for signing my official correspondence. . . . Consequently, I have not been informed about the details of its purchase."

Hey, that sounds good, Father. You follow that right up with another smart move, go on the offensive and act indignant: "In no possible way is it to be assumed that someone had commissioned Löv to purchase the fountain pen in the ghetto, and certainly not for a price of one hundred zlotys."

Your use of the word "someone" makes no sense at all, for earlier you had written that the people in your office wanted to give you the thing. Somehow or other they must have reached an agreement so that not every one of them would go out and buy a fountain pen—a crowd like that would have been too much for the ghetto. Somehow or other you (or one of your advisers) must have realized that. Anyhow, you reappear in your next sentence as the old legal expert: "As for the rest, and in view of the judicial structure of the occupied territory, it is not to be construed as a criminal offense whenever such purchases are transacted within the framework of verifiable and official orders."

So, as you must have sighed in great relief, the pen problem has been cleared from the table, and all that's left is that nonsense about the appraisal of Mother's furs, three zlotys apiece.

Now that you were back up at your castle you felt safe again, far from the ugly faces of Himmler and Bormann. You stood up from your desk; your advisers backed away in deference. Or could it perhaps have been Mother with whom you concocted your rebuttal? You walked to the window, gazed down upon your Cracow, your Poles, your Jews. The weather was unfriendly on this tenth of March, the date you composed this letter to Lammers—particularly unfriendly for the Jews in the Cracow ghetto. Could it be that the wind was wafting the sounds of shots, screams, barking dogs in your direction? Today the Jews were being driven from their homes in a brutal SS operation and transported to camps. Some women and children were shot to death; German police dogs, carefully trained, were sniffing out those who had hidden themselves; that, of course, meant their immediate death. Up at our castle, however, it was peaceful and cozy; outside, it was misty and cold, and it was that weather which provided you with your decisive inspiration. You let out a whistle, turned on your heel, strode the twenty-seven steps to your desk (what about that—I can remember exactly the enormous size of your office), and said: "Brigitte, listen to this! That's it—they'll never get us now!" You sat down, and as you wrote with your extorted gold fountain pen, you hissed out each syllable aloud: "In the Government General as elsewhere in the Eastern territories, furs were, and still are, part and parcel of the necessary outfitting of all Germans, for the winters here last five full months. The entire personnel here has had to be provided with furs, to the extent that this was possible."

You were satisfied with yourself. The bitter cold of the East would warm the hearts in Berlin.

But neither Mother nor any member of your staff was persuaded. The argument still had to be reinforced, they said. To be sure, those could serve wonderfully as key sentences, they said, but one could not start off with them so blatantly, and someone shouted, "The Wehrmacht was just issued furs recently." And someone else said that the "three zlotys" could be explained away as an error in arithmetic. Or possibly . . . You began to puzzle out what part of a fur could possibly cost only three zlotys. The secretaries were called in and consulted; they provided the solution. A receipt for payment was quickly concocted, typed out, predated; everyone was gathered around your desk, smiling happily—and when you read aloud the resulting letter, all voices repeated your words like a chorus as you scanned the text, their voices gradually growing louder and louder, for now it seemed perfect to all present: "In a final accounting, which had been drawn up in writing by Löv in his function as the representative of the castle administration, there was a line item dealing with three fox fur stoles in which glass eyes had been set. A charge of three zlotys each for these artificial eyes was recorded. The woman in the administrative offices who dealt with the bills submitted the designated amount in payment. When it was revealed through a subsequent query that the bill had evidently been misinterpreted, the correct and normal amount was immediately forwarded [*why do you call this a normal amount, hmm, Father? That's a weak point in your letter*]. In the Government General, as elsewhere in the Eastern territories, furs were, and still are, part and parcel of the necessary outfitting of all Germans, for the winters here last five full months. The entire personnel here has had to be provided with furs, to the extent that this was possible. All of these furs were obtained through regular channels and at normal prices and were paid for at both normal and regular rates. Incidentally, whatever furs were located in the possession of the Government General [*don't you mean whatever furs the Franks had left over?*] have long since been forwarded to the wool and fur collection point for the use of the Wehrmacht."

Just let those people in Berlin go on gossiping about corruption. But now Mother and your sister began yammering about how they had been left standing out in the cold, and so one more paragraph was added: "As to the purchases made by my wife and/or my sister in the Government General, the usual regulations apply, according to which every German from the Reich within the Government General has been permitted to make purchases in compliance with the general moderation demanded by the present situation [*it couldn't be better expressed, Father*], so long as the supplies were available in the Government General [*another excellent clause; but who actually had to keep building up the stock, Father?*]; this procedure is in line with practices in effect in all occupied territories, in the East as in the West, in the North as in the South." This last sentence is cleverly formulated, since it allows for gradual geographical shrinkage, until (thanks to the diminishing returns from our slaughter program) the point was reached in May 1945 when the whole German Reich simply goes up in a puff of smoke.

After Frau Mylo types one final, clean copy, you sign the letter with a feeling of accomplishment, "Heil Hitler! Your Frank." Then as you read it through you have another thought: namely, that perhaps this or that additional proof of the authenticity of your statements should be appended—that a little poem should be added. And so, in a happy circle, refreshing yourself with Polish sacramental wine and Baumkuchen (little cakes a mere fifteen inches high each; I have a photograph of a feast at the castle in which every guest is being served an individual cake like that— may I squeeze that information in here? And we know how much you liked to guzzle wine consecrated for the mass), you begin your verse. When the group effort is finished, you write the final version on a fresh piece of paper with the gold ghetto pen:

> *In the castle at Cracow, at Kressendorf,*
> *In Munich and Berlin, at the Schoberhof,*
> *We hear everywhere the selfsame yell:*
> *"I need a pen quickly, and I really mean schnell!"*
> *The spark is struck, we are soon all afire*
> *To bring the GG his heart's desire.*
> *But the powerful hand of our lord and master*
> *Breaks all the pen points—it's a dreadful disaster.*
> *To forfend any similar repetition*
> *We seize today's chance and escape our perdition,*

By presenting our boss with this gold fountain pen.
May he wield it forever and ever. Amen.

What is the poet trying to tell us with this verse? The first two lines show that the dedicatee is the owner of several properties, a total of five, a mythical number. After a straightforward listing of them in the first two lines, suddenly the drama begins and culminates temporarily in the word "yell," and the plot is driven forward by means of active verbs (e.g., to "strike a spark") cleverly used in the passive voice. "GG" is doubtless an abbreviation of the dedicatee's honorific. It is probably meant to indicate a title of office, a supposition bolstered by the pre-positioned definite article. The power of this GG is symbolically elucidated by the vibrant image with its strong allusion to a Germanic sword: "But the powerful hand of our lord and master / Breaks all the pen points. . . ." On the one hand, the potent syntax of this sentence strikes the eye; we are surely to assume that a certain volatility in the nature of the dedicatee is being evoked. On the other hand, the terms "lord and master" and "powerful hand" are meant to make it clear that we are dealing here with a poem from the so-called "epic of the Third Reich. . . ."

Okay, okay, Father, I'll stop. But the poem is genuine. Your letter is genuine. I can believe you, I suppose, when you object that the poem really came into being without your knowledge, that there really was a presentation of a gold fountain pen. Nevertheless, as I know your life, as I know your character, my version of the events seems more likely. That's the result of the extremes to which you took things.

Where should I go with you now? Should I go on tormenting you in your terrifying eternity? I know you don't want me to stop, especially not now when I could be describing how nobly you arose and departed from Poland in order to deliver your four great speeches in the Reich. You're cross with me, aren't you, because I go on needling you about those lowlife affairs with eggs and furs and refuse to dwell on the things you consider more immortal.

Oh, something else, Father. At first, Krüger seemed to be unable to appreciate his good fortune. Himmler ticked him off with a telegram: "Dear Krüger, I learn from a letter of yours to SS Obergruppenführer DaLuege that you're having difficulties now because of the Sonderdienst. I must now tell you in all seriousness that you finally must stand up for yourself in this matter. The Führer's decree has been signed. You are State Secretary. You are now in the saddle, so please finally ride the horse yourself."

The horse, Father, was you. They rode you to your ruin. But many a one who sat on your back was ridden to his own death, too. Above all, those you were obliged to throw. Like Lasch. How the story of my second father's death gives me the creeps still. By the way, in forging your diary later, you have the wrong date. He wasn't shot as early as May 6, 1942, on the orders of Himmler; he died on June 3, 1942, at 4:45 in the afternoon—a time of day when most other people are simply enjoying tea. My poor Daddy Number 2, who liked to seduce secretaries and, every now and then, Mother. I have a photo of him: a watered-down version of Fred Astaire, dancing in the woods at a picnic outing, with a snappy little handkerchief in his breast pocket, a soft double chin, eyes bulging out. How they must have been bulging when he learned in his cell at Cracow or at Breslau that his final moment had come. "In one hour I shall be no more," he wrote to some sweetheart at home, a pistol on the table in front of him, sent by Himmler with his comradely greetings, suggesting that he might please execute himself. Or I might select the other version put forward to explain his death; it seems to me more plausible: two SS men block the door, then enter. They always murdered in pairs; that seems to have been according to regulations. Was it so they could impress each other?

Lasch writes: "After settling all other matters, I am sending my final letter to you so that I might be with you at the hour of my death. It will be agony for me, this necessary departure after a deed that cannot be undone. But believe me, it is the best for me. Now that misfortune has befallen us, there is not any possibility of going back." The following is clearly directed at you, Father: "I have been abandoned and betrayed by all; in my despair, I know I have done much wrong and would in any case have faced harsh punishment." Father, that's beginning to sound like a business deal, his final piece of business: you're going to kill me (or I'm going to kill me), but I have not been legally sentenced to die and will therefore not leave behind the humiliation of it for my wife and family to bear.

Lasch is sitting at his little table, working on his screwy language and thoughts on the Acquittal First Class he has awarded himself. Can you appreciate his situation? He continues: "The whole thing, of course, has been dreck, a filthy mess. [*Can you see from his use of the word "dreck" how the fear of death has seized hold of him, your blond rascal? His urge to stay alive has suddenly and powerfully re-emerged; he realizes that a couple of truckloads of Polish art are not worth dying for when you're only thirty-eight. For a few seconds his imagination is filled with a shower of little exploding golden balls, the fireworks of hope that Himmler will come in laughing and smiling, take away the pistol, slap Lasch heartily on the shoulder, and say: "It was only a joke, my dear Lasch, only a little test. The truth is, we intend to put Frank in this cell." But nothing has changed, and he goes on writing.*] Others have profited from it; I myself never have, but it seems that I must bear the responsibility and now atone for it. . . . Yes, it is better to die than to live without honor." Father, you always thought exactly the opposite.

The letter continues, sweet and sappy, with hearts and flowers, anguish and eternity, just the way Germans writing in that stupid German style have always checked out from life. Then suddenly he tosses in a sentence that like a sudden flash of lightning reveals how outrageously people under threat of death were prompted at that time to testify against other members of their own family: "I have forgiven my parents, for they were only tools of fate."

What a picnic a writer could have with Lasch's last months,

Father. Those scenes where the blond rascal of a Governor has frantically gathered up his loot to ship it out of the country; this mad pursuit of secretaries, pressuring them to sleep with him; the woman who betrays him out of jealousy with her phone call to the SS; my pious Father in a truck full of Madonnas, carpets, furs, canned goods, only a hundred meters to go before reaching the border between the Government General and the Old Reich; the call from SD Security Headquarters, Cracow, to the border guards: "Stop him!"; the gate is lowered, the SS pulls up; naturally it's night—night has a monopoly on such scenarios—and naturally it's raining. At the same moment, Lasch is in his governor's palace, is lustfully abed with his new catch, huffing and puffing; the jealous secretary has opened the service door for the SS, goes up with them; he hears the boots of the SS outside his elegant chamber; the bimbo steamily involved with him sits up and then climbs up and off him; the SS enters the bedroom.

"The whole thing went so incredibly fast," said Lasch's deputy years later. "In a split second he was arrested and dragged away by the SS."

That didn't bother you. You had enough to do just protecting yourself. And so my second father sat in his cell and wrote: "How I would have loved to experience the German Reich in all its splendor and glory after the war." And then comes another sentence of the sort that always annoys me, in your prose as well as in others'; hardly have you finished detailing your woes when you turn the tables and play the hero: "How glad I would have been to die the honorable death of a soldier at the front." Father Lasch, I don't believe you. When I consider your deceitful, money-grubbing life, I'm certain you would have sold the collective food supplies of the German Army to Armenia in a second. But dying an honorable death? No, really not. Maybe you could have performed the miracle (which would probably have made me ultimately prefer you to my Daddy Number 1) of selling the plans for the disposition of troops at the front to the Russians, or the plans of attack of the Seventh Airborne Troops on the Irkutsk Basin; you could have hocked the poison-gas grenades which the honorable German generals so humanely intended to use to annihilate the civilians of Leningrad to the Hungarian peasants for exterminating moles. But that you yourself would ever have pressed the butt of a rifle against your own soft, white shoulder—oh, no.

Father, in a single respect Lasch is one up on you. After the war, a married couple and their two daughters were trying to trace him; he had once helped them escape from Radom. They said, "Dr. Lasch greatly aided us and two other people and did so with total disregard of Nazi principles. We shall always think of him with great gratitude." I've never held in my hands any evidence like that about you.

You're roaring down there in your cauldron, claiming that I have; screaming that I'm lying. Me, lying? Yes, I'm lying. You're right. But calm down. Here's something that I don't want to suppress: a song for you, written by Richard Strauss. Yes, Strauss sang a song, *for you*, and accompanied himself at the piano. You were standing there next to him, in his home, struck dumb in your vanity, flattered by the fact that this world-famous composer, for you alone, *only you*, had made up this little ditty and turned it into a song. You hum the melody and I'll recite the text:

> *Who enters the room, so slender, so swank?*
> *Behold our friend, our Minister Frank,*
> *Like Lohengrin sent by God, our Master,*
> *To save us all from every disaster.*
> *And thus I laud, I praise, I thank*
> *Our noble friend, good Minister Frank!*

What's he thanking you for, Father? I have yet to discover the exact answer to that. What I do know is that it was Strauss who once wrote that nauseating open letter in which he demanded the expulsion of Thomas Mann from Germany. So my rough guess is that you as Minister issued some order or other paving the way for this great friend of yours to circumvent a bureaucratic obstacle or two.

By the way, here's something that will bug you: the catalogue of the works of Strauss makes no mention of the grand "Hymn to Reichsminister Dr. Frank." I daresay you would approve the Strauss estate's coughing up the musical notation for this masterpiece so that it could be sung as an encore after each Strauss opera production.

Back to Lasch. He's still sitting in his cell; he's still alive. And he writes, "Now the end is near. Himmler is waiting. Farewell . . . farewell. . . . Your Karl."

What a reassuring feeling it gives me to picture the SS entering the cell just as he is writing his next-to-last sentence. Now just guess, Father, who suddenly appears on the scene? Right. Good old, dear old "God"—the words you crooks were always prepared to spit out at a moment's notice, God packaged in saliva. "God bless you & keep you." Did he only have time to write an ampersand because the SS were already snarling at the door and had already released the safety catches of their pistols?

What traces are left of Lasch? An urn arrived weeks later, perhaps from Auschwitz, perhaps from Breslau. It was buried in the Waldfriedhof in Munich, right near where Mother also reposes. Do you suppose that the two of them, sharing the same birthday, are now joined together beneath the sod? Probably not. All the mourners knew perfectly well that what filled that urn could never have been the real ashes of Lasch. Both you and he were tossed to the winds.

So all that finally remains is a thumbnail biography, put together by two historians, Präg and Jacobmeyer. When I match up your two careers, it would seem in truth that the paths of two authentic bums managed to cross each other in life.

Lasch, Karl, Doctor of Political Science, Doctor of Laws. Born December 29, 1904, in Kassel. Wilhelm-Gymnasium; banking apprentice, passed examinations, received his certificate of maturity. Studied economics (Cologne). June 1, 1928, in the auditing department of the Klöckner Works (Castrop-Rauxel); graduate degree, Doctor of Political Science; January 1, 1931, fiduciary for economic matters in Kassel; implicated in several civil suits on account of financial irregularities (inconclusive); March 18, 1932, oath of disclosure (bankruptcy). Winter semester 1931–32, law studies (Munich), working simultaneously for the Allianz Insurance Company. Party member (NSDAP) since June 1, 1931 (No. 547640). June 26, 1933, temporary director, and since October 1, 1933, chief business manager, Academy of German Justice; February 12, 1934, director of the Academy. December 1934, promotion to Doctor of Laws, partially by virtue of credits earned through the irregular use of prize essays lifted from the files of the Academy of German Justice (inconclusive party-court trial). June 10, 1936, chief of the Office of Justice for the Reich. December 28, 1939, Governor of the district of Radom [*it's astonishing how quickly you brought Lasch in; your own installation as Governor General dates from October 26, which means that after a mere two months you two crooks were together, setting yourselves up for the plunder*]; August 1941, Governor of the district of Galicia; September 30, 1941, party-court trial because of various irregularities (quashed by a decree of the Führer dated April 27, 1938). January 24, 1942, committed to detention by the German Special Court in Cracow; May 9, 1942, charged by the Attorney General at the Special Court in Breslau (verdict demanded by prosecution: death sentence by reason of corruption, criminal foreign-exchange dealings, black-marketeering, etc.); June 3, 1942, executed on the orders of Himmler, without judgment having been rendered.

Now enter Uncle Marian. This good man from somewhere in the employ of the IG Farben Industries in Frankfurt, whose little beard and whose hair, graying at the temples, made him look like one of those display-window mannequins that are used to lure old gentlemen into buying stylish suits, that lover of garlic with schnapps, this Uncle Marian of mine came to a wretched end in prison because, pressured by Mother, you had brought him into the GG as your authorized representative for the textile industry. And lo and behold, this good man of industry really made hay in his new role, but with his old code of ethics. Himmler's informers checked him out and discovered that in the first year alone he had made a profit of one million zlotys.

Beyond merely making money, he also knew that he had to catch up in other respects. He and Aunt Else, his wife, Mother's sister, wrote you on December 23, 1941: "Your kind invitation to stay at Belvedere Palace in Warsaw was a pre-Christmas treat for us. The rooms as they are presently decorated are fabulously beautiful; we had to walk through them again and again, admiring everything. . . . I have already seen many beautiful things in my life, but what I got to see in the Belvedere is really something special. Only a true gentleman knows how to furnish his rooms so elegantly and with such rare connoisseurship. The discreet atmosphere in every room would please the most discriminating taste. . . ." One can already hear the greed dripping from his pen, greed for a life equally beautiful, equally discreet—it's crazy but it's true. One can only be grateful to Himmler for snatching Uncle Marian away. Of course, it was only as a substitute for you. Reichsführer Himmler really did a great job of terrorizing our relatives. Uncle Marian, whom I knew only as a photograph in a silver frame on his widow's writing table, whom for decades I thought of as one of the few innocent members of our clan, died like a dog a mere three years after having so admired your elegant and lordly taste. He was sentenced to four and a half years' imprisonment on account of black-marketeering. He suffered from heart trouble, got no medication; the good man couldn't even beg the guard for his evening garlic clove. They just let Uncle Marian starve to death.

Can you recall driving with Mother past the prison in 1944 in your official Mercedes and Mother whining, "Hans, can't you really do anything for Marian?" You sit there in silence. You don't utter a word. You puff on your cigar. Maybe you're silent because you know that whomever you help stays on the death list anyhow.

When Dr. Losacker, your Polish Minister of the Interior, was being hunted down by Himmler because he had actually gone out and picked a fight with the SS in the GG, he was warned by a friend in either the foreign or the interior ministry that he'd better get himself onto a train at once and not even think about returning home.

Dr. Losacker had organized and was present at a meeting of Polish landowners for the purpose of arranging a modus vivendi between landowners and occupiers. Krüger got wind of the meeting being held at one of the estates and committed a true atrocity in Himmler's name. Scarcely had Dr. Losacker left the meeting when the SS arrived and executed all the landowners. They waited for him to leave in order to create the impression that the Minister of the Interior had himself set the trap. When Dr. Losacker heard about it, he dispatched cars with loudspeakers to drive throughout the area denouncing the SS crime, in Polish, as an act of terror. It's obvious, Father, why Himmler was in a rage after that.

Even faced with his awful predicament, Dr. Losacker went to your castle and left a message in your office (you were at Kressendorf at the time) informing you that he was being sought by Himmler and asking you, please, not to try to do anything to help him.

"Why did you do that, Dr. Losacker?" I asked him. "Surely my father would have been able to help you."

He hemmed and hawed, and then he told me candidly, "If your father had interfered, if he had stood up for me, I would have been a dead man."

He is the only courageous man I ever discovered in your circle. His friend the Secretary of State helped him go into hiding in

Berlin and through tough telephone negotiations arranged with Himmler that instead of being executed, Dr. Losacker would be sent to the front as a member of the Punishment Battalion.

Considered in the light of your noninterference on this occasion, you actually did some good for one human being.

Gift-Wrapped Poles

I beg your pardon, Father, let me correct myself. There were others you helped, of course. On the one hand, there was the Deportation-of-Poles Program; on the other, you personally developed your Presentation-of-the-Poles Program—for a select group of friends, naturally.

Were the Poles in question sent out as gift packages with little ribbons tied around their heads? Or were they delivered on a leash by a GG policeman? Such as, for example, the one you sent to your friends the Gulbranssons, who thanked you so heartily for the gift, thus revealing that there was a period in the lives of this brilliant artist and his wife, Dagny, when even they took leave of their senses. "Dear and Most Valued Herr Governor General, We were so happy when the Pole arrived Sunday morning and in such good condition. . . . He makes a most proper impression and is already hard at work in the garden."

Olaf Gulbransson himself writes, "Bronislav is like a present from the Promised Land. Dagny and I breathed such a sigh of relief. You know how tormented we were by our former drunkard. That one drank up all his earnings, sixty marks from us, as well as his pension of another sixty. He would begin drinking Friday afternoon and by Monday he was still drunk. Aside from that, he had such a poisonous personality, a class-conscious rowdy, constantly arguing with all our neighbors. And he was often so nasty to my Dagny. . . . Thank God I didn't know about it at the time. I would have finished him off with a quick uppercut to the jaw. And I'm so unhappy when I'm in prison. Oh, how good Bronislav is for us! He is capable, industrious, has high cheekbones, a true White Russian type; but his father is from Posen, and so he is really German. His way of speaking is calm, slow, East Prussian. He could be my brother. I didn't tell him that, didn't even let him notice anything. But we exchanged a reassuring glance of recognition when we first met—or so I believe."

A letter like this really hurts me, because I love the drawings of this man so much, because I remember how he once illustrated Ludwig Thoma's *Lausbubengeschichten* in a way that practically makes the text superfluous. And then for him to be capable of writing a letter like that. Yes, it's full of his charm, full of his touching Norwegian idiosyncrasies in handling German grammar (which I have edited out here). But how could he have been capable of writing you so snivelingly from his home on the Tegernsee, this Norwegian colossus who exuded human warmth, who turned the coldness around him into coziness? How could he have written, "Whom have I to thank for this piece of great fortune up here on my hill? I do not know how I should phrase it. Dear and honored neighbor, I can only shake your hand with both of mine and say with all my heart, *mange, mange tak!*"

So much warmth and sincerity for a gift-wrapped Pole.

Of course you also had us in mind when you were shipping slaves from your private empire. It continued to cling to me: in the fifties, when I was at boarding school, we had to learn this little poem about good manners that contains the lines:

> . . . *Off the table with your feet.*
> *Don't crumble your bread, don't gobble your meat*
> *Like some Polack or some Tartar*
> *From Galicia. Please act smarter.*

Now back to you. Can you remember Petro Polyniak, who, according to a confidential evaluation drawn up for Mother, came from a petit-bourgeois family but whose subservience nevertheless made of him a "practical, neat, and willing" servant? Well, you couldn't make much of a splash with someone like that; but on the other hand, he "would doubtless be qualified to deal with the furnace and attend to other such household duties appropriate for a male" at the Schoberhof—not at the castle in Cracow. But this Petro Polyniak, because he was of petit-bourgeois origin, had one dreadful shortcoming: "He has had no experience in serving at table and must be trained."

Do you remember Anna Wuzk? She earned ten marks more with us than Bronislav did at the Gulbranssons'. She was with us from October 25 to December 28 (the year is missing); then Mother probably got fed up with her. Did she survive? What did she think of the Franks? I'd like to be able to talk with her now. Or with Johanna Nadritzna; the only thing I've been able to discover about her is that she was issued a coupon for clothing at Resettlement Camp 94b in the district of Saxony. Who was she? Who is she? Why can't I still rid myself of a sort of nagging inferiority complex whenever I think about these former "employees"? Why does a guilty conscience like that always have connotations of something obsequious in the minds of us Germans? What good would meeting them now do for me, when all I could do would be to sit there with my dachshund eyes and feel guilty?

I needed to do only a little investigating before my suspicions were confirmed that the pay of these house servants had something highly illegal about it. Mother was clever; she decided that Poland was our personal, free-of-charge reservoir of servants. Two months before you had to escape from Cracow, your office manager was obliged to write Mother: "I have been able to ascertain that your desire to continue employing Polish and Ukrainian workers at the Schoberhof but at the same time to have them reported as being employed in Cracow is no longer permissible."

All Poles looked alike to me. I seem to recall that we addressed all servants as Johann. And I still remember what fun it was for me, as a little squirt, to always be yelling "Johann" when we were at Kressendorf. Obediently, "Johann" would come climbing up the stairs toward me. I would watch him through the railing; when he reached the top he would politely ask me what I wanted by saying the one word "Please?" Whereupon I would crow "Thank you" and run into the nursery, laughing.

I think Mother put a stop to that—or was it that I just began to get bored? The one thing I really remember was an intense feeling of triumph from giving orders to grown-ups, coupled with a strange sense of guilt. I assume that my feelings were similar to yours as the Governor General? We both knew we were doing wrong; and when Mother admonished me or when Himmler, Krüger, and Hitler (or later the International Tribunal at Nuremberg) took you to task, we both had to eat crow.

Our personnel were more courageous than we were. The household help saw right through your nouveau-riche nonsense. It must have been something unforgettable for the chef, chambermaids, nursemaids, and kitchen help, that scene with Mother hammering her fists against your chest in front of all of them and attacking you full of tearful rage, "Hans, tell them they finally must begin calling me Frau Minister!" That's something that must have really embarrassed you—in contrast to revelations about Poles and Jews and how they were being treated.

You would have bitten your lips to shreds for shame if you had known when you were still alive, and weren't hearing it from me now for the first time, what our servants were capable of doing to Mother in retaliation. "No, I'm not going to tell you," my nursemaid Hilde says to me forty years later. "You have to," I reply. "No, no, no—I promised my son that I would never tell any of the Franks." We are sitting with our third bottle of red wine. My old nursemaid is riddled with cancer; neither of us knows that in a few months she'll be dead. But now she's still quite alive, and the wine is bringing the truth out of her. She begins to tell me. We are sitting in her garret apartment in Josefsthal, not far from the very spot where old Farmer F., on his Haflinger horse, had surrendered the Alpine fortress of Josefsthal to the army tank full of GIs trembling in their boots.

Okay, Father, let me tell you how much our household personnel truly hated Mother. She had invited all the big-shot Nazis from the whole district to an elegant dinner at the Schoberhof. Nurse Hilde comes into the kitchen and the chef asks her, "Are you eating tonight with all those fatheads?" "No." "Really not?" "*No* —how many times must I tell you." "And the children neither?" "No." Nursemaid Hilde begins addressing him angrily in Bavarian dialect while all the rest of the kitchen staff stare at him. The chef squints at her intently once again and says, "It's okay, then," takes the elegant Polish Meissen porcelain terrine, has the serving maid fill it with his delicately spiced cream of asparagus soup, puts the bowl on the kitchen floor, unbuttons his fly, and pisses into the steaming soup in a steaming stream, shakes off the last little drop—and the whole kitchen staff is rigid from shock. Nursemaid Hilde looks as if she's going to faint. The chef raises the terrine from the floor, puts it into the hands of the serving maid, and says, "And now you're going to serve this to those people in there." Between gasps of horror come the first giggles, which after the soup plates are cleared from the table turn into fiendish laughter. The chef is literally on his knees in front of the stove, holding his stomach. The serving maid had come in with Mother's words of praise: "Tell the *maître* that the soup tasted delicious, absolutely delicious."

Such were the Franks at the zenith of their careers. Naturally, I spent a lot of time hanging around in the kitchen. I liked to be with the staff. I wonder, did you ever have a key and take a peek into the great big cupboard on the second floor of the Schoberhof, the one where Mother hoarded all that coffee and flour and chocolate and sugar and candies and tea and all those other things the big shots could still manage to get hold of during the war, just as if it were still peacetime?

Our relatives, evacuees from Munich, living in our chauffeur's little house, were mercifully granted a few crumbs from our table, but they had to put up with me staring at them as they sat there trying to eat their fish. Nothing gave me more creepy fun than to stand there silently in the doorway with unblinking eyes watching my uncle, aunt, and male and female cousins eating their fish and trying to pick fish bones out of their mouths. They didn't dare tell the little fruit of the Minister's loins to get the hell out of there. I guess it was no big surprise for them when, as a dessert treat, I hid in waiting behind the garage for one of the cousins and then whacked him with a fence picket, driving a rusty nail into the back of his neck. The nail went in deep, but it was not life-threatening. The image of the round, red hole in the tender neck of my little cousin is still as vivid in my memory as if I had been examining it under a microscope day after day, all my life.

In your Reich, holes at the back of people's necks came from bullets, and that gave you something to worry about. No, Father, it wasn't the fact that it was happening that worried you, but that Hitler's SS was making it happen without you. And so you said to yourself, If there are going to be crimes, then please, let them be committed in my name. Things couldn't be permitted to go on like that any longer. Yes, you had some really big things to worry about. The SS would not murder people in the legal way, the way you wanted. The atmosphere simply would not become more "German"—or rather, it did become more German, i.e., more corrupt. Every single department in the Reich decided it had to have a hand in your government, because nobody could take you seriously. Speer once called you an idiot in a conversation with Hitler. And so you had to go and stand in front of your paintings, your handsome Raphael youth, your *Lady with the Ermine*, as a source of courage to inspire you to do what as a German, as a genius in legal matters, you simply had to do: show some authority.

You picked up a fountain pen (legally obtained?) and decided to impale your archenemy Krüger on it. He happened not to be in town at the time, and in letters you could show a lot more courage. "The consideration of very urgent police matters in the Government General will be on the agenda of a meeting at the Castle in Cracow at which I expect to see you. I have set Friday of this week as the date for this meeting, 11 a.m. This notification is tantamount to an official order. May I request that you not underestimate its importance."

Boy, you really got him with that, Father. There's not even one "please," not a single "would you." The memo is hard-hitting. Yep, that's the kind of Führer the GG needs; our Führer needs a strong Führer like you in the GG so that he can have his backside free for dealing with Russia. Let me take you firmly by the hand now; we have two more days left. As we stroll together on the ramparts of the Wawel, we can prepare ourselves carefully to put one over on Krüger—and to put him and Himmler and the whole SS finally in their places. We're going to do all that by using the icy voice you always liked to use when you talked about inferior Poles and Jews who have no right to be alive. With your cutting and "ice-clear" (one of your adjectives) reprimands you will truly force Krüger to his knees.

Oh, Father, my Father, how you have disappointed me. How my ears still burn when I read what simple tricks Krüger used to make a fool of you on that Friday at 11 a.m. On the other hand, I must thank him (hey, Krüger, can you hear me?) for the notes he jotted down from memory, minutes that I consider absolutely trustworthy. I know about things like that because I have been secretly hidden for a long time in every corner of your thoughts and feelings; and I know what a pigheaded coward you were at every confrontation, and . . . well, read it yourself, and tell me from your cauldron down there whether Krüger wrote the truth or not.

He was the typical German murderer, the kind we love so much and would have been so happy to bless with a good pension, if only he hadn't preferred to be listed as "missing" after the war was over. (Some people claim he committed suicide; but, Father, I can smell a rat: he's still alive somewhere, unrecognized.) In his notes taken from memory, Krüger establishes the following: "The discussion was carried on in such a loud and emphatic way on the part of the Governor General, who was obviously overexcited, that the numerous gentlemen in the anteroom were able to sense the violence of this meeting. . . . During the nearly one-hour meeting I myself spoke very calmly, matter-of-factly, and precisely, which doubtless must have annoyed the Governor General in the extreme, since he allowed himself to make utterances the emotional quality of which can unfortunately not be duplicated here." Father, you hothead. When you were still a lawyer, you almost always possessed the same mannerisms of ironical coolness and self-controlled superiority that Krüger boasts of. "The shorthand notes I took during the meeting may well have contributed further to his state of excitement, since he referred to them as inappropriate and told me that under no conditions would he acknowledge the authenticity of any such minutes drawn up for the Führer without his signature."

Man, how you're beginning to twitch. How this handsome murderer has got you sizzling like a French fry. And you can't stand the cold way he stares into your bulging eyes, which must have been rolling back into their sockets the way they did at that "comradely interrogation"—or the way they will five years later on your walk to the gallows.

"His uncontrolled behavior, which I am tempted to compare with that of a person of sanguine disposition, made it difficult to derive any kind of useful intelligence out of the conversation—insofar as one can refer to this confrontation as a conversation." (That's also well expressed, Father.) And now he gives you another kick in your fat ass, so that practically nothing is left over from the person you prepared yourself to be when you gazed at the

Lady with the Ermine, seeking inspiration. "Since the meeting took place without witnesses, it may be that the Governor General in pursuing the matter, will contest the points as outlined here (in the way peculiar to him), as being either inaccurate or subject to his own different interpretation."

He was right: you were a master of denial. May I remind you of Professor Kubijowic, the leader of the Ukrainian National Committee? One of your men once asked you how he should behave toward him. Your answer: "I don't know this man." Your chief administrative officer drew your attention to the fact that the professor had visited you only a few days before. Raising your voice, you answered: "Please take note of the fact that this gentleman is unknown to me." That was a lie, and you know it.

But now back to your painful row with Krüger. You began in a slightly nervous tone of voice, "I shall not, here in this room [*what you meant to say was "here in the GG," not your gigantic office where you were sitting at the desk and had to watch this goddamned Krüger taking his writing tablet out of the briefcase he had brought along, and then taking his fountain pen from the inside pocket of his jacket, when you hadn't even gotten through your first sentence*], let myself be interrupted in any way or by anyone [*it is a pleasure to see how elegantly you are constructing your syntax*], and least of all by you [*Krüger darts a quick look at you, but then lowers his gaze to his fountain pen and presses it to the paper a couple of times to start the ink flowing*], and I shall absolutely not tolerate any attempt at forming a government within my government, especially not by you—you who are subordinate to me. [*You had really prepared this part of your sentence terrifically well— a smart uppercut. You raised your voice to the decibel level where you could be certain—for you knew the acoustical conditions in the castle—that the secretaries and gentlemen in the next room could hear in amazement how you were reading the riot act to the chief SS and police leader, Himmler's intimate friend. I'm still here, peering over your shoulder, even though we are unfortunately obliged to hear at this very moment that that bastard Krüger is now repeating your last words, muttering them as if he were a stenographer taking dictation: ". . . subordinate to me . . ." The SOB is looking at you, and you catch yourself making an involuntary pause, fixedly gazing at his fountain pen to see whether he has caught up with what you're saying. You're afraid, you're sweating profusely; you shift awkwardly to a tone of irony.*] I regard your actions, if they are to be understood at all, only as an expression of sudden nervous strain, something that is, of course, understandable after two years of such intense work [*that is good, Father: put him down as a neurotic case, as someone sick, perhaps as an effeminate non-German; that would be something this SS jerk could not endure. Keep it up*], as an indication of momentary upset [*that is a lousy touch; you should have followed through on the neurosis theme and finished him off*], something produced by your heavy workload. [*The bastard is already writing again, then stops, looks up at you; you are still sitting straighter in your chair than he is—make use of it.*] These repeated missteps of yours recently, particularly in the past half-year, must be regarded as ill-bred impertinence, something I can no longer endure. [*Once again your voice grows a touch more shrill; you're imagining how the gentlemen on the other side of the door, in their admiration for you, are nodding at one another.*] Whoever dares to stir up agitation and discord in the well-ordered structure of my Government General [*very good, very good—it is yours, the GG*], for that person [*well . . . what, Father? Blow him away. Send him home to the Reich. Have him arrested*] there will no longer be any room for cooperative work, and any such individual would simply be hitting his head against a brick wall. And furthermore I must forbid, in the most decisive way possible, the constant interference of any and all central offices in Berlin in matters concerning this Reichsnebenland."

Krüger is mumbling your words back to you: ". . . must forbid, in the most decisive way possible . . ." Father, it's all going downhill now; you're squawking, in a weaker and weaker voice. Krüger takes careful note of that, grows more confident, until in your despair, having just emphasized that there was "an irreparable split" between the two of you, you suggest that you could draw the line, consider the matter closed, and re-establish the former state of mutual trust. What was really happening here was your attempt to make that famous comradely gesture with which you crooks strove not only to conceal your crimes but also to restore your fraudulent masculine image.

But Krüger, ice-cold to the tip of his fountain pen, retorted, "Considering the incessant reprimands and the suspicion cast upon me during this discussion today, I am in no position to give any answer at the moment, since I am honor-bound to first report to Reichsführer Himmler what has happened at this meeting."

At this moment a look of horror must have burst through that shiny porcine face of yours, for Krüger takes pleasure in noting for Himmler in his minutes of the meeting: "This was clearly something that made him lose his balance."

Cowardice is pulsing in your veins. Krüger is in hot pursuit; he wants to cut the GG puppet from his strings once and for all. He suggests (that clever bastard) in a very calm tone of voice that since you, the allegedly so powerful Governor General, had appointed him to his post as the chief SS and police leader (you had no other choice in the matter, to be sure; but that was another clever dig on his part), you could now demand that the Führer remove him, Krüger, from office.

Now you've really been knocked back on your ass. So that is what has come from your so boldly planned, your grand reckoning with Himmler's representative, his own Johnny-on-the-spot. Krüger knows that you couldn't even get a toehold in Berlin. Seen from a different perspective, your isolation from power could have redounded to your honor. For example, you could now be free to fight effectively for the opposition in Poland and for the Poles. But your pathetic answer forces me to switch with pleasure over to Krüger's side. You: "I would not even begin to think of burdening the Führer, who has greater worries, with matters like these while the war is going on. If, however, we were not at war, I would resort to other measures."

How cowardly, Father, how infinitely cowardly you are. Krüger immediately delivers the mortal blow: by remaining silent. He lets your words echo away in your gigantic and pompous office. What a disadvantage such big spaces are for people who cannot fill them. Krüger's final point in his minutes: "I responded to his last remarks with silence." There you sat now—you, the puppet, the person Krüger from then on always referred to as the "jumping jack."

Three years later you were part of another dialogue. Party member Masur had informed you that certain expressions were being used about your predicament.

You: "What expressions?"

Masur: "That the Governor General has been let go, that he's been dropped. Secondly, in this connection, the expression 'puppet' has been used."

You: "They said I'm a puppet? What does that mean?"

Masur: "The picture I get from that is of a man sitting up at the top somewhere but who has no real say in anything."

You: "Anything else?"

Masur: "That's about it."

That hits hard. It even gets to me. God damn it, you puppet. Temporary address: Castle, Cracow. Then later, puppet with new address: Nuremberg prison. What an edifying spectacle: the person who always had the word "law" in his big mouth was finally snapped up by the law. Whereupon the puppet, suddenly so little and pious, was obliged to defend his own empty head.

Lilly and the
Lawless State

Four years before your final battle, millions of corpses had begun crowding in on you to such an extent that by 1942 you had dug out your little diary, your own personal one, and written: "I am very sad, in fact in despair, about the path our German legal system is taking. More and more we are developing into a wicked and violent police state. This is not good [*what an understatement, Father*]; it is threatening the Reich. Even though I must admit that during wartime all formal matters of systematic government must defer to the necessity of absolute, totally obedient, and disciplined unity, law and justice nevertheless constitute a holy and eternal concern of the commonweal, a creation of the indestructible racial character of our people. One cannot overestimate the sense of justice of our people [*but certainly that of its legal minds, Father*]! For that to thrive, there must be a clear zone of action for judicial power, one in which the government may not interfere. At present, all of that is gone."

Father, dear Father of mine, I would be prepared to argue seriously with this passage in your diary, but also to believe you, despite the awkward words with which you are mourning the screwed-up state of justice, if only you had not prefixed those words with this paragraph, written on that very same night: "History will record what I, alone, as the Governor General have accomplished in the Polish East since September 1939. I have established a great, strong, well-integrated Reichsnebenland under the most difficult material, political, and human conditions. It is worthy of recognition, and I am proud that the Führer has also acknowledged and confirmed this. My official diaries have already reported on my activities in what was formerly Poland."

And then, after that, those sentences of yours about injustice being on the increase in Germany? Didn't it occur to you that your grief and then your boasting about your accomplishments in Poland don't exactly fit together? My God, what a perfect addition to the political guardians in Germany you would be now. This almost schizophrenic sanctimoniousness—how I hate that in these people now! Incidentally, your self-congratulatory description of the GG isn't correct, either. You were perfectly aware that there was not a chance of your being given a free hand to govern the GG the way you wanted to. You knew that the real power was in Himmler's hands, that it lay with Krüger, that all the ministries of the Reich had a hand in your government and could do as they pleased, and that you were only distracting yourself with pomp and pilfered luxuries from the crimes committed against Poles and Jews that your administration was covering up.

The unity of administration, with you at the head of the three powers—that was your dream, but you never succeeded in maneuvering it through politically.

And how does this German man, so deeply concerned about the state of justice, continue his diary entry? "But one event seems to me worthy of note within the framework of this diary: Lilly has reentered the realm of my psyche. [*Does that mean that your lamentation about the lawless state one paragraph earlier wasn't so important? The score is now 1–0 for Lilly against the Lawless State. Such were the rhetorical bloopers that show how shallow your concern for justice really was.*] A few weeks ago she told me in a letter that her only son was missing in Russia. . . . Consequently, we met on May 6, 1942, for the first time in twenty years. In Bad Aibling. At her home. Immediately we burst into uncontrollable flame. We were reunited once more, so passionately that now there is no turning back. . . . On Monday, May 11, we were truly reunited in Munich— and the same thing, all day long, on May 12." It must have been great, Father, to be sleeping again (or for the first time?) as a forty-two-year-old with the love of your youth. You had about four and a half years more to live, by the way. Surely I will learn (if I go on reading this passage) more about your erotic feelings, about your unrestrained joy, and about the other things that knocked you for a loop, until your greed was finally satiated; about the bliss of finally embracing the true and only beloved instead of Mother's body bursting its seams. The Governor General's travel uniform lies in a wrinkled heap in the armchair; for the first time you neglect to safeguard the crease in your trousers. I read on in your diary. Let's have it all. You, married to a tough-as-nails woman from Forst, someone you haven't been in love with for a long time, if you ever loved her at all; you, Governor General and Minister of the Reich without Portfolio; you, guarantor of justice. Let me read on about your love. . . . But I'm already stuck: "It was a solemn and transfigured reunion of two human beings who ignited one another and whom nothing could restrain for long." Why do you have to suffocate this stormy passion with such a stew of words? Who else do we discover there, squashed between your two naked bodies? Well, who else but the Shining Light on High? "May God give His gracious assent to our union."

He probably did. But then, the Lord God (who had played along without showing any mercy, right up to the gas chambers) simply did not reckon with Mother. Scarcely had she heard about your wanting a divorce when she began a fight to the finish. Lounging in your bed of lust and writing in your diary, you didn't have the slightest notion of what was coming: "Soon there will probably be all kinds of big and little problems to solve. But we have given each other our hands and our hearts. This time it must finally, finally happen. For our mutual love is older and greater than everything that came later. And it is deeper. And purer. A song of happiness chimes within me. My Lilly is back again! My good, dear Lilly"—who was probably no longer much concerned about her only son.

He, incidentally, must have died a terrible death in the Soviet Union, an unknown soldier. He was twenty-two. Lilly wanted you to pull strings and arrange for a search through the missing-in-action files. How grotesque that the two of you got together over the body of her dead son.

From the beginning, the reason your early love affair with her had come to naught was your own cowardice. Yes, of course, she was the child of a stinking-rich banker; and of course, her father behaved in the conventional nineteenth-century manner when he forbade his daughter to go out with a poor jerk whose father had been a lawyer expelled from his law society, who sat around for most of the day in the saloon on the Schellingstrasse and raised chickens at home. (What a cackling wedding that would have been back there in 1920!) But you didn't fight back; you simply put up with it. All you did was hang around outside their Munich villa, a coward with bloodshot, burning eyes.

Father, I'll grant you this great love of 1942. Long after the war, Aunt Martel happened to be standing next to a tall woman waiting at a bus stop, who happened just then to be speaking with an acquaintance about you: "If I'd wanted to, I could have married Hans Frank." It was Lilly.

They say that your photograph was in a frame on her bedside table until her death in 1973. The picture is gone. Your letters to her are gone, too—something I regret, because those letters, particularly the ones from the prison at Nuremberg, were probably more honest than that pompous drivel you fed to Mother and me. And yet one of her female relatives whom I located years ago said, a little bit poisonously, "Lilly never had the guts to visit him in Nuremberg."

It would have been a howl, Mother and I sitting on one side

of the visitors' room, waiting to be conducted to our last conversation with you, and Lilly waiting on the other side—almost
as funny as the idea of the Tribunal approving Alfred Rosenberg's
petition for you to defend him. Just imagine this game of musical
chairs between dock and witness stand, first you, then Rosenberg,
then the other way around—funny, funny.

The game of musical chairs that entered your life with Lilly
was quite something, too, at least according to what Mother discovered from the stars. She had your horoscope read, presumably
by Frau Obermeier (who, amazingly enough, as I discovered, at-
tended an astrologers' seminar in 1944. In the middle of the war.
In Germany. What a weird world). If one bears in mind that you
had already kicked the bucket by the end of October 1946, it's
rather ironic to read Frau Obermeier's 1942 prediction: "In 1946
the sun enters a union with Venus, which indicates that true
happiness is to be found only after then. At the same time, the
waxing moon, which in the years following 1946 will be in the
ascendant, indicates a fundamentally new departure in life."

Your residency in hell might also be described that way. That
lady astrologer had quite a sense of humor: "Until that point,
however, Mars will be in opposition to the House of Life and bring
along with it the most severe stress and battles with others and
with oneself. In other words, the message for Hans is that he must
see to it that he endures until 1946."

Or was Frau Obermeier a democrat in disguise who wanted to
strengthen your criminal determination so that you would be sure
to end up before the Military Tribunal? I liked her; I stayed
overnight at her house when we visited you in Nuremberg for the
last time. Either she must have been secretly overjoyed with her
right-on-target 1942 horoscope, or else she must have scratched
her head a little in embarrassment when Mother, silently and with
pursed lips, held the horoscope under her nose.

Mother's success back then had to do with her influence over
Hitler—at least that's the way she saw it in 1942, when she read

you Obermeier's next sentences: "At present the waxing moon is in the sign of Libra in the tenth field. This is very important in public affairs as well as for strong professional connections; in others words, Hans cannot be overthrown."

Well, such jubilation! Poland would remain ours. I already saw myself with the little scepter in my hand, dressed in my little plaid suit, walking along behind my ermine-draped parents—when suddenly Mother brought things to a stop. For the thing she could least endure was what Obermeier was predicting for Hans in her next sentence: "In May, Mars will be above the moon. Great excitement with (or because of) women." Well, now, that brings us right back to your diary entry: "My Lilly is back again!"

It was really one helluva situation for your beloved GG when you entered Mother's room on May 18 and revealed "the most gruesome things" to her, at least according to her precise recounting of the story in her letter to Hitler or Lammers or Bormann—in any case, to one of them, which means to all of them. These "most gruesome things" had to do with nothing less than the annihilation of the Jews. You confessed to Mother that you were part of a criminal regime and, in order to save Mother and me, had to "make the greatest sacrifice that a loving husband can ask of his beloved wife: divorce."

So that's where we stand: you exploit the hideous extermination of human beings as a ploy to obtain a divorce, because (and you were quite at liberty to say so) you harmonized so much better with the girlfriend of your youth than with this remarkably greedy, unerotic creature named Brigitte. Mother wiped away the news about mass murder like a drop of wine from that French mahogany table, and in doing so gave the postwar German people a good example to follow. The only thing important to her was to prevent the divorce.

But the rotten thing about Mother is that after writing to them about those "most gruesome things" she had learned from you, she adds this phrase in parentheses: "(Details later, but only in

private)." Which amounts to telling them that she was planning
to tell either Himmler or Lammers something like this: "Well,
Herr Reichsminister, the things I hear about conditions in that
Auschwitz place of yours! Now that's just hard to believe—the
things my husband was telling me: He says the Jews have to take
off their clothes and that two thousand of them are shoved into
one room and then the gas is turned on, and that's it. Could that
really be true? And he says that they whip them and beat them
and torture them; and my husband tells me that they cut off their
hair and smash out their teeth for the gold and—oh, by the way,
their clothes are all collected in piles; would you know if by any
chance I could get to take a look at those piles? There must still
be some nice materials there, and underthings, too. . . . But I'm
getting off the subject. So, then, Herr Reichsminister, can you
believe all that? And that's why my husband tells me he wants a
divorce. That's not having much faith in our final victory, now, is
it? That makes such a terrible impression on everybody."

After the phrase in parentheses ("Details later, but only in
private"), Mother lured her correspondent on with the words "the
utter abyss!" She really could be satanic. Yes, go on, hit her, down
there where you boil together. For decades I've been seeing you
that way, wedged together, thrashing, clawing at one another,
spitting, biting each other—what a sweet pair of parents. Mother
goes on in her letter by saying that during the past few days you
have been in a rather unstable mood—something not so hard to
understand, after all, speaking man to man: having to lie there
next to your old woman in those beautiful Polish beds up in your
castle, while the Lilly you so passionately yearn for is unable to
come to you. A hard test of patience for the old groin. I can
understand that. While Mother was in there copying from her
private diary for her report to the super big shots: "I wrote in my
diary: 'Dear Lord, protect him. What is our fate to be? Have we
come to a great turning point in our lives? I fear we have. Dear
God, give me the strength and the power.' " That must have

sounded good to the big shots. Mother was clever, and yet she reacted just as grotesquely as you did, as all of you did, the way people are still reacting to all that horror. Mother goes on: "Hans has all of my pity. I suffered so dreadfully that by May 19 I simply had to pour my heart out to another human being; I could no longer endure the burden of suffering alone. Can you imagine my terrified astonishment when my confidante wondered aloud whether there might not be another woman in the picture? That would make the whole thing too much like a romantic novel."

What a sweetheart Mother must have been. To be able to reduce murder and mayhem to part of the plot of a "romantic novel" and suspect that a woman was behind the whole thing. That's the way all of you were; that's the way we are now: genocide reduced to a muddled story about two women. Mother became more and more of a bitch, began to shadow you and send her mob of women friends out after you as spies. You go dashing around through the Reich, through the GG, in your automobile and your private railroad car, until you're fed up with the whole thing. Then, on June 3, 1942, the two of you performed the following classic dialogue in the music salon of the castle (incidentally, in the presence of the Beautiful Madonna). Mother enters. You do not come toward her. You had her sent for, perhaps by my very own Johann, though this time it was for real. So Mother comes in; Father is standing at the grand piano (you had a theatrical way about you—you stood there as only Chopin could have stood).

You: "Tell me, Brigitte, how long have we been married?" Mother is nervous, no question about it. For a long time she's known all about Lilly. She had swiped your diary and copied passages out of it.

Mother: "Let's see . . . seventeen years."

Whereupon you (a little flatfooted, I must say): "My, that's a long time." You make a gracious sweeping gesture, the lord of the manor, and Mother is foolish enough to respond to it and sit down. You continue: "Tell me, wasn't I always chivalrous toward you?"

Mother gives one of her ice-cold answers, which must have made you falter a little: "You were in a position to offer me an agreeable life."

Flabbergasted, you repeat your question: "Wasn't I always chivalrous toward you?"

Mother doesn't budge. The tough-as-nails opponent is awakened in her: "You were generous, and I've been comfortable." (Every inch the materialist.)

You're silent. She's silent. Somebody ought to come in, sit down at the piano, and start playing; then you could sing an aria.

You had sworn to Lilly up and down that you would lay all your cards on the table—and so you said bravely, but with trembling knees: "Well, Brigitte, I don't love you anymore."

In her unexcelled style, Mother's letter to her correspondent in the Reich Chancellery continues: "I had to stop myself from fainting, my legs were weak. 'But Hans, what are you saying, that can't be true,' etc. My diary entry reads: 'He doesn't love me anymore; I don't mean anything to him anymore. The earth is opening up beneath my feet. I am unhappy beyond words.' He wants a divorce. He asks me whether there isn't someone else in my life, too [*Mother, are you still screaming from your scalding? I just wanted to stop you for a second and congratulate you on your dramatic style*]—was there someone who loves me and whom I love. And then he asks me whether I realize how often and with how many others he has already deceived me in our marriage."

My dear Father, that's really pretty strong stuff, to be so scornful and then on top of that boast about your sleeping partners like some cock-of-the-walk. Your good upbringing must have abandoned you at that moment. Justifiably Mother adds: "I am too shattered to give any kind of answer. [*Of course she couldn't, Father; you couldn't just sit there and begin to quiz each other now.*] Everything suddenly seems so disconnected, so crazy, and I truly began to doubt my husband's sanity."

The Pleasures of
Herr Governor General

What Mother does not describe in her letter or diary is
something she surely did anyhow. She began to howl.
Mother was capable of just sitting down and producing an absolutely apocalyptic sound from her well-padded wattles, from that
throat of hers always kept so nicely warm by those furs she swindled
the Jews out of—a sound that not only shredded your nervous
system (already so weak because of your bad conscience) but is
unquestionably still echoing throughout the rooms of the castle
today. We really ought to check out sometime whether this banshee
wail of hers can be heard every night bouncing off those walls.
Mother, is your voice still haunting the Wawel? Or maybe all of
you? Are you spooking around every night in your sexy camisoles,
with a rat fur over your shoulders and calling out, "Hans, oh,
Hans, why did you leave me?" And then that terrifying drawn-
out wail issues from your hollow throat, the elegant camisole flaps
about your mottled old-woman's flesh; you shriek endlessly through
the corridors, a sound that still keeps the Poles flying back into
the arms of the Catholic Church. Well, no matter. In any case,
that wail assured your victory back in 1942. "Our discussion lasted
but a short time. After perhaps one hour, however, he apologized
for everything, was so charming to me, and a scene of reconciliation
followed."

That was on June 3. The next day Mother's diary reveals these macabre lines: "Again Hans calls me into the music room and informs me that Lasch has shot himself to death. And, totally incomprehensible to me, he declares that the divorce is now no longer necessary. Evening harmonious." "Evening harmonious"! —what a pair of words with which to put your mutual friend Lasch, my second father, to his final rest!

On June 5 (during the night you must have realized that life with Mother truly wasn't much fun any longer) you were a real bastard to her. But there wasn't much else left for you to use to scare her away for good. She had swallowed the genocide story without blinking an eye; Lasch's suicide was unable to make her evening disharmonious; the only thing left for you was to pull political rank on her. Mother's diary: "Hans very upset with me. Said I was to blame for his unhappiness. Someone had told him I was not a good National Socialist; and he made it look as if they had advised him to get a divorce."

My dear Father, Mother was a step ahead of you in a flash, as usual: "I am staggered, cannot understand a word of what he's saying, but declare myself prepared to be divorced immediately if they demand it."

First-class move on Mother's part; so now you had to come clean. If you'd had one, you'd have had to produce a telegram from Hitler and read it aloud—for instance: "Dear Frank, Can't stand it any longer, conduct of my war suffering, don't understand why Brigitte not National Socialist. Stop. Request you dispose of her immediately. Where 200,000 eggs? Heil Hitler. Your Hitler."

But you didn't have a telegram; so what was your solution? Right. Another one of those shitty reconciliation scenes which probably cost some Pole or Jew his last family treasure. Mother writes enraptured: "June 6. Hans came and brought me a wonderful piece of jewelry as a talisman to make up for all the suffering he had so inexplicably caused me."

Hitler bent over his desk again, studying the progress of his war; the German armies took courage again; and for better or for worse, you could hardly keep your hands away from Mother's breasts the following day. Mother described it delicately to the big shots in Berlin: "Hans professed his love to me. In the evening [*you took quite a long time professing your love, didn't you, Father?*] the Slovenian minister of war was with us, and we spent a harmonious time together." Sounds like a pretty classy threesome. All the time Lilly must have been down in Upper Bavaria, fuming with rage.

But now you had your official life to deal with. I wonder if the Hitler Youth noticed the secret grin on your face when you spoke to the kids: "When we look back at what the German leadership has accomplished in the last three years in this territory, and when we compare the filth, destruction, terror, feebleness, the wretched conditions, pestilence, and general ruination that we inherited here with the shining image of healthy order, of a life that is unfolding here everywhere, even as a blessing for the foreign population of this territory [*fabulous how you can turn the Poles in Poland into foreigners, Father*], then, my young friends, you can appreciate how our work is equal to the test of the most critical, the most uncompromising judges. Today we can sense a new clarity, an austere purity in this land."

How could you stand the stress? Caught, as you were, between your official lies and your private lies? Caught between a woman you don't love but are married to and a woman you passionately desire? It was too much for you. Most of all because, God damn it, you couldn't get a divorce from that female. What kind of justice is that? you asked yourself. Hey, yes, right . . . then you finally caught on. Exactly, what kind of justice is that? Where there's no right to get a divorce, there's no justice at all . . . and you were up and away. You gave your four speeches in the Reich, the ones you praised so highly to yourself—and not a soul realized that the whole thing had to do with getting a divorce from the old lady.

I, at least, can't explain it on any other grounds, can't explain

Hans and Brigitte Frank at Cracow Castle in 1942, with myself at the age of three in my checked "pepita suit."

My father giving a salute, somewhere in Poland, either after an appearance as speaker or following his review of the troops on the occasion of his birthday.

My father, gun in hand, during a visit to a weapons factory in Poland.

MUZEUM HISTORII FOTOGRAFII (CRACOW)

The first sample of oil pumped from the ground in Galicia in autumn 1942 is presented to the Governor General in a little bottle. Galicia, given to Russia as part of the 1939 partition of Poland, was swallowed up by the Government General after Hitler attacked the Soviet Union in 1941.

MUZEUM HISTORII FOTOGRAFII (CRACOW)

Himmler, Goebbels, and Frank (facing camera, left to right) with Mussolini (back to camera) at Hitler's Obersalzberg retreat during the Italian dictator's state visit to Germany in 1941.

The "Frank postage stamp," a British counterfeit smuggled in to incite dissension between my father and Hitler; only the Führer's portrait, of course, was permitted to be used on stamps.

Left to right: Italian Minister of Justice Dino Count Grandi, Hitler, my father, and Minister of State Meissner in the Reich Chancellery in Berlin.

Himmler during a visit to my father at Cracow Castle in June 1943.

Even before the Cracow ghetto was walled in, innumerable laws against the Jews were promulgated and posted. Here, "Jews are forbidden to enter the parks."

Jews in Cracow, forced to leave their homes and move into the ghetto.

ABOVE: My father standing on the steps of Kressendorf Castle, his weekend retreat near Cracow. BELOW: At the Cracow railway station on March 13, 1943, my father extends congratulations to the one-millionth "guest" worker sent from Poland to Germany to satisfy wartime needs. My father gave him the pocket watch, but a short time later, on the train, two SS men took it away from him. The worker himself jumped off the train and survived.

MUZEUM HISTORII FOTOGRAFII (CRACOW)

My father (in dark glasses) during a recess at the Nuremberg trials.

My father after his suicide attempt in May 1945, following his arrest by U.S. troops.

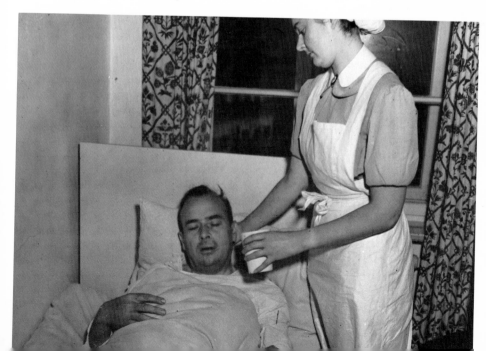

The U.S. hangman Woods
in Nuremberg, 1946.

Hans Frank shortly after his
execution at Nuremberg,
October 16, 1946.

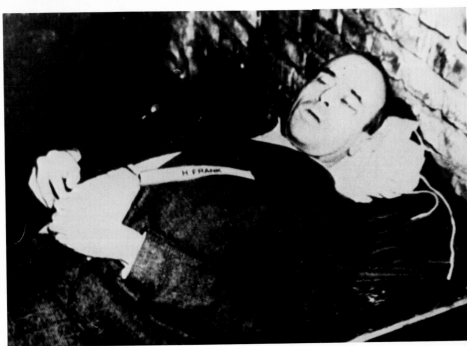

why you suddenly came up with such sentences as the following between June 9 and July 21, 1942, evoking great applause at the universities of Berlin, Vienna, Heidelberg, and Munich: "The legal mind will always recognize that war takes precedence over everything else. [*That was still a judicial cliché in Germany; but now you suddenly got downright bold:*] However, I am of the opinion that even during wartime, when all our sensitivities are at such a high pitch, the people's sense of justice demands above all the strictest observance." And then: "I believe in the possibility of constructing legal security in its broadest sense within the framework of authoritarian governance." And then you were even more to the point: "I believe in the possibility of uniting authoritarian governance and judicial independence."

I can see you now in your cauldron with a proud look on your foolish face. You are listening reverently to your own words again. They constitute the bread of charity in your damnation. So I'll toss a few more crumbs of it at you: "A people cannot be ruled by force; the lives of a people without justice are something unthinkable." "Justice is therefore not only a treasure of trust between people and leadership, it is also a guarantor of freedom." And what comes now smells to me as if it were being directed at Mother. Well, maybe not. For once, I'll let you enjoy a tentative moment of courage: "But freedom brings with it the possibility for spiritual development."

You're leaning dreamily at the edge of your cauldron. Yes, Father, you should have said that from the very beginning, should have been fighting for that very thing.

After this first speech in Berlin on the ninth, you had your "so-called one-minute conference with Bormann," according to Mother's tattletale diary. I'll have to put my imagination to work again and see how it might have gone. Naturally, the big boys had heard about your speech in the great auditorium at the University of Berlin. Bormann was sent in the name of the Führer to confront you, and he wasn't much concerned as to the whereabouts of those two hundred thousand eggs. Instead, he doubtless gave you some solid advice couched in polite language.

Bormann: "The Führer heard about your speech yesterday."

Frank: *"Jawohl."*

Bormann: "The Führer does not find it proper for you to be delving into abstract ideas about justice during this serious period."

Frank: *"Jawohl."*

Bormann: "You're getting me all mixed up. So then, the Führer . . . etc. . . . . delving into. . . . Instead, he would like to have morale-building speeches from his leaders."

Frank: *"Jawohl*—although I would like to add, Herr Reichsleiter, that we are dealing here with only closed sessions at the university."

Bormann: "Do you think we don't know that? The people, however, are perfectly satisfied with the justice system they already have. The will of the Führer, that's their justice. It's what you said yourself everywhere, ten years ago. Heil Hitler, Frank."

Is that the way it went? And then off you dashed to Lilly in her featherbed. Okay, I'll grant you the pleasures of Lilly. And maybe you did give those talks just to impress her. You could never get your mind off Lilly after that. Mother had to entertain Edda Mussolini all by herself at Kressendorf Castle—which she doubtless enjoyed doing enormously, of course.

On June 13 and 14 our housekeeper becomes your accomplice. You tell her about Lilly and that you are getting a divorce. But then on the next day Mother is able to report in her diary: "Hans came from Kressendorf in a good mood, talks about how sorry he is that Lasch is dead, that 'good blond rascal,' as he always called him. Hans was very tender with me."

Free pussy time for our Hans! Daddy Lasch is dead. But, Father, apart from that, where was your deep grief about the sad state of justice in Hitler's totalitarian Reich? Still, that must have occurred to you, at least occasionally, as you were tossing around in those various beds, because on July 1 you were capable of speaking beautiful sentences such as this one from your Vienna speech:

"There can be no Reich without justice; there can be no justice without judges; and no judge can proclaim justice without the genuine power that has been granted him from above."

And you're even more precise in the words you spoke against Himmler; that "comradely interrogation" must have still been bugging you: "With all the zeal of my convictions I must insist, over and over again, that it would be bad if police-state ideals were to be implicitly equated with National Socialist ideals and at the same time completely to replace our ancient German views of justice." The record shows that your comments earned you "long and stormy applause."

Those were tricky times for you. What with Lilly and Krüger, Brigitte and Himmler, eggs and furs, what with your rudimentary ideas about justice popping up again, you had to find a new path to happiness.

On July 7, a week after your speech on behalf of justice, decency, and morals, you climbed into Mother's bed and said: "Brigitte, I demand a divorce. There's nothing physical left between us. My needs are being completely taken care of by Gertrude and Lilly." Those words were damned filthy, my dear man—really unusually filthy even for you.

After that, you found yourself immersed again in speechifying—your target this time, Munich. In the Auditorium Maximum you uttered, among other things, the following remarks, perfect examples for showing what a swamp you and your cronies had led justice into: "It is not possible for a judge to be a danger to the Reich." And: "Advocates of the law bear within themselves one of the holiest ideas of the community of our people—namely, the idea that the other party must always be heard, that no one should be condemned without a hearing."

That hardly applies to Jews and to the reproach lodged against them that they are Jews, does it? In those cases, it didn't seem necessary for "the other party" to get a hearing.

What really bugs me about you at this period is the chutzpah with which you take your trips from a raped country into the Reich as the Governor General and have the nerve to talk about "justice" to people there; then you return to the GG and get the murder machine going again. Remember that special New Year's Eve in 1942, when we were celebrating the upcoming year at the Schoberhof? Your staff were calling you from Cracow to wish you Happy New Year and you said this beautiful sentence: "I request you kindly to delay death sentences until I have returned to Cracow." In that connection, how about one more sentence from your speech in Vienna: "The more human a state, the more German it is; the more just a state, the more indestructible, and the greater a Reich is, the greater must be the sense of justice in the minds of those who would designate themselves as responsible for that Reich."

Wait a minute—I'm wrong. You went on to Heidelberg this time, and there, on July 21, 1942, you suddenly said something quite remarkable at the university: "We have taken precautions to see that nobody is convicted unless he has had a hearing, that nobody be sentenced unless he has been able to defend himself. May a benevolent destiny preserve this for us."

How's that—what did you say, Father? You "have taken precautions"? Did you somehow achieve that mighty goal somewhere between Munich and Heidelberg? Did Hitler suddenly appoint independent judges in a wild rush? Or am I supposed to be reading between the lines again, doing what you cowards expected of their progeny? Am I somehow supposed to see acts of political resistance between the lines; resistance to the gas chambers between the lines; resistance to the German addiction to whipping children against the wall between the lines; resistance to splattered brains between the lines? A life lived between the lines—a hero's life.

No, Father, I don't believe in any hidden acts of resistance on your part. I believe that your "so-called one-minute conference" did not take place on July 10 but after your first three speeches, on July 20 in Munich, or on the morning of July 21, and that

Bormann said to you: "My dear Frank, of course you may give your speech in Heidelberg; but in the name of the Führer, forget this nonsense about justice being threatened. And let me assure you, the judges themselves don't want any independence."

And, blissfully mindful of your handsomely paneled railroad car, and of your many gorgeous uniforms, you murmured, "But of course," and defended yourself by saying that you only wanted to protect the lawyers a little who were being given such a hard time by the SS "Black Corps"; and besides that, you said you believed that "the unity of the Reich and its judges has been completely achieved," all of which so perfectly explains the sentence quoted above, and all the ones you spoke later in Heidelberg. One of those sentences, also from 1942, is particularly inspiring: "There must never be a police state, never! Every fiber of my being rejects that."

Now, I think, would be the ideal time to launch a real attack against Himmler, and describe the conditions and the murders in the concentration camps, the way you described them to Mother. But no; the only thing you care about is the prestige of your German twisters-of-the-law, all of them, from the top of your administration on down: "Therefore, as a National Socialist and as the leader of the German defenders of justice, my job is to protest these constant attacks and insults to justice and to the guardians of justice."

Father, you can relax now. Your remarks met with total success in the postwar Federal Republic of Germany, where the judges themselves forbade any legal proceedings against their own reputations and former activities. Only one of them was ever arraigned on account of his activity in the Third Reich, and naturally he was exonerated. I can see you now, smirking happily at that good news; German Federal judges have brought you home again. They arranged for you to slip out of Woods's noose; they led you by the hand from behind the black cloth in the gymnasium at Nuremberg, and they brought you with them into the new democratic state.

They have engraved forever in their memories the following sentence from your Heidelberg speech, because it evokes so glorious a portrait of them (you wrecker of language, you parasite): "When the judge, dressed in his judicial robes, resplendent with the majestic symbols of the Reich, appears in the courtroom, there must radiate from him that strength which through the centuries has illuminated our people's pathway and which signifies that justice and righteousness alone form the foundation of the state."

After delivering these mighty words you drove home to Mother. There your words were considerably clearer: "I demand a divorce. I need a right to my life, too. I've taken care of you long enough. I need Lilly's strength." And when Mother was all set to break out in her banshee wail again, you uttered the first words truly worthy of that infernal realm to which I condemned you long ago: "You're clinging to me like any ordinary Frau Meier to Herr Meier!" For so prominent a family as ours, that was the worst possible insult. If you had said instead: "You're clinging like Reichsfreiherr Baron zu Rüdenhausen to his Princess Adelgunde Sayn-Oppenstein-Wittgewitzka," then Mother would probably have stopped her howling, looked up at you with joy in her tear-filled eyes, and asked, "Is that really true?"

But as it was, Mother capitulated. She wrote to Lammers or someone: "After that remark, I gave him his freedom." Father, you made it. The Meiers saved you. But then what did you do with your victory? Nothing. After a short spell you knuckled under again, and your rattletrap wedding coach continued on its bumpy road. Why did you cop out? Could it be that Lilly had an even greater appetite for Polish furs? At least Mother was already well supplied.

Your four great speeches on behalf of justice—the ones you and your lawyer, Seidl, kept dwelling on with such pride at Nuremberg—they were nothing compared with your terrific speech a few days later in Lemberg (i.e., Lvov). You gave it on August 1, 1942, the first anniversary of the annexation of Galicia to the

Government General. There were honor guards, Ukrainian and
Polish delegations, and reviewing of the troops. You didn't take
Mother along; she would have been incapable of exuding the
appreciative glow you always valued so highly in your audiences—
the glow that your German listeners so willingly displayed this
time too, when you said: "It is impossible to thank the Führer
enough for having entrusted this ancient nest of Jews, this Polish
poorhouse, to strong and capable German muscle—to people who,
with shovel in hand and supplied with insect powder and other
necessities, finally made it possible for a German to live here in
comfort."

You could play Chopin so beautifully. You loved Beethoven.
You were friends with Richard Strauss, with Hans Pfitzner. You
had tears in your eyes whenever you read Ludwig Thoma's *Christmas
Stories*. And you were capable of speaking those words? These
words? "It is clear that we, above all we in the Government General,
we the venerable troops experienced in bringing a conquered land
back up on its feet—it is clear that we appreciate what the Führer
has given us with his gift of the District of Galicia, and I'm not
talking here about its Jews. Yes, we still have some of them around,
but we'll take care of that. Incidentally, I don't seem to have any
of that trash hanging around here today. What's going on? They
tell me that there were thousands and thousands of those flatfooted
primitives in this city once upon a time—and there wasn't a single
one to be seen when I arrived. Don't tell me that you've been
treating them badly?"

And what does the official account record about the reaction
to these words on the part of all the generals and German officials
present? "Great hilarity." How can language permit such abominations? Why didn't your fat mouth rip apart when you shaped
those words into such horrifying phrases and vomited them out
between your lips? I can imagine your cheeks suddenly inflating
after that last sentence, as if puffed out by a sudden excess of
atmospheric pressure, and then exploding. The "hilarity" in the

hall stops, turns into screams: the flesh of your cheeks hangs down from your skull in strips; your upper and lower jaws are exposed; the teeth in them seem gigantic. Blood runs down all over your nickel-plated, hot-shit uniform. Your hands grasp for your face; your tongue swells and explodes; spurts of blood splatter the people in the front row, where Governor Fischer is seated next to Frau Governor, and Frau Governor gets covered with most of it. Now you double over, because you can already feel what's coming: from somewhere deep inside, your neck inflates in a split second and makes a screeching and hissing sound, like the sound we can hear nowadays at a gas station, the sound a tire pump makes when you hang it back on its hook. You grab at your carotid artery in your neck, which is just on the point of exploding, and . . .

But nothing like that happened; you simply continued your little speech: "My God, when I write my memoirs someday and describe how I entered Posen with my five men in order to fulfill the Führer's task and establish the Government General—what I saw then can't be described. All those Jews running around everywhere, so unbelievably disgusting that we were surprised the earth didn't stop turning [*again the official account records "great hilarity"*], Jews of such hideous repulsiveness. . . ."

Several swinish sentences later (yes, that "comradely interrogation" must still have been bugging you), you can't stop yourself from saying: "We feed the population to the extent we are able to—I can't grind any grain if I can't get it to grow from the ground. The chickens are well behaved, and we have enough eggs." Father, you'll never get rid of that obsession. Bormann must have asked you about the missing eggs after all.

The boys in Berlin probably took your law-and-order speeches too seriously—that is, they misunderstood you. If they had been in your audience at Lemberg, things would never have come to the pass they did. Hitler, that snake in the grass, sat down and wrote a letter which turned out to be one big surprise for you: "Reichsminister Dr. Frank, in order to be able to devote himself

more intensively to his tasks as Governor General, has requested
my permission for him to resign from his Party offices. I have
complied with this request. I appoint Dr. Georg Thierack as the
new head of the NS Rechtswahrerbund," the National Socialist
Association for the Preservation of Law.

That must have made you mad as hell. In addition, he even
gave Thierack the Academy for German Justice. How were you
supposed to refer to yourself from now on in your speeches? It
had always been so impressive to be able to say: "I, as Reichsminister, Governor General, head of the National Socialist Rechtswahrerbund, President of the Academy for German Justice, etc."
With one stroke of his pen Hitler shortened your speeches.

You must have been anxiously sitting there on the edge of your
seat in Cracow; but no news came over the ticker tape about the
GG being taken away from you, or your private railroad car, and
all the rest. Nor, for the moment at least, could Hitler care less
about your problems with women. Nevertheless, his directive must
have really bugged you. So you wrote Bormann that you had never
requested them to remove you from any of the Party offices. Then
you wrote something else: you sent in your letter of resignation.
If all that was left to you was half your titles, then it would be
better not to have any at all.

Now that must have upset Hitler, because he immediately lowered the boom on you and issued a ban against your making any
more speeches in the Reich. The only place you were permitted
to go on squawking was in the GG, as the Governor General. No
matter; it was now your turn to sit down and concoct a real
showstopper of a resignation letter. You went to your desk at
Kressendorf and in your bloated style formulated a document for
posterity, your political testament, and signed it in your own hand.
It begins with a sentence that pulls the rug out from under everything: "In consequence of the events of recent weeks, I have
declared to the Führer, per memorandum to Reichsminister Lammers, that I shall resign as Governor General, since his trust in

and approval of my performance have been withdrawn." After this lead-in, you begin, despite your long-winded meanderings, to generate some surprising truths (at least for those days): "The expansion of the sphere of authority of the executive branch of the police—which in the latter's hands is now subject to the most arbitrary abuse—has progressed so far that one can now speak of a total disenfranchisement of our National Socialist citizenry. When things have come to the point we find them now, when any citizen can be taken to a concentration camp without the possibility of self-defense and kept there for any length of time . . . when things have come to the point when security of life, freedom, honor, honest gain, etc., no longer obtain, then, according to my firm conviction, the ethical relationship between state leadership and citizenry also disappears entirely."

There follow a few platitudes about the state of justice; then you make a big deal out of your work as the GG, and then continue, using those awful superlatives of yours: "The Government General is today the most enlightenedly led and the most securely administered territory, and from it has redounded to the German Reich, in its difficult wartime mission, the most incalculable support." (Imagine my calling you "the most-hanged criminal.") In any case, you are approaching the end of your testament, you blabbermouth. But instead of adding now, "Dear Herr Hitler, I can no longer go along with your swinish regime; the security of justice means more to me than anything else"—instead of that, you go back to the beginning of the document and write: "The only condition under which I could remain in my post as Governor General would be if the Führer himself were to express his most emphatic trust in me and my future activities as Governor General."

And so he did. At least he muttered something or other in response to your seductive calls for reassurance, something that made you happy. It makes me happy, too, because now you were absolutely certain to get that noose around your neck. Mother has described for posterity how you drove up to the house, beaming from ear to ear, sprang out of the Mercedes, and, like a boy, ran up to the door of the Schoberhof: "Brigitte, Hitler is letting me keep the GG!"

That, then, was the conclusion to your battle for a state of justice. How grandiose had been the final sentence of your letter of abdication written at Kressendorf: "I salute it [*you probably meant your government and all its murderers and thieves—in a word, your German administration. Or did you mean something else?*], and a single glance back upon our Government General will be enough to justify our conviction that we have not lived in vain."

That regime cost plenty of other people their lives, however.

Tête-à-Tête
in the Salon Car

Your own life was running out faster and faster. To be sure, you succeeded, thanks to SS General Bach-Zelewski, in getting rid of your closest enemy, Krüger; but apart from that, what was the good news?

Filled with envy, but also heroically, Mother wrote you: "You are taking trips to the Reich in your private salon car just to satisfy your physical needs, while the best of our people are sacrificing their lives." And even when you weren't satisfying your physical needs, your concern for Poland was not evidenced in any very strong way. Once more, Mother held under your nose the things she had experienced with you: "One little adventure among many. We were driving from Kressendorf to the theater in Cracow, exceeding the speed limit. Two poor Poles got run over; all one could see was how they were lying in the street all tangled up in their bicycles, and you, the great 'father of the country,' simply kept on going without the least concern for those poor people!"

Because the divorce has finally been initiated, you are taking revenge and accusing Mother of having written from Kressendorf to all kinds of women friends, saying that her Hans had fallen out of favor with the Führer, that he had nothing more to hope for, and that if he continued to just hang around, the Führer would even take away the GG. Witness: Grandma. Well, it was enough to drive one nuts the way the two of you dragged everybody into your divorce.

Now you play your last trump card. Mother was faced with a clause in your lawyer's deposition claiming that her incessant talk about your sex trips, your bad odor with Hitler, and your loss of authority in the GG had "not only been the severest blow to the personal honor of the Governor General but had also shown contempt and undermined his public reputation in his role as the chief administrator of the Nebenland of the Greater German Reich, as Reichsminister, and as leading functionary of the Party." It was a sign to Mother that she was about to be out in the cold and had better start looking around for warmer clothes for future eventualities. But of course she already had plenty of furs for that.

After she got herself warmed up, she fought back. She simply swept aside the divorce litigation and your foolish posturing as the Governor General with the remark that your behavior was the "consequence of a psychosis which, in turn, [was] the consequence of the sexual adventures of my husband." So that was your reputation in Berlin—a man whose pathetic orgasms had evidently destroyed his brain. You struck back violently, spread the rumor around that Mother had probably had an affair with the recently rubbed-out Lasch, after all. In Berlin you told the super-krauts that your wife was solely responsible for the undermining of your authority role as National Patriarch.

Now, that assertion vexed Hitler, for as the German people still recall with gratitude, Hitler was very chivalrous toward ladies. Your divorce proceedings began to grind to a halt. Here I must insert for your delectation a revealing passage from Mother's letter to the super-bosses. It shows that Mother was prepared to pull out all the stops. She began sniffing around as a real Aryan was supposed to: "On August 28 I came by chance upon my husband's diary, which was kept in a place accessible to anyone." Well, Father, what do you think of that? Where was your diary? Did you keep it right inside the front door, in place of the guest book, wide open? Or maybe in the kitchen with a little pencil dangling from a string, just in case our maids or the chef might have had a sudden idea they wanted to jot down? Well, where was it? Mother lets us in on its whereabouts: "in his night-table drawer, which doesn't even have a lock." Naturally, Mother, this makes it public property.

"I read the remarks he had written in it and was very unhappy." Wait, Father. Mother is being very candid here (presumably with Lammers) and, in a very well-bred fashion, spreading your most private thoughts around: "When I took a closer look at the diary, I could tell from the fresh ink that he had recently been adding things to it, frequent exclamations like 'Lilly, where are you?' or, 'Oh, Lilly!' He probably had even showed her his diary. I found the whole thing so childish that I took pity on him in his delayed adolescent love."

Mother makes a point of reporting that between April 28, 1942, and March 12, 1943, you made fourteen trips to the Reich in your private railroad car, for a total of 170 days away from your job to spend with Lilly and others.

And she still has a few more arrows in her quiver. After you put forward additional grounds for divorce, she inquires sweetly of Hitler's chief of staff: "Aren't those perfect examples of the legal hair-splitting that the Führer is fighting so hard against? My husband, of all people, who I always thought was supposed to be the first man of law and justice [oh, Mother, you bitch] is capable of using those very tactics? That cannot be normal." And Mother closes: "The one message to take from everything I have said is still, as it always has been, that I do not want a divorce and that someday my husband will thank me for that!"

And you? It's November. A cold wind is blowing. The English Garden in Munich is bare and autumnal. People are looking healthier, because they're no longer as fat as they were. The people of Munich are sticking with Hitler just as much as they ever were. And here you are, walking hand in hand with Lilly through the

English Garden. You don't see Aunt Margot, who is following you,
having been put on your tail by Mother. What a touching soul
you are this moment, liberated from us, from politics, from your
crimes—or so you seem to think.

It's just Lilly and you together, two souls as one, the way it
never was with Mother. Yes, it must have been hard to get married
when you were really in love with someone else. And now the
love of your youth is back with you again. You're all dressed up
in your snazzy best, and your heart is beating just like a high
school boy's. You stroll past the Haus der Kunst, through the
arcades; you approach the cathedral, the Frauenkirche. I'd give
anything to have heard what you were saying to each other. After
you were dead and gone and Lilly was still alive, she always refused
to let me visit her. You wanted to bury your guilt in a new and
happier life; you wanted to forget the whole Third Reich in an
ardent embrace that would obliterate everything else. What were
you two talking about? About your future after the war? Did you
still see yourself as boss of the GG? As a Minister of the Reich?
You step through the portal of the church, you walk down the
nave; you don't care who sees you. Aunt Margot was there, she
saw you; but you simply never thought Mother would stoop so
low. Neither did I. Here, at this moment, I'm entirely on your
side—but probably only because the whole thing is so crazy. You,
the Governor General, walking hand in hand through Munich in
broad daylight, your fat lips parted, smiling so happily. Yes, Lilly
had a—what would you call it?—a "most infinitely, most sexually
radiant effect" on you. You proceeded right to the foot of the
altar, looked deeply into each other's eyes, like two sheep, and
then you, you married man, you father of a family, produced the
little box that was burning a hole in your jacket pocket and opened
it. Margot could see exactly what you were doing, that good soul,
Mother's trusty comrade. You took out a glorious diamond ring,
which probably cost the GG treasury about twenty-five thousand
marks. She, in turn, produced a kitschy opal ring. Then you placed

the diamond on her right ring finger; then she, in turn, placed the opal on yours. Aunt Margot couldn't suppress a gentle sob. Then the two of you went into a deep-tongue kiss. You united yourself in marriage before God.

Oh, yes, and with the blessing of Lilly's father. Just now, it occurs to me again, you master of sleaze, that before this touching ceremony you and Lilly had stood at the grave of her father. Margot had been there, too, but she couldn't get close enough, so she asked an old woman to tell her what she had heard, someone who was tending the nearby grave of some deceased relative or other. "What a crazy bird!" the woman began. "First, the two of 'em stood there like a couple of fish, not sayin' a word, then all at once the fat slob takes hold of her hand, raises it up, talks right to the grave. 'Father,' he said—or anyhow that's what I heard— 'Father, here I stand,' he said, 'with your little girl.' Well, that's what he said; then he said, 'With your daughter.' He said, 'I beg you'—yeah, he was talkin' to the grave again—'I ask you for her hand in marriage.' What a jerk, lemme tell you! 'I ask you for the hand of your daughter!' I thought to myself, This war is driving everybody nuts. I got up off my knees and tried to look him straight in the eye, but they just kept starin' at the grave like in a daze, it made me feel real creepy, and then the gentleman, he was dressed to the nines, I have to say that for 'im, she too, tall lady she was—the gentleman anyhow went on talkin' to the grave: 'I feel in my innermost soul that you have given us your blessing for our eternal union.' Pretty nice, huh? Then they went into a big kiss, and afterwards sprinkled holy water on the grave with a sprinkler—and after that they walked away, clingin' and huggin' each other."

Aunt Margot was shattered, but she continued her pursuit of the blissful couple in a taxi—or was it on her bicycle? Or maybe Mother had a car at her disposal? Anyhow, there you were, a bigamist in your soul of souls. You were sad and happy at the same time; when you were with Lilly, you didn't give one shit for the rest of the world. If it hadn't been for all that blood on your hands, if you weren't so deep in it, right up to your elbows, if it weren't dripping from your arms, I could have said to the two of you: "Get you to your marriage bed, make love in peace, rejoice, be fruitful and multiply."

For her part, Mother was livid. She kept on staring at the photograph of her competition. She must have tried in vain to convince herself how ugly Lilly was; but the fact is, Mother, Lilly was beautiful. And she was not a whore. So how could you get to her? How? You can't do it simply by cutting her face out of the photograph in which she's sitting next to your mother on the lawn at Kressendorf, drinking coffee (I'm looking at that very photo right now). No, it had to be something else. What sort of inspiration might occur to a true German woman at that particular historical moment—just as it might today, when the fat is in the fire? Right, you've got it: the lady could be a Jew.

Yes, Father, now you're freezing. It's true, Mother actually denounced Lilly as being half or quarter Jewish. If she ended up in a concentration camp, so what? What then? Well, Hans would come back to me, that's what.

But it didn't work.

All this time, now that you were in possession of Lilly's soul, you were making arrangements to find a secure and official position for the rest of her. So what does the potent lord of the land do in such a case? He makes a contract of employment, "to go into effect beginning September 1, 1943. Frau Lilly G. is to be employed in the office of the Governor General and will become a part-time employee in the office of the personal assistant of the Governor General." (Sounds as if you dictated that in bed.) You were so generous: "Frau Lilly G. forgoes all monetary remuneration and the equivalent of her salary will be donated, for charitable purposes, to the winter relief drive."

Scarcely had the news reached Mother's ears when she metamorphosed into a veritable Fury, determined to do Lilly in. If she couldn't get her as a Jewess, then she could call up the equivalent of a total military alert. Mother fanned the flames, and lo and behold, your man Eisenlohr was soon compelled by the authorities to write "that the employment arrangement concluded on 9/1/43 with the central office of the GG must be dissolved effective 9/1/44, in consideration of the demands of the total war effort and national security."

So much for Lilly's contribution to the winter relief fund. Her removal from official service in the GG presumably shortened the war by several years. You were sour as an old lemon. Your only recourse was to another flight into lyrical effusion. On a picture postcard you wrote to your Lilly: "We shall be together again at the lakeside. And our life together will grow in intensity, and we shall endure in the face of all adversity. My Lilly! Remain at my side! May my pains be consumed [*or did you write "consoled"? I can't decipher it*]. Day and night I am with you, my Lilly—for eternity!" You had to face your real eternity a mere three years later, Father. Your execution made it possible for you to signal your arrival in that eternity with a little strangled whistle as the noose closed around your neck.

Before that event, however, and under the protection of Hitler (who put a real damper on your divorce), Mother—now you're freezing in your cauldron again, aren't you, Father?—undertook a nocturnal attack upon your very own person. In Munich she furtively stole into the train in which your private car was coupled (the mere reminder of that event makes you shiver). It was winter, but Mother's jealousy kept her toasty warm. Doubtless she also let loose a couple of anti-Bolshevist exclamations by way of camouflaging her identity in the jam-packed passenger compartment. (Later she recalled the moment: "How the smell of those people distressed me!" Incidentally, I pause to remark that I never heard her say anything against the Jews themselves. That was a field reserved for you to plow deep. In the art of verbal annihilation, which preceded and then accompanied the physical annihilation, you were infinitely more inventive than she was.)

Mother waited until the train got to Freilassing, then burst forth. She sprang from her seat, dashed onto the platform, and ran to the very end of the train where your car was located. There were SS men everywhere, but she had her Frau Minister's pass with her. (Here it is in front of me at this very moment; how sweet she looks in her photograph, so good and maternal, hair parted in the middle and lacquered on the sides.) The last extension of this Pass Number 1337 reads, "Valid until December 31, 1945"— but after May of that year, the pass didn't do Mother much good, as you can appreciate from your knowledge of recent history, Father. That in itself was enough to make her object vehemently to the unconditional surrender.

Well then, Mother stepped right through the guards who were supposed to protect you from any and all attacks. I always approved of these bodyguards, by the way. Death in a rain of bullets or by hand grenade would have been too gentle for you, too sudden, and too quickly over with. There was a point in time, back there in 1943, when, as a little wicked water sprite, I sat on your shoulder and took care to see that nothing of the sort would happen to you before you got properly hanged, and to ensure that you would get a full and unadulterated taste of the fear of death before it happened.

Mother rushes from checkpoint to checkpoint, getting ever closer to your private car. She shows her pass one final time and is then ushered by a slightly astonished guard into your car, where she is received by a very astonished adjutant. She stops him from warning you, rushes huffing and puffing (after all, she was already forty-seven years old at the time of her Freilassing spurt) to the door of your sleeping quarters, and tears the door open. The adjutant's words, "But Frau Minister!" stick to his throat. I wonder exactly what Mother had been expecting to find? You on top of

Lilly? Lilly on top of you? Gertrude and you with the Polish countess?

Poor Mother, such bad luck again. You were lying there asleep, alone. The ruckus she made in breaking and entering awakened you; you turned over in bed; she turned the light on; the train started moving again. "Brigitte, is it you?" Not a very inspired opening sentence for such a gifted orator as you—but I'll grant you the disadvantage of the light glaring in your eyes and your sleepy stupor. Mother stood there a little sheepishly; naturally she didn't want to be deprived of the rich figments of her imagination. You caught on quickly enough, and donned your dressing gown (silk, of course). Since your hair had begun to thin a bit by this time, I can hardly portray you as having a snarled mane, tousled and messed up from the pillow; no, it was just stringy. You probably had bad breath, too. Mother began with a litany of lies, none of which rang true. The adjutant had withdrawn at once; you pushed her back into the drawing room, where you then made a terrific scene—this time you had the advantage over her. Then you went back to bed.

That was a bad move on your part. Mother just plunked herself down on an armchair instead of retreating and began to pull that same old trick which always got on my nerves when I was a child and later as a teenager, all those years I was compelled to spend with her. First, she began to whine softly and then, growing louder and louder, to howl like a coyote. (For a moment your adjutant seriously considered putting in for a quick transfer; it was still a long way to Vienna.) I picture you tossing back and forth on your bed in agony, for Mother was a genius at varying and modulating the sounds she could produce, though there was nothing at all like a lullaby in either the pitch or the volume of that instrument. Then she stopped. On the other side of your mahogany wall you imagined her fumbling for her little hanky, finding it, blowing her nose, and letting out a big sigh. Then the performance started all over again, up and down the entire scale.

You lay there in your bed, enraged and growing weaker and slacker by the minute. The adjutant brewed a pot of tea, which Mother accepted with a big, noisy sob. The train rumbled on gently—much more rhythmically than today, Father; today the tracks are all smoothly and boringly welded together. And you, how lucky you were this time: Lilly did not come to meet you in Vienna when your private salon car arrived.

It's pretty obvious that you two were never able to forget this painful nocturnal episode. It underscores for me something that Father O'Connor said later: "Even in prison he was still frightened of your mother." Were you afraid she might howl even outside the window of your Nuremberg cell?

Yes, there were plenty of painful things about Mother as far as you were concerned. But there were also a few things about Lilly, too, one of the minor ones being that you had to wear that effeminate opal ring she had given you as a token of your rediscovered love. You had to take such precautions so that Mother wouldn't get to see it! On the other hand, Lilly insisted, of course, that you wear it everywhere in public. She had a cunning side to her, your Lilly did. It could be said that you bounced back and forth from one dragon lady to another, though you must have taken considerably greater pleasure in chasing the latter naked through your salon car. True or not, I can at least imagine such scenes, especially after hearing from those who knew you so much admiring testimony about the "Great Stud of the Eastern Territory."

"Then You Are
My Mortal Enemy"

"What disasters are still to come my way, I do not know. All signs point to an attack and a battle to the finish," you wrote to Mother, in the hope that she would not want to be with you for that final battle and would let you go. You tempt her as follows: "You should not come along with me into the darkness ahead. God be with you, Brigitte. Give me back my strength. Release me . . . and grant me salvation [*those three dots are in your letter, you theatrical genius*]. My life must take on a clear sense of direction. Or it must end." Those last two words you wrote in a tiny hand—such dramatic desperation. Mother did not retreat: "Dear Hans, You have lost all your senses again and the demons have taken hold of you." Mother means the demon of sex. After this introduction, she goes after you with hammer and tongs: "They tell me that the Führer will put up with this only a little while longer, but I would like to tell you that it is the *Lord God* who will put up with it only a little while longer."

You were mightily afraid of both of them. The Lord God had already been drawn into your bigamist's nest, and now Hitler was playing a very serious game. Mother writes you in horror: "In November you, along with several others, were supposed to be awarded some kind of Order of the Red Cross. When Hitler's State Minister Meissner delivered the proposed list to the Führer, he approved all of them, except that he did not give his permission for you to be among them."

To her great dismay, the Frank family was left standing there in the cold without the Order of the Red Cross.

Things got worse. Mother had her spies everywhere. Even the Führer had no inkling of how helplessly he had been delivered into Mother's hands. "When Minister Meissner composed the texts for the Führer's New Year's telegrams and brought them to him, all of them were worded identically for those who have positions equivalent to yours. The Führer let them all stand as they were, but in your case he himself crossed out two lines of personal greeting." The Frank family was shocked. You were shocked. Everybody around you was shocked. You wrote Mother in your corny way: "At this terrible time, at this epochal moment in our history, when entire worlds are reshaping themselves into new constellations, I must be prepared for the worst." While one might think that you are conjuring up here a terrible vision of human bodies, your awareness of what was going on at Auschwitz and Maidanek, the only thing that follows this prophetic bombast is another request for a divorce. Then you reach new heights of literary bathos: "I'm standing at the end of all my battles. My time has run out. I must now stride toward the eternal sun, filled with clarity and inner strength. Brigitte, how far removed I am from everything . . . how far removed. . . ." (Those little ellipses are also verbatim.) You seem to be emulating the performances of the great German actor Heinrich George, whom you saw during the same time at your Cracow theater. Your mawkishness ascends the scale: "Everyone who belongs within my circle is now cast into misfortune." Go on, Father, cap the climax: "May God illuminate your pathway: you shall never encounter the same me again. . . ." (Ellipses yours again, Father; and something else interesting: that colon in your sentence.) Thereupon, Mother must have said something like, "The hell I'm going to let myself be forced into a divorce with such baloney," and then she said: "I'd rather be the widow than the divorced wife of a Reichsminister!"

When Mother dumped that cold water on your idiotic posturing with that down-to-earth, realistic remark, you must have suddenly looked like a real jerk in that amateur Hamlet pose of yours, peering out from the theater wings up there on the Wawel. So you threw in the towel right away; maybe it was that very remark of Mother's that inspired your famous two-liner: "The play is done. / I'm going home." You can just imagine how Mother's female troops gathered around her in the living room at the Schoberhof and dissected the next document she received from your attorney, the one containing the unique sentence: "The destiny of the Reich demands that he [*that is to say, you, Father*] must be placed in a position where, with his final strength and the rare capacities with which he has been endowed, he will be able to serve the Führer and the Fatherland in a dignified and unperturbed way, supported in this enterprise by a new and revitalized private life." Imagine that being recognized as sufficient grounds for divorce. But that was the remarkable thing about those times: when it came to death sentences, the German courts had long since forgotten all human justice, but it was different in the case of divorce. Naturally, what griped Mother most was that she no longer was able to skim off the cream from the GG during your marriage crisis. She cleverly misrepresented her dilemma in being forced to give way to others now, as follows: "I think only of Kressendorf. Certainly, it is a state-owned property, but look at the people taking advantage of the place now and profiteering from it! He knows exactly why he wanted to have me only as a guest there. He knows I would have put an end to such goings-on long ago."

In spite of it all, the two of you did engage in one final bout of sexual intercourse on the night of January 3, 1943, at the Schoberhof, at least according to Mother's big mouth. Perhaps it was on that occasion that she issued a special order for Aunt Margot to be present in the room. Yes, naturally, of course that's the way it must have been, just so that Margot could testify in court: "Yes, Your Honor, the Herr Governor General was lying naked on top of Brigitte. I was so surprised that I let out a scream. The Herr Governor General turned his head toward me and cursed me—I hardly dare repeat the words he used—he said, 'You shitty pack of women!' That's exactly what he shouted."

No, Father, I simply can't hide it from you. You'll have to hear the way Mother set up her whole scenario about proving that Lilly was Jewish; you can practically smell Mother's hate from her totally messed-up grammar. She wrote to a specialist in racial law: "Don't you believe that I could find out whether the grounds for suspicion—and by the way, they have been voiced by others, too—regarding the Aryan origins of Frau G.? Is it permissible today for a woman with a hardly unequivocal life-style, has she the right to inflict upon me such unhappiness?" She brewed everything together in one pot and then wrote to Lammers, or someone: "What I am most concerned about knowing is whether it may actually be true that you, Herr Reichsleiter, doubtless in the name of the Party, or that Herr Reichsführer Himmler, or even the Führer himself, has demanded that I divorce my husband."

That, in turn, enraged you so much there at your castle that you summoned up your courage and initiated the following telephone conversation with Mother. Can you still remember it, Father?

You: "Then you are not in agreement about a divorce, Brigitte?"

Mother, very cool and standoffish: "I shall continue, as I have before, to do everything I can to save you from your own unhappiness. I consider this my holy mission."

Something like that can put one in a pretty rotten mood, wouldn't you say, Father, especially when one is so hot to hop into bed with someone else? And so you answered ironically: "Yes, there's no doubt about that."

Then she retorted something I mustn't quote, at the risk of committing libel; and then it's your turn again. Rebelliously: "I am determined—" (Hold it! I have to interrupt the conversation here and set the scene properly. So far, I've made it a production

number somewhat beneath your customary level. You were sitting
at your desk up at the castle, a desk as big as Hitler's at the Reich
Chancellery; lying before you are the important memoranda concerning the promotion of the German Alpine Club in the GG
[that's a fact; that's what you were actually occupying yourself
with]; the room is pleasantly warm; the old imperial Polish flags
are hanging at either side of you from the lofty walls; you have
breakfasted well; the previous night, Nursemaid G.D. had submitted to your will. My God, were you potent—but why did you
have to blab everything to everybody? Even Mother could get the
news in Berlin; no wonder she was so aggravated. Lilly at the time
of this phone call was very close to your thoughts, in spite of your
nocturnal bed-hopping. Now you may continue.) "—I am determined to relinquish to the Führer all the power of my offices if
that's what it takes to achieve my goal."

Now you convince yourself that you can actually hear over the
telephone the thud of your wife as she falls in a dead faint. You
hope that Mother has cracked her skull open on the marble floor
of the Schoberhof. But no such luck—the woman from Forst
remains as hard as steel and straight as a ramrod. Mother answers:
"That doesn't surprise me—you've already had your lawyer tell
me all that."

I can see you clenching your fists—the goddamned woman
simply won't let you go. You say: "Are you going to take all the
responsibility on your own two shoulders, then?" That was pretty
weak, Father; it shows you've already lost. You couldn't dream up
a better ploy?

Mother: "The responsibility is yours, for you are not only sacrificing me to this woman, you are also sacrificing your career to
her."

Mother, I love you. How clearly you were able to demonstrate
how frantically Father clung to his satanic job.

Please excuse my little explosion there, Father, but the fact is
you are really getting weaker and weaker in this vital, this central

conversation that took place not so very long before the end of
your life. The only thing you have left is that empty bathos of
yours: "Then you are my mortal enemy." How you two must have
truly hated each other.

You lost this one, my friend, my Father, my Führer. That
umpteenth offer of yours to resign from all your posts was presumably brushed aside by the Number One Führer with a tired
and trembling hand. He snuffed out your attempts at flattery with
some nonsense about war and peace and duty; or perhaps he was
even more direct and asked you please to be so good as to keep
it in your pants and stop trying again and again to throw away
your brilliant career as a master criminal. Anyhow, you struck the
flag and capitulated, at least until after the war was over, and had
your lawyer write Mother another letter: "On behalf of the plaintiff
I withdraw the petition. In the matter of the resolution of his
matrimonial status, the plaintiff relies for the present on the fairness
of the Führer. The legal separation of the plaintiff from the re-
spondent, however, is not affected by this decision and shall remain
in effect. Nor does the plaintiff relinquish his right to an eventual
divorce."

As to your "legal separation," not a chance. No sooner had you
knuckled under than, presto, Mother was already turning up again
in the GG with empty suitcases to be filled. In spite of your so-
called separation there was still plenty of room for us there. Now
you had the old lady back in the neighborhood again. In retaliation
you had the wheels of your rumor mill set in motion. In turn,
Mother felt obliged to turn up the heat on you and sent a nice
letter to the sanctum sanctorum in Berlin: "You will have been
informed that my husband withdrew his divorce petition on June
7. During this period and without my having been able to defend
myself, certain individuals have started spreading the most evil
statements about me in the form of rumors. My honor as a woman
has been attacked [*Mother herself must have grinned when she wrote
that last sentence, because she crossed it out*]. They persist in naming

me in connection with the recently passed-away Governor Lasch. [*Oh, Mother, you know that my second father "passed away" as a result of his corruption. He was executed by the thugs of the very man to whom you are pouring out in such confidence all your heartache.*] They claim I dealt illegally in furs and diamonds with him; and as if that were not enough for them, they are also beginning to describe in detail a relationship between us of an immoral character. Even my children are being besmirched; it is claimed that my youngest child was fathered by Lasch."

Well, then, now I feel that my honor as a child is being attacked. Tell me, Father, did you sire me? Or did Lasch, that rat? Or Schmitt, that godly man, that authority in constitutional law? Or did all you gentlemen of the law beget me in some wild quadrille?

Mother paints a pretty picture of you in her letter to Himmler. Particularly perfidious is the part where she lets the people at the very top of the totem pole know what you've been saying: "He says he cares about nothing anymore, that he'll do whatever he wants to do and that nobody is going to tell him what he can and can't do, not even the Führer."

The sacrament of marriage was certainly held in high regard by you two. It's a fact that from now on you forbade your retinue, your servants, your advisers, your adjutants, to refer to Mother as your wife, your "Frau Gemahlin." Hitler must have heard about that, and it must have made him start trembling with rage. He was simply unable to continue his annihilation in peace.

On July 29, 1943, Mother was guarding the Schoberhof like a Cerberus. The local farmers must have thought the American GIs were already coming, so they greeted us that day with a good deal less respect than usual. A convoy of vehicles rolled up that day, raising a cloud of dust. Heavy Mercedes cars and trucks stopped in front of the house, more or less surrounding it. The dust settled slowly. It was an insufferably hot day; it also happened to be the day on which a group of antifascist children belonging to the Communist families living in Neuhaus (at least that is what I

gathered later from Mother's tirade) pushed me into a huge clump
of nettles near the beach in Finsterlin. The only thing I had on
was a little pair of swimming trunks, and I let out such a tremendous scream that some grown-ups appeared at once and pulled
me out. Even today, whenever I feel the need of a shot of adrenaline,
all I have to do is conjure up the image of those poisonous green
nettles. I swelled up to the size of a real he-man, at least
temporarily.

At that very moment, Mother was receiving your emissary. He
had various lists in his hand and was demanding the immediate
surrender of books, underwear, shirts, all kinds of other clothing—
and of something else very strange: "personal art objects." I must
insist that you let me in on exactly what those were, when I come
someday to visit you in your eternal flames. According to testimony
given later by Farmer K.'s wife, Mother supposedly shrieked so
violently at your errand boy as he was standing in the doorway
that he instantly turned around and disappeared with his lists,
cars, and trucks in the direction of Schliersee. Mother was still
standing there, snorting in her triumph, when they brought me
home and laid me at her feet, red as a beet and unconscious.
Scarcely was I put in the care of a doctor when Grandpa arrived,
babbling and with an equally nettle-burned face and swollen, bursting hands. It seems that when the first Mercedes sped by, he was
so afraid that it might be his son (that is to say, you) that he
leaped into a roadside ditch that was also full of nettles. Waste of
effort.

Out of revenge for Mother's behavior, you immediately reduced
her household allowance to two thousand marks. At first she ranted
and raged, but then she thought up an idea that put a heavy burden
on the fateful battle for the defense of the Fatherland. "I was
advised," she wrote to a confidante, "to turn to the Führer on
the subject of the household allowance not being paid to me in
full, for the Führer is my husband's only superior. No matter what,
I shall not be satisfied with two thousand marks." The upshot of

all this was probably that on the same evening the victory fanfare was played on the Reich radio network, the following words were spoken: "The German Wehrmacht announces that the Führer has decided from now on to increase the household allowance of Frau Brigitte Frank. Führer, speak and we shall obey."

Was it that, dear Father, which prompted you to insist that they give you a quarter of an hour radio time at least once a month for rebuttal? You could have waged your marriage battle most energetically over the airwaves. Once a month you could have publicly denounced the profligate habits of your wife, Brigitte; you could have enraged her marvelously by following that up with a sigh of love directed at Lilly, such as "*Je t'aime.*" You could have continued: "Lilly, my sweetie-pie, my little beddy-bye, my one and only—drift to me on the banks of the Vistula, waft to me in my castle on the Wawel. Come to me, you buxom lass." And you could have finished off with a little poem:

> "*The Jews have been ashed,*
> *The Polacks are trashed,*
> *We're safe and we're warm.*
> *Let's fuck up a storm!*"

Mother would have exploded. However, your ambition to be a radio announcer was instantly shot down, for by this time Hitler had really had enough. He put a stop to your divorce.

Mother was delighted. Now she insisted that you assume all her legal expenses. That, in turn, provoked your countercomplaint that in the course of your marriage you had bought her "fourteen to sixteen valuable fur coats." I'll never be able to escape from those furs! It seems you won't, either. What was it you told Mother's lawyer after your refusal to pay that gentleman his substantial fee for representing her and after he said to you, "The legal fees in the divorce case of a head of state surely deserve to be fixed on a somewhat different scale from the divorce costs of a baker, even a rich one"? (I like that.) You told him: "Just have her give you one of those fur coats." (Now that's the way for a great head of state like you to talk.) The lawyer had been clever enough to hike the amount in dispute up to one million marks in consequence of your contesting Mother's insult to you as head of state and claiming that she had ruined your reputation in the eyes of your subordinates. The lawyer, in any case, courageously concluded the conversation with the remark: "At least the baker Herr Huber immediately pays what he owes."

Bravo! I love it. I can see you there, licking your wounds in a corner, you, the Herr Reichsminister and Governor General. The only thing left for you to do was to give the lawyer a very head-of-stately word to the wise on his way out the door, and to tell him that you planned on keeping Mother's furs until she returned Lilly's opal ring to you. The head of state scampers as in a movie through the rooms of his castle like a petrified mouse being pursued by a cat, just like in a Tom and Jerry cartoon—a fur coat over one arm, with Mother screeching behind him, breathing down his neck: "Give me that fur coat, give me that twenty-third fur coat of mine! It's my most favorite, my most beautiful, my best-fitting one of all of them!"

So Mother was able to remain the Frau Minister, the Frau Governor General, after all. Soon thereafter she approached you with some touching words about your separation: "Considering the momentous and terrible events taking place all around us, and in view of the possibility that fate could soon affect us in a highly personal way, let us for the sake of the children try one more time. I offer you my selfless friendship."

Father, do you think Mother was suddenly seized by an attack of moralistic fervor? Or did she perhaps realize a lot sooner than you did that your lives were really washed up now, that both of you had become guilty, that you had sucked the good life out of the torment and death of millions?

You didn't catch on to anything. You continued to pursue a

hot and healthy career centered on your groin. Stupidly, directly, right to her face, and in an incredibly insulting way, you answered Mother's proposal at the castle. You were standing about three feet away from her—and God knows, if I had been there with the huge diamond sword I used for lopping off the heads of nettles, I would have sliced right through you when you, still the great head of state, said to her: "Yes, I long for another human being, especially now that I'm growing older. But you, Brigitte, cannot be that person." Bingo. Good thing you had only two and a half more years to live.

You continued to have Lilly for the needs of your heart, and the rest of you. But the end of the GG was quickly approaching. Mother wrote you this prophetic sentence on August 5, 1944, even if she's really only talking about problems with the telephone: "Unfortunately we simply cannot get Cracow any longer. That worries me."

Lilly must have loved you, at least if we can believe her letters to you: "I am constantly with you in my thoughts. You accompany me on all my paths, in everything that makes up my being. [*Father, you're beginning to infect this woman's way of expressing herself. At least Mother, no copycat, stuck to her own unique style.*] You, my own Hans, my happiness and good fortune, my life. I love you, unutterably, and I am ready for any sacrifice."

The commas before and after "unutterably" please me. Lilly had such a dramatic flair. Her relatives tell me that she took total command over you, poor fellow. And maybe the whole thing might have worked out if you could have kept yourself in check, stopped trying to be such a show-off and tyrant.

Your and Lilly's love for each other was truly unique. The time was July 1944. The German Reich had shrunk back to a more normal size, and the German Wehrmacht was showing its heels on every front, when Frau Mylo, your secretary, brought the mail to your office at the castle, presorted. She was permitted to presort as long as it was not personally addressed to you. But as Frau

Mylo told me decades later, she had unfortunately opened by mistake a telegram that had been directed to "Herr Governor General Reichsminister Dr. Hans Frank, Castle, Cracow," your thrilling official address. Frau Mylo came into your office with the packet of mail, and as she handed it to you, she was most embarrassed and begged your pardon for having opened the telegram. But, she told me, you seemed totally relaxed and reacted jovially after reading the short message. You told her: "Don't worry about it at all, Frau Mylo." When she recited the nine words of the telegram to me, I suddenly suspected that I had not only had a second and a third father, but also a second mother, someone altogether unperturbed by the millions of war dead, by the fact that her own son was missing in action, and by the abominations committed in the concentration camps that she had learned about through you (don't deny it). Despite all that, her zest for life oozed from the telegram she sent from beautiful Upper Bavaria. "Summer, sunshine, shimmering lake—where are you? Your Lilly."

What a perfect model of a German woman. We who are so alive are always the stronger ones. This left Frau Mylo speechless— but no doubt gave you a little tingle. You probably noticed Frau Mylo's shock, didn't you? That might explain the preposterous way in which you left her out at the fifth anniversary celebration of the GG when you presented little gifts of golden rings to your faithful female co-workers—whether they had performed for you in the regal Polish beds or not. These rings had presumably been made by the last Jews in the ghetto, who were permitted to live a couple of days longer for that reason alone. You gave a ring to each one of these women. They still wear them today, completely oblivious, regretting nothing. They show them off with pride and will take them to their graves on their dead fingers. The only one you didn't honor with such a gift was Frau Mylo.

Fear Grows

At the high point of your divorce proceedings, somewhere in 1942–43, Mother wrote that you had evidently become schizophrenic. I don't want to believe that was true. If I have to have a criminal for a father, I'd just as soon not have a psychotic one to boot. It was only the fear in you, fear that began to curl the hair at the back of your neck as the battle lines came closer.

As I follow the entries in the official diary of the great statesman, I can see, above all from your incidental remarks, how crooks slowly but surely begin to register true anxiety.

On the other hand, there was still enough going on to make life in the GG pleasant for you. Let's run through some of the events. For example, on September 20, 1942, you are crowned as the Harvest Festival King and that evening have the pleasure of seeing *Cavalleria Rusticana* in your Cracow theater. A day later you come on heavy again, and at a meeting of the Hauptabteilungsleiter, your departmental chiefs, tell them that the independence of the GG vis-à-vis the powers of the Reich must be maintained and add, "I shall put an end to all the atrocity propaganda against the GG and the Governor General himself!" Then, twenty-fours later, you order someone to revise a piece of theater criticism in your Cracow newspaper that you happen not to have liked, and then you record your satisfaction in having finally been granted the strengthened security police command escort you had so long hoped for (which, of course, had nothing to do with the theater criticism).

On the twenty-fourth you must arrange for Polish musicians to take over the orchestra spots of the German musicians who had been conscripted into the army. Some time later, in Nuremberg, you will be lavishing praise on your all-Polish orchestra and hoping to prove thereby what a great friend of Poland you were. But maybe the Poles don't quite see it that way, and for good reason: You summon your advisers to discuss "which individual categories of the non-German population" should be provided with gas masks, and determine that the others will simply have to die. Then you have a great moment in your feud with Krüger. It seems that he has arrested and locked up an official named Szepessy on the grounds that, among other things, he had shaken hands while saying good-bye to the Jews on the Jewish Council. So you retaliate and have Szepessy's wife brought to your office so that Krüger is obliged to repeat his accusations in her presence. Beautifully done, Father. Then, because the Nuremberg Trials are still in the far-distant future, you are bold enough to sign, on October 2, 1942, an edict against the overattendance of health spas by Poles.

You get all hot and bothered writing a letter to Bormann on October 23, telling him that you had not resigned voluntarily from your Party offices in the Reich, but that Lammers, in the Führer's name, had forced you to do so. On the same day, you play chess like an imbecile against Grand Master Bogolwubov (h5 to g5 is what you should have played). On the twenty-sixth you praise the "financial clarity" of the GG economy (what a crock); you play the heavy in the battle against the Jews by issuing a decree against the legality of their giving sworn testimony, basing it on the grounds of racial inferiority. On the thirtieth you give a speech to the mayors and other officials in Brzesko, praising the "severe, but just and impartial, German leadership." A day later in Cracow, you open an art exhibition, "German Artists Look at the GG."

On November 20 you are obliged to listen to your President

Naumann announcing that in this year alone 360 million eggs have been recorded as laid by Polish hens (something that must have given you a tiny twinge), and you voice your gratification in learning that two million Poles are going to be excluded from the standard food rations for consumers when new ration cards are distributed at the various workplaces. (What do you suppose might have happened to those two million Poles? Did such a question ever enter your mind?) On the twenty-fourth you tell your lads that because more underhanded tricks are being pulled on you, you are again going to offer the Führer the chance to accept your resignation. The Führer, of course (there must have been a pile of filled-out forms in Berlin all ready for you), refuses to accept it, which prompts you to reply: "I can see in the repeated rejection of my resignation a renewed proof of confidence in me, and I am henceforth firmly determined to uphold the authority of the Governor General in all situations and to make absolute and ruthless use of the powers that were invested in me at the time." (You received those powers in October 1939; so much for all that blather.)

On a following Monday, your nonstop motor-mouth produces this phrase: "This human matériel of Poles and Ukrainians," thereby upgrading those inferior races a notch. Does that imply that you received news from the front that things were not in the very best of shape there? Then, the following day you threaten to resign yet again, because this time you have been told to relinquish your jurisdiction over the Eastern Railway System and transfer it to the Reichsbahn. You get the bad news on December 7 that unfortunately there are still some Jews alive who have fled into the forests and joined up with the Underground. On the other hand, you are enraged when you learn on December 8 that two thousand Jewish construction workers have been "transferred elsewhere," causing a reduction in building activity. The fact that "transferred elsewhere" means to death camps was something of no concern to you. At the same meeting where you learn these things you also take up a decisively negative position concerning a reduction in the bonus for officials of the GG. Then you discover that for a whole week you have to deal with the problem of how to deprive two million Poles and Ukrainians of their food ration cards; but more important to you that day is to decide which uniform your driver should wear.

On the seventeenth you have the statesmanlike idea of creating the "Dr. Frank Prize" for German authors to promote literature about the GG. Just imagine, you might have invited back Thomas Mann to participate, or even little Bertie Brecht. Then it seems you must have been staring at the map to see how far the Russians had advanced by now, so you quickly decide to permit your Poles to enjoy some "light reading for their entertainment." Were they instantly persuaded to cease all resistance after getting your little books in their eager hands? But then you quickly show them that book reading is only a temporary thing, for on December 19 (the season of Advent makes every German pious and compassionate) you say in an address to the police battalion: "In several years Poles will no longer be in existence." In the evening you celebrate at a pre-Christmas party with your officials, and all of them agree with you when you praise the reconstruction work of your administration as an effort to raise the GG out of "Polish rubble and Polish rabble," whereupon Bühler, in the name of all the other thugs, assures you of "our fidelity to your personal leadership," which touches you to the core. On the other hand, you demonstrate your own pigheadedness by criticizing Hitler's pigheadedness in the matter of your divorce and make it clear that you wish to participate in the celebration of the tenth anniversary of the January 30, 1933 Nazi takeover only "if the Führer wishes the presence of the Governor General," something that naturally would ruin the celebration for the Führer.

On January 25 you again have to assert your authority when, without your receiving any notification, an order issued by Himmler is carried out—namely, to send to concentration camps or to shoot immediately and arbitrarily movie patrons, schoolchildren, and pedestrians. It isn't the fact that the SS is doing this that enrages you, Father (I've gotten to know you pretty well by now) but the fact that they don't think it's necessary to inform the GG puppet ahead of time. May I quote here two of your grandiloquent sentences that follow some extensive preliminary garbage of yours: "It is out of the question that directives of the Reichsführer regarding police and security-force operations be carried out by circumventing the very man whom the Führer himself has placed in his office; for such a step would render me completely superfluous. Nevertheless, I am happy to hear that the action has been taken anyhow." That's right, Poles are dead and you're not superfluous.

Two days later the matter of abandoned Jewish property occurs to you. Someone or other had done something naughty to the owners of this property, as you so amusingly put it in your speech at Lvov. One and a half billion marks seem to be ownerless and unclaimed, and that's something to make you smack your fat master-race lips. Himmler is licking his chops too, of course. I can see you grinning, for I know that at some future love fest between the two of you, you'll be the one to win the loot. Yet at this time, you are still uncertain. But you have not yet lost that heavenly sense of humor which was so much in evidence when you were giving your speech in Warsaw on the occasion of the tenth anniversary of the Nazi takeover. (Hold it—does that mean that Hitler *did* shit on you after all by not inviting you to Berlin? Oh, a wound like that naturally hurts; but your sense of humor, as I said, was not to be diminished by such a trifle.) Remember? It was your speech about "the German city of Warsaw, in which allegedly one million Jews were living at one time." How deliciously hilarious, my dear man. And now for the first time you get indirect aid from the Soviet Union on account of the situation at the front. You conjure up their atrocities; you praise your government as being "an incomparably humane regime"; and here for the first time the foreign ethnics are called upon to contribute their "obedience and devotion to our common European goals." What's that? A common Europe? I believe I can discern hints of the worsening war situation, am I right?

Still, something that overjoys you, despite that, is the news on February 2 that a Baedeker guidebook is to be written on the GG. In between times you experience a blackout or two, as is confirmed by the minutes of your governors' conference on February 22: "The Herr Governor General cannot understand what the SS— as an arm of the party, that is to say, in its capacity as the Waffen SS and thereby a part of the Wehrmacht—has to do with the management of estates in the GG." Forget it, Father.

March 22 is a red-letter day for you because, as the Father of the Country, you have been informed exactly how many human beings you actually govern. There are 14,471,000 of them, not including a single Jew; otherwise there would have been many more than 17,000,000.

On April 15, your overflowing love of mankind proves itself again to be as strong as an ox, as does your sense of justice, when you say, "These mass executions without trial, executions in which sometimes the occupants of entire towns are killed, are impossible in the long run," which brings you a few minutes later by strange indirection to the surprising question as to whether the government buildings themselves are actually secured against attack. Bühler, to your horror, says they aren't.

On April 20 some Poles make an attempt on Krüger's life. They're not successful, which elicits from you the stinking lie "Thank God," and then a little later you learn that an assassination attempt on you has also been planned, which would have crimped your style a little, on which account you attempt to banish such danger with the suggestion of replacing the "P" on the armband of Polish compulsory laborers being sent to the Reich with the Polish GG coat of arms—whereupon evidently the Poles, out of their minds with happiness, call off the assassination, so that you ultimately find it to be a superfluous expense when on May 3 Director Scharrer of the Mercedes Works personally brings you a new armored car. What a bit of luck that no one can shoot a bullet from the street right into your fat face any longer; and so in your relief you get fresh and saucy, and in the government session you reject the "atrocity propaganda" directed at you from the Reich claiming that "a perpetual feast" is going on in the GG; then you must have cast one more glance at the progress on the front, for in a flash you issue a decree stipulating that at least eighty percent of the food ration for Germans should now be available to productive Poles.

Let me catch my breath. . . . Now, what is that supposed to mean, a "productive Pole"? Does that mean that there were also goof-off Poles, or had all of them already been exterminated?

Let us now continue our mad dash through the account of your public works.

Because of the situation at the front, you now began to think a good deal more about your own stomach. On May 5 you expounded on the management of the Kressendorf estate. Were two hundred thousand additional preserved eggs hovering before your greedy mind's eye? Or did you see yourself, surrounded by the surging Soviet sea, comfortably and self-sufficiently running your state-owned estate and driving in your armored Mercedes from one row of sugar beets to the next? Perhaps it was this figment of your imagination that caused you for the nth time to retract your offer to resign in a message to the Führer. Thank God you did, for now you were still around to experience from your exalted position the discovery by the German troops of the slaughtered Polish officers in the Forest of Katyn. The first thing they probably did was to flip over the corpses in the mass grave and check to see whether the Germans themselves might have executed the twelve thousand Poles. That substantial number had a rather familiar ring to it for them, and also the way the mass grave was dug. God damn it, is it possible that some SS unit had gone and

259

lost the body-count report? However, with a great sigh of relief, they found enough proof that this time, for a change, it was the Russians. And so you promptly commissioned a novel with the working title *Katyn: The Fateful Path of Twelve Thousand Poles*. How touching, Father. At a special discount the Poles could probably have gotten a copy of the Polish translation, with your own picture on page 3. Shortly after reading your entry about Katyn, I discovered what I thought might be references to your now-no-longer-latent homosexuality. That would have pleased me; at least it would have been an indication of one human trait in you. I discovered in the table of contents of your diary, as edited by Jacobmeyer and Präg, the beautiful and mysterious sentence under the date May 21: "Frank orders the dispatch of a memorandum to Obergruppenführer Höfle in re: the clash with Höfle on account of alleged [*here it comes, Father*] improper treatment of an NSKK* man for Frank's own personal purposes."

That sounds downright mouth-watering, Father. Is this the way the memo to Höfle might have read? "Dear Party Comrade Höfle, The NSKK man bent to my will on my castle ramparts. I needed this, he needed that; it was a matter of firming up German national traditions in my own particular way. It was an intoxicatingly phallic night; on bended knee, I can warmly recommend this man to your attention. Variety is the spice of sex, or as Horace said long ago, '*Ovum est enim.*' In any case, I announce herewith my visit in the near future to your NSKK company; perhaps the two of us will find some fun-loving lads, dear Höfle. Heil Hitler! Your satiated Frank." It's now obvious why the whole NSKK company was withdrawn from the GG on the very same day, as was reported in your official diary. But now you were on this new amorous tangent, come what may; and with moistened lips you visited a French prisoner-of-war camp where the inmates had already been confined for a pretty long time. (I don't understand why the

---

* The NSKK was an elite Nazi corps of drivers/chauffeurs.

Germans get so hot and bothered about the length of *their* imprisonment in Russia.) Well, no matter—those boys were probably much too emaciated for you. You preferred instead to spend May 25 in celebration of the Ostbahn, the Eastern Railway System, "one of the life-giving arteries of the German victory," as you called it. You forgot to mention that it was also one of the death-dealing arteries. Did you arrange for announcements like this to come over the loudspeaker: "Everyone out, please. Travelers to Auschwitz and Treblinka are now requested to disrobe. In the name of the Ostbahn President we wish our passengers a pleasant final journey. Please close the cattle-car windows; the train will depart immediately"?

On May 26 at Radom, you again addressed some very clear words to all of Poland: "I also say that for every German who is murdered here the Polish race must atone." On June 10 you had the Jews in your sights again, referring to them as "the greatest peril." At about the same time, your vanity was flattered when counterfeit GG postage stamps showing your face instead of Hitler's somehow were put into circulation. Hey, you finally made it. Even if they were faked by the English, who cares?—the face on the stamp was yours. On June 18 you had the pleasure of hearing that one million fewer people now lived in Warsaw. All of you knew, of course, that it was a result of the extermination of Jews, but no one said so. Instead of that, your Governor Fischer gave voice to this charming suggestion: "The population could be reduced even further if the ghetto were finally to be totally demolished." You must have felt another tiny twinge of discomfort when you heard him then refer to "the catastrophic decline in deliveries of milk and eggs." That made you irate, for whoever dared to clamp down on your eggs was someone you had to track down and get rid of. A bit later the record reveals that you said something positive about the Soviets for the first time: "It is outrageous that the Government in Berlin can send only a handful of men, give them orders to exterminate fifteen million foreigners here, and then expect them to remain in this territory without additional security. When the Bolsheviks plan to annihilate people, they send at least two thousand Red Army troops into every little village where the people are to be exterminated. But to send us only ten thousand police troops for the whole GG, and then order us to finish off fifteen million people . . . that just can't be done."

It's sentences like that one which brought about your death. And I go on living with them.

You don't even appreciate the bitter irony in the fact that on the very same day, you learned that Hitler had appointed you President of the International Center for Legal Studies. After these triumphs you went to the Warsaw Opera and spent a pleasant evening listening to Wolf-Ferrari's *Il segreto di Susanna*. On the following day you showed your best side as a master of realpolitik when you entered a strong plea on behalf of the continued starvation of the people in Warsaw. You said: "Hungry people inevitably consume a large part of their total energy simply in order to satisfy their hunger." June 23 is the day of your victory over Krüger. In Himmler's field-command headquarters you had a meeting where there was no longer any talk about such things as missing furs, millions of diverted eggs, or the corrupt Franks and their relatives. No, things had changed. Even Himmler himself had begun to be scared shitless whenever he took a look at the front lines. Killing Jews, well, that was fine and dandy; that was humane work. But as to our continuing to slaughter our beloved Poles, maybe we should wait and take care of that after the war. It would seem that your sanctimonious policy of enticing the Poles over to your side seemed to be having some success after all. Krüger was called on the carpet, and how you must have enjoyed that. This time, you were sitting at the table with Himmler, and Krüger was standing and "being advised in the sharpest possible manner to cooperate loyally from now on with all service organizations of the GG." Hold on—I left something out. Comradeship was always held in high esteem by you comrades-in-murder, so the phrase quoted above naturally should read, "to cooperate loyally and in a comradely way."

> I once had a splendid comrade,
> A better one's not to be found.
> Standing with rifle at my side,
> He shot down all Jews far and wide,
> As if they were no more than beasts, etc.

Well, does it sound familiar? However, when you started crowning your victory with a little too much laurel, it was Himmler's turn to demonstrate to you what German prose, as opposed to lyrics, can accomplish: "Dear Fellow Party Member Frank, You pride yourself in having attained one of your greatest political successes during our recent meeting. I should like to disabuse you of this impression and point out to you that I am as resolute as ever in my determination to take all measures that seem proper to me. And that includes those in the Government General."

That must have left you sweating blood up there in your castle, and with a fresh realization of what a flop you had been (despite your alleged victory), and of where the real power lay. Well, get moving, then. Either throw the shit right back in their faces, or write a friendly little letter in reply as a diversionary tactic before you head for the Italian border. Or here's an even better idea: join the Resistance Underground. What the hell, you say? Too far-fetched, you say? Forget it. So, instead of even entertaining such a possibility, you returned to the daily round. Chief Customs Officer Tachmina found himself having to pretend to be overjoyed on June 7, the occasion of his fiftieth anniversary of service, when he personally received from your own personal hands your own personal picture with your own personal signature. That was a most appropriate gift, for neither he nor his customs officials had ever bothered to inspect our salon car or all those automobiles with this and that crammed into them or all those "personal objets d'art." And while we're on the topic of art, by the way, it seems that you and the others had been helping yourselves again, whereupon chaos broke out in the art market and heated verbal exchanges concerning missing art objects were heard. Mühlmann (your and Göring's art—i.e., art theft—agent) resigned in a flurry. And that prompted you, quick as a wink, to disband the "Office for the Cultivation of Old Art"—another glorious euphemism. Aha, so that's the reason Mühlmann didn't clam up when he was testifying at Nuremberg but instead described in detail the excessive and elaborate demands you put on him to furnish your castle and palace rooms. In a speech you gave on June 23 you revealed for the first time the true motivation behind World War II when you offered your opinion that the war was being conducted by Hitler "in order to get culture back on its feet," culture which rested on the two cornerstones of "freedom and faith." (Dear Father of mine, you evoke such grandiose ambitions.) On August 2 you heard about the fall of Mussolini and said the following: "The ultimate lines of combat have been clearly drawn: on the one hand, the Swastika, and on the other, the Jews." Since it had dawned on you by this time that somewhere out there other nations were pressing mightily against Germany, you once more made it completely clear that "we here in the GG are a completely unique structural entity, one I have built up to be totally distinctive, and to which the Führer stood as godfather during its genesis and which he sustained through its critical times. The GG has taken shape as a unified and integrated state and has developed completely independently and self-sufficiently as a *Nebenland*—a semiautonomous neighboring country—of the Greater German Reich."

Field Mowing—
Heads Rolling

Y ou thought that this idea of splitting off from the Reich was a pretty bold stroke on your part. Your next idea had to do with places outside your borders. The eastern front had gotten a few versts closer in the meantime, and the mass murders in the camps and elsewhere that had never upset you before appeared to you now as the one little blot on your political escutcheon. You had to see about expunging it in order to make yourself acceptable in the eyes of the world as a head of state for the postwar period. Thus spake the GG, in a public address: "If I am supposed to accomplish something in this territory with a mere three thousand men available to deal with sixteen million non-Germans, then I must rely on the indigenous people and their strengths. Consequently, I can hardly wish for the extermination of this people. It is insane to mow down this land with scythes. I say, if there is mowing to be done, then let it not be heads but fields. . . ." But suddenly you must have discovered a few friends of Himmler sitting in your audience, so you immediately inserted: "What happens with these people after our victory is of no importance now; it is what happens now that is important." And then as an encore, you add a final quick little word about the Jews: "The National Socialist Party will unquestionably outlive the Jews. When we began here, there were three and a half million of them; now, all that is left is little more than a few groups of Jewish laborers. All the others have, shall we say, emigrated." Funny, funny, Father.

Farther and faster you speed toward the final stages of your life. It is incomprehensible to me. Did you never pause, never stop, never weep from the sheer horror of being you, and of what you did?

Professor Kubijowic, a representative of the Ukrainian National Committee, now began to make demands about this and that, but he was temporarily permitted to survive. He even received a photograph from you, personally signed. (What a nice gesture it would have been for you also to present Hangman Woods with your photo, personally signed.) As he took his leave, the Ukrainian gentleman doubtless kissed your photogenic image once or twice. You ordered him to report to his compatriots about the "enormous sacrifices of the German people." Scarcely had he scuttled away with your picture when you already had inscribed and signed another portrait and presented it to your chief press officer, Olbricht. A scene of such poignant intensity, the way you were distributing pictures of yourself in a foolish frenzy. Could it be that for one second you began to realize that only the gallows could do justice to your depravity, and therefore you said to yourself that at least your likeness should be preserved (in the form of photographs of that solemn mug of yours), that your words and deeds should best be forgotten? For example, your words in reaction to the mounting number of attacks by the Polish Home Army. (Their determination still makes me happy today; I rejoice when I remember how those Poles would simply and finally not put up with you Germans any longer.) Your official diary refers to the problem this way: "The Herr Governor General, of course, voices his dismay that in certain instances individuals are being arbitrarily shot; on the other hand, he is of the firm opinion that henceforth, in view of the mounting insolence of the Poles, stern examples must be set." And what did SS Oberführer Bierkamp say to that? Was he somehow scared off by your "of course"? No, he simply saw it as a bit of lip service on your part and added his own view of the matter: "As to industrial workers who order their co-workers to sabotage factories—such people must also be gotten rid of, immediately, on the spot." Father, take careful note of his use of the little word "also."

By October 10 you had grown weary of the whole thing. You put your signature to the "decree concerning the method of combating attacks against the German economic buildup in the Government General." That had a lovely ring to it, but the only thing it really meant was that from now on the court-martial procedure of the security police would involve not only sentencing but also the carrying out of the sentence. Quite a picture that summons up for the accused: the German judge with his rifle at the ready, giving the verdict and then tolling the death knell. And you actually dared to portray yourself at Nuremberg as a friend of Poland? On October 19 the racially pure SS Oberführer Bierkamp reported that his agents would be lying in wait at the factories. If they caught an agitator or a saboteur, "he would be sentenced immediately and the judgment would be carried out by means of a rope." (Would the scenario go like this? "All right, boys, clear off the work benches here so we can reach those hooks up there. . . . Just a little bit more . . . so, now it's okay. . . . Comrade, toss the rope over that beam . . . that's right. . . . And bring that chair over here, and when I shout 'In the name of the German people, on your mark, get set . . .' then you kick the chair out from under this swine of a Polish agitator." Naturally, there would be a break during this typically German judicial proceeding so the Polish factory workers would be forced to witness the execution.) This remarkable man Bierkamp was followed at the meeting by an equally amusing speaker, General Sommé. This unquestionably God-fearing man proposes, "as measures to be taken against further attacks," that "we could forbid all civilians from putting their hands in their trouser pockets when they're in public." He actually said that. That's the German Wehrmacht for you, 1939–45. Sommé must have been so scared out of his wits when he was in the GG that his Adam's apple began bobbing up and down as uncontrollably as your eyes used to whirl in their sockets. All of you knew, way back in your tiny brains somewhere, what a criminal war you were conducting. Here we have the *ultima ratio* of your strategy for the invigoration of European culture: civilians must keep their hands out of their pockets. Concealed weapons, you know.

("Reporting back, General Sommé. Just saw four more Poles with hands in pockets. Executed them on the spot. However, General, I must draw your attention to the fact that a serious influenza epidemic is causing a lot of sniffles at present. Seems the victims were only clutching their handkerchiefs at the moment of death."

"Makes no difference, Lieutenant—better to eliminate four cases of the sniffles than to overlook one with a hand grenade. Continue your executions!"

"*Jawohl*, Herr General!")

What was it you did on the evening following this conference among such highly talented individuals? Naturally, you went to see *Fidelio* again, the opera with that wild bunch of singing prisoners. Maybe it was your favorite opera because there's a governor in it and he brings freedom to the heroic tenor. You loved playing the role of that Bavarian King Ludwig II and having operas performed only for you and a few of your elect. Your patronage extended even to Nursemaid Hilde. (This time it was Mother's turn to be as sour as an old lemon.)

Then there came a really bad day for you. It was around the time when Poles were being shot down like game, probably the same period of time that the Italian author Malaparte describes in his book *Kaputt*, where he writes about your trip to the Warsaw ghetto and describes how you would shoot at Jewish children. Just prior to that episode, Malaparte has Mother kissing your hands at the Belvedere, "those soft, white, tender hands." After the war Mother would rotate like a turbine on her sofa whenever she came to that passage in the book. How she would foam at the mouth and scream that it was all one big lie and that you never even knew how to shoot a gun and that you had completely normal hands. Mother would turn to me and announce: "We *never* shot at Poles, or at Jews." Inevitably she would follow that up with the story about the Poles who begged you with tears in their eyes for permission to go along with you when you were leaving the castle and going home to the Reich. And after I had swallowed all of that crap, nodding my head in agreement, I would get as a kind of beddy-bye snack the statement from her that neither she nor her husband had been enemies of the Jews: "Why, we even had Jewish workmen at the castle . . . at least until that wicked Krüger stole them from behind Daddy's back."

Then I would wonder vaguely once again how all that information could possibly fit together. On the one hand, you were always praised in our family with the standard cliché, "Father was the most powerful one of all in the GG." But on the other hand, how could this man Krüger simply have come and taken away your own private Jews and have them dragged off to be gassed in a concentration camp? It made no sense.

Yes, I know, Father, I didn't yet know much about how difficult it was to be a politician in your sense of that term, about how all of you just had to keep your mouths shut, even though you knew all about the murdering. You kept your mouths shut for the sake of a greater goal—even when that greater goal didn't amount to anything more than a handsomely paneled salon car.

Well, back to the point. On that really bad day I started to recall for you, a letter was brought to you from Count Ronikier, the presiding officer on the committee of Polish representatives to the GG, the one who made his participation in your Harvest Festival dependent on certain guarantees—for example, that his compatriots would no longer be shot to death in such an arbitrary fashion. What a meddling son of a bitch, you said to yourself. Your face was flushed with your murderer's blood. What the hell. The Count has got some nerve, for the love of Christ almighty!

What goddamn presumption, the filthy Polack! And to think that you, the Governor General, were such a friend of Poland. Something like that was just going too far. Your Chief Administrative Adviser, Weyrauch, was probably proud of you. Now that was the way a genuine German should talk. We'll never let ourselves be blackmailed by those Poles. In a shrill, stentorian voice you ordered Weyrauch to "inform Count Ronikier that he has until eighteen hundred hours today to decide whether or not he is going to take part in my Harvest Festival with the other members of the committee! If he refuses, I shall not hesitate a second before dissolving his committee!" That's tellin' 'im, Father—although if you could have managed to be realistic for once, you would have had to admit that there were only a few people like the Count to take it out on, people who were just a little bit premature in waking up out of their collaborationist dreams as the Russian front drew closer. Nevertheless, the Count's letter was courageous. Above all, the Count was stubborn. And so you had to disband the committee. But now the question was, where are you going to get your new minions, others prepared to work with you now that the GG territory was getting smaller by the hour? Yet you did manage to find a few; let's call them the Volkssturm of the collaborators, the very last gasp. (Those same people were wandering in a daze around the Schoberhof in March 1945, the very image of woe.) At least you could still afford to scream at little Weyrauch. Here are your very words: "Under no conditions am I prepared to have German authority challenged, not even in the slightest." Seconds later, that must have seemed just too ridiculous to you; either that or Weyrauch wasn't your typical cringing German coward, after all. He barked back at you that your phony rhetoric was just not good enough, that you'd have to say something a little more substantial. "What do you mean, 'something more substantial'?" you muttered. You repeated what you had said before and then, without any transition at all, screamed at him: "And tell that Count Ronikier that if he's so outraged about the shooting of Poles, who after all have been unmasked as members of the Communist resistance, then I, as the Governor General, am a great deal more outraged at the shooting of almost one thousand Germans. And tell the Count to be so good as to keep his hands out of his pants pockets—tell him that!" (But Weyrauch was really no fool and talked you into removing that last sentence, so that it doesn't actually appear in your diary.)

Harvest Festival time. Polish peasants, thoroughly frisked. The poor folks, can you imagine what they had to endure after the war merely because they had honored you with their Harvest Crown? Either you had been eating chalk by the handful the night before, to make your voice sweet and refined like the Big Bad Wolf in the Grimms' fairy tale, or you had been listening to the calamitous morning news about the situation at the front—in any case, you were full of praise for those little peasants (did you actually put that crown on your head, or was it just sitting on the table in front of you?); you praised to the sky the "industrious and clean work" of those Polish peasants. Isn't it odd that you and your kind were always going on about "cleanliness"? Perhaps in the last analysis it had something to do with the unending filth that all of you had on your hands. You kept on praising them and their culture. After all, wasn't that the very reason we were at war? You praised "the calm, steady, culturally pure development of the population in the GG." What a wonderful achievement, Father. The number of living Poles was indeed growing smaller and smaller, but for all of that, more and more cultivated. The final product would perhaps have been a single individual Pole who could recite all of Klopstock's endless *Messias* without a single hesitation and eventually whole passages from the novel you were planning to commission on the slaughter at Katyn—or, even better (which would surely have been your preference), three hundred days' worth of entries from your official diary.

On October 26, 1943, it was time again for another celebration. This time it was four years of the GG. Among its many great accomplishments for the Reich you emphasized the four hundred thousand liters of brandy per month that you regularly sent to the Wehrmacht, that is, to the front lines. This could explain quite a lot. Perhaps all this time we should have been ascribing many a German hero's death to total inebriation and alcohol poisoning. For example, "He died a drunkard's death for Volk and Vaterland"—that would be a more honest version of the telegrams sent to the bereaved parents. Announcements made by the Oberkommando of the Wehrmacht about "staggered front lines" or "battles swaying to and fro" would have taken on a completely new meaning. If I had suggested such a thing to Mother after the war, she would have darted like a weasel from her sofa and gone into a fit of feverish speculation about your having actually been a Soviet spy who caused the collapse of the eastern front with his fifth-column trafficking in brandy. "Bring me my typewriter right now," she would have said. "I'm going to write a letter to the Kremlin to find out if I can get a widow's pension from them for the equivalent of a Reichsminister's wife." And she would have typed a letter beginning: "Most Honorable Herr Joseph Stalin, May I presume on your precious time for just one moment? . . ."

October 27. You were delivered from evil. Himmler called off Krüger—naturally, under the disingenuous pretext of needing him as a general for his new SS divisions. The truth of the matter is that Himmler was now practically shitting bricks. Is it true that you bums really wanted to give the Poles one more chance for survival? Sure you did. The fortunes of war . . . well, they weren't on your side now. Which is why you became even more transcendental in your personal philosophy. You wanted to ensure a more secure arrangement for yourself in the hereafter. And so you issued a dinner invitation to all the German Catholic priests and Evangelical pastors in the GG. Only one showed up: Father Burger, and what a gift of God he was for the Catholic Church. A representative of his class, so typical, so German, so infinitely far removed from that stubborn, brave, and blessed Father Rupert Mayer.

The two of you had a conversation that, if it had been written down and performed on stage, would have driven the Vatican Bishops' Conference in its rage to the point of exorcism. Father Burger was stationed in the arch-Catholic city of Cracow; every day he encountered Karol Woytyla (later Pope John Paul II) on his busy rounds. He knew how pious the Poles were; every day he saw St. Mary's Church overflowing with parishioners. And after some phony introductory pieties about having nothing against the pastoral care of Germans in the country, you asked this man of God about his connections with the Polish clerics. "Your Eminence [*which was probably the way he began his answer to you; what is certain, however, is the rest of his indignant reply*], I entertain no connection whatsoever with Polish clerics." "That's fine, that's fine," you doubtless answered, and then urged him to take a more comfortable seat, perhaps to enjoy a sip of brandy with you, which the pastor accepted with gratitude. And then this true messenger of God proceeded to denounce his Polish fellow priests: "Based on my experience, I have the feeling that the Polish clergy exercises a considerable influence on the activities of the Underground Resistance." If the Lord God had already known then that the cardinals were going to be electing Woytyla from Cracow as the Pope, a powerful bolt of lightning would have zapped down from the battlements at that very second and toasted and charred Father Burger to a crisp. He would have been nothing more than a little pile of burnt crumbs at your feet, and you would have called in Adjutant Pfaffenroth and said, "Have Father Burger swept up at once."

But as always, the Lord God laughed up his sleeve as he observed this little scene between you and Burger and was, as always, delighted to see what a glorious success he had made of his murderous little race of Germans. For Father Burger (surely by now already on his way to be canonized, since the Church will never abandon its obedient clergy) really got going—but unfortunately not the way he would like to get going. What actually seemed to be bugging him was that he couldn't manage to get hold of an official car for his pastoral duties, "even though, Your Eminence, I have all the appropriate papers."

"You haven't? So what?" you asked yourself. "Has he already been studying the new Baedeker on the GG? Does he only plan on being a tourist in my empire? That seems to be a fairly secular preoccupation for a priest."

But that's not at all what's on his mind. In reaction to your raised eyebrows—or was it your flared nostrils, your earlobes, the curled pinkie of your right hand? whatever—in reaction to some kind of lofty, patriarchal gesture of yours, Father Burger enlightens you: "It is an insufferable situation that whenever a German is murdered in this country, a Polish priest has to celebrate the funeral mass."

Did that knock you for a loop? Father Burger meant it in all seriousness.

History is silent on whether he got his car or not. Still, what images arise: his automobile stops, Burger jumps out in his priestly regalia, rushes up, whirling the holy-water sprinkler in the air and threatening his Polish colleague with it, that inferior priest who is just about to give a dead German his final rites.

Apart from what is revealed in the official minutes of this momentous meeting, perhaps you also enjoyed a pious conversation about whether a new kind of coffin might be developed for the unfortunate murdered members of the master race, one that would permit the dead man to hold the rosary in one hand at his breast, the other, the right hand, raised in the "Heil Hitler" greeting, and at the foot, naturally with your own personally inscribed dedication, a photograph of you. Then you suddenly switch to a topic closer to home, prompted by thoughts of your sexual prowess, and tell the stenographer to be sure not to omit that part of your conversation in which you requested Father Burger "to do everything possible in [his] sermons to instruct German women in matters dealing with their moral behavior," because "the enormous increase in the birth rate of illegitimate children is causing [you] great concern."

It must have really griped you that as lord of your own domain you still had not been able to introduce the *jus primae noctis*. Was it because you knew there would be resistance from that prudish Hitler—and perhaps also from married German women? You would have had so much to offer those new brides in that castle of yours, bulging with "personal objets d'art." Before the priest left, you had one more inspiration, which occurred to you when Father Burger came to his final lament about being the only true German Catholic priest in Cracow and you remembered how shoddy he looked in his personal appearance when he arrived. He must have licked his little red lips when you, his great patron, informed him that you would place at his disposal choir robes and church vestments "so that the services in German churches in the GG could be held in more fitting fashion." And where did you get hold of all those garments, Father? "From supplies stored in the castle," of course. What? Why? Where? Do you mean to tell me that your servant Nickl also had to keep a selection of church vestments in constant readiness for you? Were they hanging in your closet next to your Nazi service uniforms? Did you say to Nickl, "For my morning coffee I would like to wear the great Te Deum robes with those glorious tassels, and get the Sancta Mater ready, too. Please serve my coffee in that communion chalice, the one with those unique Renaissance decorations. My egg is to be brought to me on the Veit Stoss paten . . . yes, yes, the gold one . . . you know, the one my wife picked all the pearls out of. Oh, and one more thing, please have the great Cracow crosier placed at the table opposite me"? Is it even possible that you received Father Burger in one of your priestly robes?

Finally,
an Assassination
Attempt!

The appeasement policy toward the Poles that was supposed to guarantee the survival of you crooks prompted you at the beginning of 1944 to set up something you had the audacity to call "off-limits areas and regions set aside for labor recruitment." What phrases. They remind me once again of those magnificent laws you promulgated for the protection of marmots, by which I mean to say that those Poles who were still left alive—mercy upon mercy—finally achieved the distinction of being regarded at least as animals. On January 14, 1944, you uttered your famous "mincemeat" sentence. I have been sitting year after year muttering that sentence to myself and trying with all the power at my command to lower myself to the level of your mind and soul, trying to imagine myself in your shoes and being capable of uttering that despicable statement in front of human beings: "Once we have won the war, then for all I care you can make mincemeat out of the Poles and the Ukrainians and anything else hanging around here."

Needless to say, you're begging me not to quote you out of context. That's what all of you bastards say if anything as terrifying as those words has ever once crossed your lips or flowed from your pens. You still say it today, here in Germany. What you said later in your speech, in fact, makes the whole thing actually more disgusting: "But at this moment in history the only important thing for us is to succeed in keeping the almost fifteen million people who are organizing themselves against us under control, quiet, occupied, and disciplined. If we are not successful, then at least I will be able to say triumphantly that I have killed two million Polacks. But meanwhile the important question for us is whether the trains will still be able to get to the eastern front, whether the state monopolies that produce five hundred thousand liters of vodka and millions of cigarettes will still be able to function [*I was right; why are you mentioning all that schnapps again? It was a totally drunken soldateska, wasn't it, that was supposed to defend your GG against the Soviets? By the way, congratulations on the hundred-thousand-liter increase—was that the "miracle weapon," the Wunderwaffe, that Hitler had been promising?*], whether agriculture and the other means of food production, our source for the forty-five thousand tons of grain we have already delivered to the Reich, will be able to be secured. All that is quite a different matter."

Evidently fear had reached your nostrils, was crawling up to your eyelids, had taken hold of your hands, made you wake up every morning in a terrifying depression. It was angst deep in your breast, as if a doctor had just told you, "Inoperable cancer, Herr Governor General." More and more frequently you would catch yourself reminiscing about the time when you were not yet a criminal; you probably yearned to be back in your student days. How you must have trembled when you were alone—in the bathroom, before the mirror that still reflected your unlined face, still sleek and porky as a well-fed pig. Murder puts on weight. And then your voice . . . you had to clear your throat more than ever before you spoke. Often you would stand rigid and silent at the high windows of your castle and stare out. You dusted off your Catholicism and brushed it up so that you could find out to what extent prayer might anesthetize your fear. Yes, Father, even your hectic coupling with Lilly or Gertrude didn't help you. The Polacks were getting more insolent. The Russians were coming closer, and the GIs and Tommies too, behind you in the West.

And then came January 29, 1944. That evening you were in your private railroad car headed for Lvov. "At 23:17 hours, kilometer 22.3, there was a muffled explosion caused by the detonation of an electrically ignited device. A section of track approximately one meter long was destroyed. The explosion took place directly behind the rear axle of Salon Car 1006, which was violently shaken by the sudden air pressure. Salon Car 1001 was immediately derailed but continued to jolt and bump over the railroad ties and roadbed, as did its auxiliary car immediately behind it. The chief steward of Salon Car 1006 pulled the emergency signal immediately after the detonation, but the locomotive engineer had simultaneously felt it and of his own accord applied the brakes at once and brought the train to a halt."

Those moments must have been almost as bad for you as the ones two and a half years later in Sergeant Woods's noose. My favorite scenario has you in Car 1001; I prefer you there so that your filthy soul can be shaken loose and launched a few meters out of your body. Just at the moment of the explosion you were walking from mahogany table to mahogany sofa; there was a bang; the car was lifted off the tracks; the unexpected sound of axles scraping along the gravel of the roadbed reached your fat ears. You fell to your knees, put your arms out to brace yourself, cowered there like a whipped cur, and were shaken from stem to stern. You wanted to scream, but your position as the Governor General somehow prevented you. Yet there was still this horrifying fear— and then you were suddenly flung forward when the brakes were applied. Your shoulder and one fat cheek scraped over the mahogany floor; you let out a loud groan; your whole body was thrust forward, and you began to slide head first into your mahogany wall. Your head snapped backward, while your body, thanks to the weight of two hundred thousand black-market eggs you had stuffed yourself with, continued going forward; your head was bent even farther back, presenting a taut neck. . . . (It was only after the war and after your execution, whenever I used to hike from Schliersee to Neuhaus, hopping from one railroad tie to the next, that I would inevitably have this image of your body bouncing along the tracks in your salon car.) You lay on the floor and listened to the shots being fired by the Poles who had opened fire from the edge of the woods after bringing the train to a halt. You were glued to your mahogany floor; your brain itself turned into a smooth chunk of mahogany, and just as dead; maybe you mumbled a prayer at that moment to your Beautiful Madonna, or one to the Black Madonna of Czestochowa; maybe a thought of that nimble Father Burger flashed through what was left of your mind, knowing that your assassination would naturally be a great treat for him, that he would rush to the scene in his new official Catholic GG car, his elegant funeral vestments folded neatly in the backseat, his smoldering and ever-ready censer on the front seat next to him—he would careen through the night in the direction of Lvov just in order to be the first to place his finger on the dead brow of his master. That would have done a great deal for his career in the postwar Church. I can hear him now: "You are being blessed by the priest who laid the Governor General to rest."

On the other hand, however, you may well have been proud as a peacock that at least one starving and decimated Polish re-sistance group deemed you worthy enough of going to the trouble of putting a bomb under your ass and blowing it sky high. For the Frank clan the attack was also something of a blessing. For decades afterwards we were unable to conceal a certain pride in the knowledge that even before the attack on the Führer's life you were honored by an assassination attempt. With this awareness swelling my little breast, I was able to go to school a quite different lad from all the rest.

Car number 1001 comes to a halt. You stand there erect, like a real man again; you clear your throat (to see if you still have a voice left) before opening the door, and then reveal the full stature of your statesmanlike self-control and ask: "Is anyone hurt? Heil Hitler." (I add that little touch to my scenario because all your life long you managed to say the wrong thing.) Then you all drove back to Cracow, where you arranged for safer transport by plane to Lvov. How I would like to have met those four or five Poles who tried to blow you off the face of the earth; their fate would interest me. Although I doubt I ever will, I'm still grateful to them for not having got you and that your crooked life came to a more appropriate end in the noose, in accordance with the law and following a just sentence. Damn it, how exactly did that rope feel? I must know. Did it feel rough, or did the soft black hood under it make it feel gentle to the skin?

You recovered quickly from the shock, and by February 1 you were already back at work, recording the transfer of all art treasures from the Office for the Cultivation of Old Art (that title would be much better if we could add the word "Pillaged" before "Old") to the castle administration, where they would be closer to you nouveaux riches. You also had the opportunity to deal Mother another swift blow by ordering that she could get her hands on provisions, automobiles, etc., only on your specific written authorization. Was it Mother's poisonous reaction to that alone or was it the general enmity of a world at war that prompted you to declare one day later that "because of threats to the Government General, a condition of military alert is henceforth in effect."

On February 6 you are once more granted a meeting with Hitler. You mention in his presence that "the removal of the Jews from the GG is an enormous relief to the total situation within the country." In fact, the Führer got only good news from you. Gradually he, too, was beginning to have the shit scared out of him by the "total situation," and he praised you and your administration for everything you had been able to "extract" from the land. That was (and it still remains) a good example of the euphemistic language of true crooks. As an aficionado of belles lettres, you must have appreciated that felicitous phrase. Nor did Hitler make you or your marriage battles responsible for the threatened loss of the war; rather, he "spoke about the difficult weather conditions that had been characteristic throughout the length of this war. Had the weather in 1941 not been so bad, Moscow would long since be in our hands." That observation led to your obsequious retort: "*Jawohl*, mein Führer, this filthy weather—but the Lord God is on our side," or something like that.

In a fit of vanity you dictated to your stenographer the following account for the official diary: "Our conversation lasted altogether approximately two and a half hours and ended in an atmosphere of friendly harmony. The Führer's assessment was doubtless also the same, and it was clearly his intention to establish a complete settling of differences between himself and one of his oldest battle comrades, and to officially record it in the presence of the Chief of the Party Chancellery."

This Chief of the Party Chancellery, whose name you don't even want to mention, is good old Bormann, the same one who way back in Weimar days was guilty of actually killing someone— the same one who for years now had been beating you at every game with one hand tied behind his back.

After you left the boys, you next visited Hitler's doctor, Professor Morell, who began questioning you in a conspiratorial way about what you were planning to do with those animal glands that were piling up in the GG's slaughterhouses. You patted him on the back, so to speak, and promised him, like the great patron you were, that he could have all the private parts he needed. Then your report ends: "Thereupon I returned to my private railroad car and with it left the Führer's headquarters in the direction of Berlin." What a grand and seignorial conclusion. But of course it wasn't the real conclusion—not quite yet.

Presumably because the Russians were approaching fast, you began (no big surprise) to promote the playing of chess in the GG. Your objective seemed to be to arrange things so that when the victorious Soviet general climbed out of his tank at the Cracow castle you would be standing on the entrance stairway, receive him, and say: "I open d4," in the hope that he would then report this inspired chess move to Moscow and Stalin would immediately decide to recognize you fully as King of the Reichsnebenland.

At about this time you exercised your right to grant reprieves. It had to do with the case of a Pole who had shot four Germans while he was under the influence of alcohol after suffering a nervous shock. You're furrowing your brow down there in your cauldron? I'm frowning myself up here. It seems I read that entry incorrectly. Obviously it was the other way around: you reprieved a German who, after *his* nervous shock and under the influence of alcohol, had knocked off four Poles. Since you were already in such a merciful mood, you then proceeded to call off the trial of another German, someone who had shot down a group of Jews because of their alleged "insubordination"—which is to say in plain language that he had been doing a little target practice to prepare himself for the final battle.

It began to annoy you, despite your patronage of Father Burger, that your German subjects were growing more and more pious as the front drew closer and closer: "It is a very disagreeable sight for me that we seem to be filling our Catholic Churches in the GG with more Germans than I would ever have expected."

Oh, my—if Father O'Connor had ever heard you say that! He would have made you atone for that at the foot of the gallows by rattling off forty Our Fathers, which would have given Julius Streicher, publisher of that wretched anti-Semitic rag *Der Stürmer*, whose date with Woods came right after yours, a little more time to catch his breath in preparation for the end.

Then you got the okay from Himmler to take control of Jewish property. That pleased you, the opportunity to pocket everything for the German cause, as long as you were still in command. The two of you held a discussion about "whether the personal property of the Jews could immediately be put at the disposal of the Government General." But your cultivated heart grew heavy from all these contemptible arguments about money and Mammon, and it thirsted for refreshment. That it got from your visits to your State Theater. You went to a performance of *Faust I*. It is mind-boggling, the way you managed to fit all that in—the way all of you could stomach what you did: hold debates at noon about murdered Poles and Jews, haggle in the afternoon over the property of the Jews you had gassed, and then in the evening absorb culture. (See *Faust I*: "My tears pour forth, / The earth possesses me once more.") Schedules like that generate fresh courage, in spite of the depressing situation at the front. Your GG shrank to the point where you could take it in at a single glance; soon you were able to make out the borders of your Reich from the battlements atop your Wawel Castle. For that reason your Cracow Governor, von Burgsdorff, now requested you "very cautiously to elicit to a greater degree the cooperation of the Poles in the interests of a certain mutual self-preservation." What a bold idea, with your backs to the wall. You added another clever twist to it: you decided that you wanted to establish an anti-Bolshevist Polish League, but without an anti-Jewish section. Right, Father—how could you, with so few Jews left?

Now how else could you win over the Polacks for the German cause? Aha! With a theater! A Polish theater under Polish direction had to be established. Would that be a good way to cajole these tricky people to the point where they would validate you as head of state, even in a free election? But wouldn't you know that goddamn Count Ronikier had some tricks up his sleeve, too. The theater director you came up with was obliged to inform you that it would be "undesirable and inappropriate" for you to write a foreword to the program for the first production. How I laughed when I read that, Father. What a brave man that must have been. And I'd love to have seen the expression on your face. He just plowed right ahead and dumped on your fat face, on you who thought you had the automatic authority to write anything any-

where for any reason—he just dumped a load on that miserable
hollow rhetoric of yours. I'll bet that news got things stirred up
again at the castle. Your face must have been purple, your movements spastic. You kept on shrieking imprecations, while behind
it all was fear. I can feel that fear in you now; I have long since
been able to reproduce it in myself, anytime. I have known you
so long and so well. I crawl into you, I feel with you, and I know
that it is precisely these little signs in you that make the collapse
of German power so vivid and pungent.

Up to that time there was nothing printed in the GG on which
your face wasn't reproduced, spewing its fetid garbage. And now
comes this Polack bastard. "I consider it totally unacceptable"—
thus begins the unusually restrained manifestation of your burst
of anger in the diary—"for the representatives of the German
Reich to be dictated to by a Pole in regard to what they may or
may not do."

Did you then start singing your defiant "Song of the Vistula"?
And did Bühler join in? And Pfaffenroth? Did they begin to har-
monize with you?

You ordered that the contract be canceled forthwith and that
the theater "revert to its status as a *Volkstheater* to be administered
by the authorities of the city of Cracow."

The Conclusion:
A Film Starring
Hans Moser

How well I know you now. How warm and secure I lodge in your brain. After your contretemps with this smart-ass Pole, didn't you feel the Angel of Death hovering through the room once again; didn't you feel his wing feathers brush your cheek? Those moments when the bowels seem to collapse—the fear of death. And then having to pull yourself together again; how wretchedly, how angrily you lashed out.

On March 4, 1944: "The Jews are a race that must be exnihilated! [*A new word you invented?*] Whenever we get our hands on even a single one of them, that'll be the end of him."

A few days later you were worrying about whether the "security measures at the castle to be taken in case of an air attack" were adequate. Did you stand on your ramparts like Macbeth and did you see Birnam Wood come sneaking up on you? Then, lo and behold, the day came when you established, once and for all, guaranteed legal rights for the Poles. Well, only in one particular regard. Or to be even more accurate, you canceled certain regulations that years before you had rejected as being a waste of paper. In any case, the execution by firing squad of ten Poles was announced publicly by means of *printed posters*. On that same day the ingenious General Sommé informed you of his transfer to the Italian front. Presumably he had to teach manners to the Allies at Monte

Cassino and stop them from running around any longer with their hands in their pants pockets.

Another of your pigheaded reactions to the war situation was the issuing of citizenship papers for ten thousand ethnic Germans, the Volksdeutsche. Actually they were in a bit of a rush and just had time to leave their little handcarts loaded, perform a lap of honor in the castle courtyard, and then rattle on westward with you shouting a "trek heil" after them. And finally—finally!—you deigned to honor Poland's highest representative of Catholicism, the Prince Bishop Saphieha, with a meeting in Cracow. (Needless to say, you were hardly able on this auspicious occasion to let loose with such remarks as you had made three days earlier when you shouted out in your theatrical way: "Whoever says, 'Yes, the Jews are gone now,' to that person I am able to reply, 'Yes, they are gone—but how, by what methods? Do you appreciate who had to perform the sacrifices, who had to surrender himself to the task?' ") You had to make it clear to Saphieha that the Poles perhaps after all did not represent a source of mincemeat themselves: "The Poles are naturally hoping for their freedom like all peoples. But freedom for the Poles in any present-day sense could only be one in which a sort of free and independent kingdom [*interesting, my dear Father: surely in your own thoughts the King would have been you*] would have to be backed up by some sort of strong, protective European power." The Prince Bishop remained cool, but your facial twitches probably increased substantially.

In other respects Saphieha was surely Father Burger's match, oozing sanctimonious words about how outraged his Polish flocks were at the murder of Catholics being committed. "I believe that many of these murders were committed by Jews," he said. (In my scenario, the Jews go up to their guards and say: "I ask your kind permission for two days' leave before I must go to the gas chamber so that I can murder a couple of Poles; they're just too anti-Semitic for me, those shitty Polacks.") This meeting showed you that even though the Church was on the same wavelength with you in the matter of anti-Semitism, it was not fighting on your side—that is, on the German side.

By now your fear had already taken on a frequently insane quality, as is revealed ten days later in your official diary: "The meeting then turned to the question of security, which in the opinion of the Herr Governor General is getting worse and worse. Recently the Resistance movement is even working with bacterial warfare." It must have been from that point on that you really began to stink, no longer just your character, but by this time even your very body. Your bathtub remained unused, and you took to dousing yourself with eau de cologne (probably from the requisitioned supplies, insofar as Mother left any behind in the GG). You justified yourself by referring to the habits of Louis XIV whenever one of your officials, gagging for a breath of fresh air, left a meeting with you. Could that, and not their love of the Fatherland, be the explanation for why day after day more and more officials of the middle and upper echelons began hurriedly departing from the GG? They preferred serving in the army to staying with you. I see you now in a swarm of dung flies, roaming nervously around the ramparts of your castle.

Despite it all, you managed to preserve your love of cultural pursuits. Reacting to the moaning and groaning of your theater people, you suggested that they provide themselves with clothing, stage costumes, and fabrics "from the Jew camps of the SS," which, of course, because of the endless stream of victims being sent to the extermination camps, were being constantly filled up with things for your theater.

Nervously you gazed out over the land, worriedly asking yourself how the Poles who still remained there could finally be convinced of the useful aspects and practical advantages of German rule. Your solution: Polish secondary schools were suddenly opened again, despite your former dictum that the Poles were expected to learn only enough to be able to serve their German masters attentively and otherwise had to toil until their fingers were worn to the bone.

And here is another very, very proud statement, which surely your lawyer, Seidl, would have produced at the Nuremberg trial as evidence of your extraordinary spirit of combat against Himmler's SS and your love of the Polish people, if he had had the time: "The Herr Governor General is of the opinion [*I must add that this was on April 19, 1944*] that within the foreseeable future the police will no longer be devoted to the task of capturing slaves." Yes, yes, Father, in the foreseeable future. When one day later destiny permits you to celebrate Hitler's birthday for the next-to-the-last time, you are emboldened to praise the GG as "homeland of the Poles and the Ukrainians." To be sure, you describe as a "homeland" the place where these people ran a high risk of being shot dead in their tracks in exchange for protection against the man-eating Bolshevists. Father, you know that your hopeless, loudmouth sucking-up to those you slaughtered simply came too late. So did that official reception of yours on May 11 for the "heads of the Autocephalic Orthodox and Autonomous Church of the Ukraine [*whatever that may have been*] and the honorable worthies of the Orthodox Church in the Government General," with whom you were at least in agreement in their anti-Bolshevist stance. You shared your lovely sentiment with them: "Stalin is the embodiment of the denial of God on Earth; Adolf Hitler is the affirmation of God." This conviction did not help you achieve much inner peace.

While you were establishing new bonds with higher powers, other Germans had more serious matters in mind. They wanted to have at least some final opportunity to indulge in a sex orgy or two (that is, before they founded the Christian Democratic Party in the new postwar Germany). The Nazi Judge Brodmann had filed suit against the increasing flouting of the proscription against fraternization with Polish women. You dismissed his complaint and proposed instead a half-assed (or should I say ball-less) idea of publishing a little manual in which the duties and obligations of a party member would be set forth precisely. Like this, perhaps? Question: "How do I protect myself from naked Polish women? Will the singing of the 'Horst Wessel Song' when exposed to a true Polish-Catholic believer with fantastic tits help me get rid of a hard-on?"

On the other hand, the birthrate of the ethnic German population fell considerably. They must have taken a good look at each other and decided that the best thing they could do was to let themselves die out. Or was it because the Volksdeutsche men were constantly after the Polish women because they hadn't yet had the opportunity of tying your little manual around their crotches? You were obliged to recognize with great disapproval that the Germans from the Reich and the German soldiers "were contributing by their behavior to a slippage of German authority." (Yes, Father, the unconditional surrender was already casting its long copulative shadow.)

You were meanwhile reducing your superior productive strength to tatters between the grinding forces of chastity and anti-Semitism. You seized the opportunity to organize an anti-Jewish congress in Cracow, in connection with which you so cleverly dubbed the city "Antisemitropolis." Your wit was still powerful, and your fear was, too; on June 3 you again gave official voice to it: "This morning I was in a mood in which I could see everything sinking away before my eyes." But you recovered and filled yourself with the hope of promoting chastity and productivity through the creation of honorary decorations in the form of a "castle ring" and a "castle pin." For three days you spoke at excruciating length about your realization that "after the annihilation of the Jews in Poland is completed, there can no longer be any talk of a Jewish future from the point of view of blood progeny," for "only here in Poland were there Jews who had any children." Again and again, your exacting gift of observation is most impressive.

Scarcely had the ingenious General Sommé cleared out when

SS Oberführer Bierkamp came up with the clever idea of sending out phony "bands of Soviet soldiers whose mission would be to conduct themselves badly."

You were already so confused from sheer panic that you next demanded at this administrative meeting the immediate withdrawal of the Kalmuck people from the Bilgoray Forest, and just as the others were trying to figure out the meaning of this illogical change in subject, you again jumped ahead and suddenly demanded the closing of all luxury restaurants. That was on July 7, 1944. At that time you had no more than ten months before your two attempts at suicide. But it was the luxury restaurants that were giving you something to worry about then. After all, they were a thorn in the homicidal eye of the bosses in Berlin. The big shots were already forcing you to cancel the performance of all those merry operettas in the GG, in consideration of the all-out war situation.

It's crazy, the things that were going on in your private Reich. The Germans there were revealing themselves in all their grandeur, slaughtering millions, raping thousands, gorging themselves with their families and friends, corrupting one another, and black-marketeering till the cows came home. At the same time there were more and more weary, exhausted, and confused soldiers. The eastern front was getting closer and closer to the western front. Obviously my fingers would itch to write an epic comparing these last months of a toppling regime with the wild and glorious demise of the Nibelungs at the court of the Huns—if it were not that such poetic language would evoke too much admiration for, and too much glorification of, true German warriorship. The truth is, we are talking here of uniquely brutal and cowardly killers.

It was now high time for each one of you to go out and get yourself a token Jew to brag about. It was high time, not to shoot that last decisive Pole, but to jot down for him your own German name and beg him to keep it in reserve as the name of his dear German savior, hold it in readiness in the event of some future emergency—just the way German doctors handed wounded English soldiers their calling cards at the battle for the bridge at Arnheim as a first step in issuing themselves their own certificates of purity, expediting their denazification process in preparation for their postwar medical careers. No, it wasn't German girls who were the first fraternizing shiksa floozies for the GIs, as we called them in Bavaria; our so-called brave soldiers were the first parasites to wriggle their way to safety. And as to those murderers in German judicial robes, they had it especially good: they were in a position to take extra precautions in exonerating themselves after 1945.

However, for your own family you kept a sharp eye out during your final phase: "The messenger will be bringing a few things" to Bavaria, you wrote on July 19, 1944, and at least for the time being we didn't have to make common cause with refugees and other sad sacks as far as food was concerned. On July 22 you announced the imminent arrival of your bread-and-butter man. But what I find particularly terrific about your letter is the news that even in the chaos of battle, culture and the arts maintained their same important spot on your scale of values. On the one hand, you said you planned to send us items of clothing "along with foodstuffs, as long as I still have the opportunity of doing so." On the other hand, it seems that you were indeed fearful of encirclement but didn't wish to let it happen without the proper accompanying music: "Senowski will be staying only another half-year. Then, as a successor to Hindemith—who is seriously ill, quite incapable of working any longer, and has already announced his own departure—I am thinking of Karajan or Mennersch."

Just imagine this scenario: Karajan is directing your state orchestra in the Soviet anthem as the Russkies come politely tiptoeing into the so-called Parliament Hall up at the castle. You hand over the key to the castle on a red silk cushion with a regal fringe to the commandant, accompanied by the opening chords of the *Eroica* Symphony. (We Germans always seem to play the *Eroica* whenever one of our criminal plans has fallen flat.) Suddenly, for the first time, Karajan grabs his back in pain, the first sign of the problem that was later to cause him so much distress. The maestro does not deign to honor you with a glance. He packs up his little baton, goes to the castle courtyard, revs up, and wings his way nonstop to Salzburg.

But back to your private and so very statesmanlike letter to Mother with its remarkable final sentence: "I am getting everything together here now. Including the fur coat." Evidently, without any consideration for the great Russian offensive at the San–Vistula Line, Mother must have specifically requested this item. She seems also to have requested another "thing" that always wore out so quickly in the Frank family (probably because most of the stuff you used to send was not of very high quality). After the first two sentences in your July 25 letter ("The situation here is getting more serious by the hour" and "I am happy to learn you are all safe and sound"), it comes: "I am sending you the girl and including some other things at the same time. More to follow."

"The girl" was another one of those starving Polish women who didn't have the strength to perform good work since Mother persisted in her tightfisted reluctance to open her food cupboards to the servants. Besides that, this Polish girl presumably didn't have enough humility at her command to say, "At your service, Frau Minister." On July 26 you continued defiantly in a letter from the Wawel: "The situation here continues to grow more serious— but our faith grows all the stronger." Now, was that already your Catholic faith, Father, or still your indomitable faith in the final victory?

It was probably faith in victory, for on August 14 you still had the ability to demonstrate a good nose for practical politics: "We hope that the Government General, to the extent that it has already fallen into the hands of the enemy [*Father, the GG had been in "enemy hands" ever since its founding*], will come back to us. No one is any longer even contemplating our evacuation of Cracow." Correction: the Polish Home Army was. And of course the Soviets were, too. The final upshot was that you were able to get away with only some food provisions and a few small, easily transportable valuables in the face of the attackers just before Christmas 1944. "It is altogether uncertain whether I will be able to spend Christmas with you this year and so I am sending several things for the holidays with Nickl. Eisenlohr will also be bringing something along."

Perhaps it was these deliveries of food and servants that compelled Hitler and Speer (unfortunately too late) to rig up a plan whereby transports were very strictly regulated. That scheme of theirs pleased me. I was so fed up by this time with those never-ending Polish geese, eggs, sausages, and servant girls. And still, we didn't want to give any of it to those refugees who were already popping up here and there in our Bavarian Schliersee Valley. It would have gone against the grain of our customary Catholic moral code and things like that—you know what I mean.

Scarcely had your boys in the administration swallowed your decree about closing the luxury restaurants when you took the next step and suddenly proposed organizing a Party Day festivity in a grand style. Instantly, even your own governors were against that.

A perfect example of the great German cause in those days was a request issued by Bierkamp to the governors, asking them "to put at my disposal German-Polish interpreters," since the interpreters who worked for the Sicherheitsdienst, the Security Service (Bierkamp's way of formulating things begins to sound a lot like you now), "have already been extensively executed." ("Where the hell is the interpreter?" "He's sitting in his office, executed." "And his replacement?" "Oh, he's already been extensively executed in his own living room." "What a helluva mess.")

Again you must have been found wandering through your castle, shaking in your boots; fear was eating deeper and deeper through your very cartilage. They found you trembling, leaning up against the eastern ramparts. They brought you happy news: in their newly conquered territories, the Russians had resorted to a brutal sort of slaughter—rather imitative of your own example—and that gave the politician in you a new straw to clutch at. Who was murdering more human beings now? you wondered. The Russians? Or was it still us? In any case, you told Governor Wächter to "condemn the unprecedented terror of the Soviet Russians" (well, well, Father, do I detect a little bit of envy there?) and "to express to the victimized population my own deepest sympathy and that of all members of the government." Their eyes streaming with tears, no doubt, the Poles listened to this message of concern from their good patriarch.

Because the front was already so close, you decided to raise the salaries of the officials and other employees in government and industry. That transparent gesture was a kind of bonus for hand-to-hand combat, Father, and those officials and employees managed to swallow even that. A race of greedy hogs, those Germans. How they rejoiced in their extra three hundred zlotys per month, even if they did have to huddle closer and closer together in their offices because the enemy was already pulling the desk chairs one by one out from under their fat asses. Or was this perhaps a clever ploy of yours to increase their future pensions in the Federal Republic? Every year that one of those officials spent in occupied Poland was figured in when it came time later to calculate the size of his pension. And an increase in salary like that began to amount to quite a tidy little sum, except that it nearly had to be paid out in rubles, so close had the Soviet threat come by that time.

Suddenly you began to talk about the Government General as "the bastion of the East." Was that the stenographer's mistake? Or did he do it on purpose? Or was it *your* mistake? Surely it should have been "bastion *against* the East." Or were you already contemplating—"I open d4"—sharing your experiences in the reconstruction of pillaged territories with the Russians?

For one moment as I read your diary from those days, I can imagine you as a happy man, gazing contentedly at the reassuring sight of those three big open tanks, finally completed and filled with water for fighting possible air raid fires. Next, I read an entry that seems to be one of those which you and your secretary fraudulently added to your official diaries later on in Neuhaus: "The Governor General ordered the art expert von Palézieux to have a precise listing of all art objects drawn up. The keys are to be handed over by Palézieux to a Pole above reproach, one who will be able to remain behind at the castle. Under no circumstances does the Governor General himself intend to remove anything that might be state property." Why this strange emphasis, little Father? Previously, at your behest, Palézieux had designated all those things as "international art objects." He had furthermore assured you in reply to some question of yours (you certainly had become jumpy) that "the food provisions for the inhabitants of the castle precinct were already secured, as were the supplies of water for both drinking and cooking."

More and more you were preparing for siege—though, to be sure, the artistic framework for the preparation was still most imposing. Incidentally, Father, "a Pole above reproach"? That's another of your remarkable stipulations. Was such a person to be an art connoisseur, or was it more important for him to be an anti-Communist? Was he supposed to be a racially pure Pole? God, how you do go on. Himmler probably thought so too, and things were getting a little tense and sticky on all sides. After all, the guy was pulling three of his police regiments out of the GG, but all your objections amounted to nothing. You were forced to see the situation he was in. Hitler was more important to him than you were. Besides that, these police regiments, daylight saving time or not, couldn't get a clear shot any longer because of the huge stream of refugees passing through. Your ridiculous fire-fighting tanks suddenly threatened to become the main battle line. The fear inside you must have been dripping with cancerous lesions by now. I can see you up on your ramparts like the Hunchback of Notre Dame, like the Elephant Man. Your fear has turned into fleshy growths. You are stinking from your putrefying snot, and my heart rejoices.

For even they are going to put a noose around your neck. They will be hoisting you up the flagpole of the castle. You howl in pain. . . . And I'm filled with an unspeakable joy that your regime is finally coming to an end, an insane sense of satisfaction that you are going to feel with your own body at least a taste of that nameless horror we caused millions of others to feel.

Emerging from your fear, but still in desperation, you were willing to grant the Poles an extra-special award. "The Poles have earned their recognition as being absolutely qualified to participate in future European cooperation." What a stupefyingly idiotic sentence. One might hope that in the second it took to utter it, you realized its and your own absurdity.

But then it was off for an evening of song with Professor Hans Pfitzner. My God, those artists. The mind boggles to think of them going along with each and every final battle of their powerful patrons, and enduring until the next tyrants are securely in the saddle. How you must have felt when on the next day the assassination attempt on Hitler's life failed. You had been hoping to escape with your life and avoid a court trial in the sudden peace that would set in after Hitler's death. With trembling hand (as I must assume) you found yourself instead obliged to send a telegram: "My heartiest congratulations and words of blessing for your divinely inspired deliverance from the hideous peril of the criminal attack on your life." Hitler was alive. And you came one step closer to the gallows. You were already trying to escape on tiptoe, so that the rope would not get a chance to begin its stranglehold. On July 26 you realized with a shock that "the Government General has suffered most decisive losses in power and space." Very beautifully put—sometimes you surprise me with your choice of words which manage to break away a little from the trite and hackneyed. But then again your stupid superlatives ("most decisive" indeed) wreck everything. That was a disability that only Woods was able to cure you of.

There now follows what seems to me to be a particularly crazed episode in the history of your collapse. You, of course, see it differently: "It is a tragic situation that on one and the same day the governors of Galicia and Lublin report to me at the castle and inform me that their districts are, to all intents and purposes, lost." Did the three of you lean over the city map of Cracow, and did you perhaps speculate about which of you was going to get which district so that each could at least keep in practice until the wonder weapon arrived from Berlin? "Small, but all mine," you must have had to admit as the days dwindled down, eventually switching into the comparative form: "Smaller, but all mine."

Now the time had come to take a serious look to see if in those five years of a just regime there hadn't perhaps been, here or there, a tiny injustice committed. For the first time in administrative session there was talk about consigning certain files and records to the fire. I deduce from the simultaneous references to the bursting warehouses of the state monopoly administration that a substantial bit of time was being set aside for that endeavor. The word was, eat well and assuage your consciences with a good bonfire. You exhibited such stature, Father, such class, such quality. That's what your incorrigible friends still claim today. They claim that you proved it once again when, according to your diary, you "expressed at this critical juncture and turn of events my gratitude and recognition to all of my fellow workers for the excellent work they have performed during the past five years, excellent and beneficial for the Reich." (I thank you very much for your specificity—I had really been expecting "for Poland" instead of "for the Reich.") There you sat, shattered by your destiny, in your purloined hall in a stolen castle in a plundered land—and where many a tear was bravely held back by those who had never shed a single tear for another human being.

You received the Polish Count Potocki. And check this one out. See how the Poles have suddenly been transformed from subhuman creatures and suppliers of mincemeat into fellow human beings. You expressed to the Count your most deeply felt conviction "that the Poles as a worthy race are in a position to make a valuable contribution to future European undertakings." It took you five years and millions of murders to accomplish that one. Count Potocki got up and left your presence. I wonder what ever happened to him.

You remained, and had to start worrying about where you were going to get the wherewithal for a future without the GG in it. Should you begin to draw on capital assets? That's not in the Franks' blood. Instead, you first sent a telex to Goebbels saying that even with the loss of your empire you still definitely wished to continue as minister and have your own administrative department. Next, since the Russians were a mere 118 kilometers from Cracow on that day, you proposed "that the splendidly conceived memorandum on the treatment of Poland and the interconnections between German policy and current Polish trends and concerns be sent to SS Obergruppenführer Kaltenbrunner." For chrissake, Father, wasn't that a little late? The next time you saw Kaltenbrunner, by the way, was when he was in the dock at Nuremberg. No doubt the two of you exchanged a subtle comment or two about your sensitive policy vis-à-vis Poland during those last hundred days. Perhaps you also got a chance to tell him about your great act of courage—that is, your final threat on August 12, 1944, to resign your post as Governor General unless (always an "unless") there was an immediate stop put to the confiscation of farm wagons that were supposed to be used to bring in the harvest, and not for the construction of defensive positions. By this time your threat to resign could hardly have aroused so much as a weary groan in Berlin.

On September 4 you managed to produce another classic example of the confusion in your anxiety-ridden head when you proclaimed to your roundtable of crooks: "I intend to direct all my efforts toward exploiting every opportunity to settle the mood of the Polish population." Those words were no longer in synch with your new image, Father. ("Well, then, Minister Frank,"

Woods mocked, with the noose in his hand, "now let's the two of us begin to settle your mood.") This new Hans Frank image of yours, however, did drive you to send Hitler a telegram on October 5 in which you proposed a coadministration of the GG with the Poles. Somehow or other, that proposition didn't reach Polish ears. Someone in your public relations department must have screwed up royally, Father. I can't imagine that the Poles wouldn't immediately break off all activities against you and your gang in the expectation of such a generous arrangement. And to think you also said in one of your meetings that "a certain humanizing, a certain Europeanizing, and a totally just and legal treatment of Polish society must now be put into effect." And further: "The theory of total annihilation, of complete enslavement, of thorough disenfranchisement is a terrible violation against the interests of our Fatherland." If properly launched, that sentence alone would have been enough to guarantee a complete acquittal for you in Nuremberg. But thank God, someone screwed up again. Your friendly comments about Poland and your critical ones about Berlin (which, to be sure, you shouted over the shoulder of your billowing leather coat as you leapt into your jam-packed armored Mercedes and fled with your "personal objets d'art") simply were not deemed sufficient to save you from the noose. So there were only two things left for you to do now: pack up your loot and your faith, and make a run for it.

But wait, one more thing. On the occasion of the opening of a training course for National Socialist Commanding Officers (how could you carry on with such nonsense to the very end? it's staggering), you still had time to utter a prayer to your German God, whose white and flowing robes were now dotted with the remains of countless little corpses and whose little beard was dripping with red blood: "Bless our weapons in this our one great final battle of the war. If, Lord, it should not please you that Germany should continue to exist, then all of us, as soldiers and men of Germany, choose to perish without a trace rather than go on living as subjects and slaves." So much for your faith. The loot was to follow forthwith. On September 9 you conferred with your bank officers about the "removal of bank note reserves and printing plates during the evacuation." Now you've got the right idea. Put the money and the art in the sacks and head for the open spaces. The trouble is, the open spaces turned into the confines of your narrow prison cell.

Before the day you actually shut up shop and fled from Cracow, you took inspiration from a 1529 document and dictated an essay about the life of Alonsa-Sposares Aquirre; you went out to greet your "good and diligent struggling people"; you viewed the hilarious film *Sieben Jahre Pech (Seven Years of Bad Luck)* starring the Austrian film comedian Hans Moser. This was preceded by a brief consultation with your comrades-in-arms about the discovery of the Maidanek concentration camp and the dispatches printed by the shocked world press; you enjoyed a performance by Heinrich George at the State Theater; worked yourself into an angry rage about the confiscation of your armored car; and dictated another essay, "On Justice" (in which you doubtless had many brilliant things to say); dictated yet another essay, this one with the title "The Orchestra Conductor"; and nine days later began even a fourth one, "On Dilettantism," by which, Heaven forbid, you certainly were not referring to yourself. It's just another of your usual blatherings that no one could possibly care less about. Sorry, I have to make that quite clear. And there's something else I have to make clear: the astonishing fact that you could alleviate your fear by writing down this stuff. It is difficult to get a real hold on you during these weeks. You were behaving somewhat absentmindedly, as if Mother had knocked you into dreamland with Lilly's talisman. I discover you now discussing of all things the issue of a special postage stamp that was supposed to appear on October 26, the sixth anniversary of the founding of the GG; dictating more of your dilettantism essay; enjoying Hitler's approval of transferring Polish volunteers into the Wehrmacht; having the state orchestra conductor Lothar perform parts of his new opera, *Brabant*, for you; and dictating again, you unbelievable son of a bitch, in the fall of 1944, your new essay, "Administration and Administrative Justice." Was it that, like so many of your companions in Nazi justice, you wanted to promote an easy transition to a university post after the war? "Let the whole world be against us, the Lord God will be on our side," you bellowed at the top of your lungs at the Heroes Cemetery in Cracow. Then you received the standing committee of the Polish delegation, and there you are again, the murderous king of the collaborators. You ooze your way into their favor; you emphasize that "I have always struggled to promote, maintain, and expand the great European cultural community." Well, please, what could possibly follow after that, you Fiddler on the Wawel Roof? In order to emphasize your love of Poland, you say: "Among other things I have established a great Polish orchestra, the Philharmonic of the Government General." "Among other things"? Among other things you won imperishable fame as the great founder of cemeteries for slaughtered Poles, Jews, and Ukrainians.

Thus passed the final days of your reign. The essays have all been written. Now fear has you in its clutches again. Where are the wonder weapons? Where is the Wehrmacht? Lammers receives a classic Hans Frank telegram in which you "reject all responsibility for the failure of the Wehrmacht to prevail in this territory." Then you lay another egg: "I can no longer demand that the few police officials still remaining here allow themselves to be shot down by the dozen." On December 9, 1944, you attend an opera for the last time in your life—in your own theater, in your own Cracow, in your own GG. The title is almost too kitschily ironic to be true, *Orpheus and Eurydice*. For nearly six years you let the underworld (in both senses) thrive in this land. Thank God I, too, was spared my salvation scene in your own personal opera.

Fear makes one stupid. It made you stupid. There you were, on New Year's Eve, 1944–45, squatting in your castle. You didn't even have two full years of life ahead of you. And in the circle of your faithful companions you were drinking champagne and thinking things over. From the depths of your armchair you began to speak: "Actually, my Government General is quite literally a neighbor country of the Reich." They all gazed at you attentively, as you wished them to do. "Actually," you continued in your shrill voice, "actually, I and my country are independent of Hitler." Now you leaned forward, placed the champagne glass from the private collection of Count Potocki on the table, and asked in all seriousness, "Why can't I, a sovereign head of state, negotiate with the Soviets? I can declare myself, along with my Reich, an independent entity and take up a position of benevolent neutrality vis-à-vis Stalin. Then his troops could march unhindered through the GG in the direction of the Reich."

The gentlemen and ladies of this intimate circle surely applauded you. You are even said to have given the order to find out the name of the attacking Soviet general so that you could initiate friendly contact. That is the *esprit d'escalier* of modern history.

"I am staggering under a heavy burden," you wrote.

And then, suddenly, it was all over.

Flight and Gluttony

Time was up on January 16, 1945. You perform your ham actor's farewell scene on the stage of the castle, and one day later, according to the diary, take your leave with great emotion: "The Herr Governor General departs from the castle at Cracow with his automobile convoy in the most glorious winter weather and radiant sunshine."

What wouldn't I give to be able to speak with those Poles who were the first to go up to your castle after your departure. I am consumed with curiosity: how did your rooms look then, in what condition did you leave them; who was that "Pole above reproach" to whom you had the castle keys given; what kind of letters, what kind of files did they find there, what kind of pictures, uniforms; did you leave dirty laundry behind; did you clean the basin after you brushed your teeth; did you take one more bath on that final morning; did you leave your shaving brush sitting there, or maybe a book on the nightstand with a bookmark in it, as if you were intending to return that evening? Was the stove still lighted in the servants' kitchen; were the dishes from your last breakfast stacked up, unwashed? Did the Wawel Castle just sit there abandoned, in total calm, for perhaps an hour, before the real owners dared to come up and take a look—in radiant sunshine and glorious winter weather?

Little father of mine, I have found another sort of diary of yours, really more of an appointment book, with a few entries in it about your last months there. Well, for one thing it appears that up there in the castle courtyard in Cracow you were burning official records. And what is it I read later, under the date of Sunday, January 21, 1945? Here it stands: "Morning—the GG, Mohr, von Fenske—burning of records." But this was not at the Wawel any longer. By this date you were already at Seichau Castle in Upper Silesia, staying with Count von Richthofen. That means that on the four days between the time you got the hell out of Cracow and this beautiful Sunday you must have been rummaging through all sorts of additional files and records that you had taken along with you. The little entry is a clue to how reality gradually filtered through those homicidal skulls of yours.

Those first days after the evacuation must have been lovely. The Herr Governor General (yes, you) did his best to forget the loss of his Reichsnebenland by reveling in some disgusting and depraved parties. They said it was such excessive gluttony that Bormann in Berlin was enraged by descriptions of it and so close to apoplexy he almost didn't live to see the end of his own power. And I can imagine that Hitler was so confused and upset about the miserable example you were setting for his embattled population that he directed Bach-Zelewsky with a group of soldiers into some wrong battle zone or other, so that the Oder-Napper sector could no longer be contained. Yes, for the past several months the army reports from the front contained some place names all too close and familiar to the Germans.

There are other entries in this appointment book (not written in your hand) which indicate the depths of your plunge and paint a picture of an almost comical frenzy of activity. "Trucks to be packed with paintings, etc." was something to be taken care of on Saturday, January 20. It would have been more correct to write "repacked," for you had already packed those trucks in Cracow. In Seichau the paintings were once again sorted through and then sent on to various destinations.

Then it was off for a weekend which you dedicated to true culture. What does the appointment book have for that Sunday afternoon? "17:00 hours. Departure of the Governor General for Agnetendorf, to Gerhard Hauptmann." That fraudulent, watered-down version of Goethe had been a friend of our family in its heyday. You remained there with him in the thrall of a lovely conversation until Monday afternoon, while the collaborators in your escape stayed behind with plenty to do: "Monday, January 22. Morning, crates brought down; evening, cars packed; 17:30 hours, Governor General returns." And what a beautiful trip you then enjoyed, as you headed in the direction of Upper Bavaria, riding in the backseat of your Mercedes, license plate EAST 23. It must have been like this: The little demon in me sprang down from your shoulders and for the last time snuggled into the deep, warm automobile robes. The motor purred quietly. (That man Schamper was really a first-class chauffeur. He could almost make one forget his low opinion of Mother; he couldn't stand her. "That rotten bitch" is what he used to call her.) I leaned against you; you were still drunk on Hauptmann's ponderous intellectual drivel. Yet you were easily his equal when it came to the art of blah-blah-blah. You were also still drunk from the champagne and carousing chez Richthofen on your stopover there before returning home to the Reich.

Those six years of rule were now behind you, and the approach of the Russian troops was causing your Reichsnebenland to crumble into little bits. But before you left for your weekend festivities, you had decided to stage one final, emotionally wrenching scene in which, if one follows the description you later wrote in your Nuremberg prison cell, everything that constitutes the good German coalesced one last time: "I was the last of my people to leave the Cracow castle, at the moment in which the Russians had already nearly encircled the city and were beginning to penetrate into the suburbs to the north of the Vistula. [*How brave, Father, how brave—like a captain on his sinking ship. And the Russians were already so close. What a hero!*] That was on Wednesday, the seventeenth of January, 1945, at two o'clock in the afternoon. [*Note well, you historians and you schoolchildren. Something like that is a moment in modern German history you must never forget—isn't that what you had in mind when you were writing, Father?*] On Tuesday, January 16, 1945, that is to say, one day before, I took a final walk through the rooms of the castle I had so carefully maintained and so tastefully furnished. [*Unfortunately, I can't suppress the urge to remind you of the testimony of some of the witnesses at Nuremberg; according to them, that business about "carefully maintained and tastefully furnished" is given quite a different twist. Your wonder-boy art expert, Dr. Mühlmann, testified that you, more than all the others, had been driven by a greedy and insatiable love for ostentation. What you really should have written if you had been honest is: "the rooms I had crammed to capacity with pillaged art treasures and furniture." . . . But let's get back to your preposterous lies.*] In that great coronation and parliament hall, with its magnificent view far out over the wonderful old city, I stood alone and considered the path that had led us here. [*Yes, dear Father, but wasn't it a little late for such musings? I can only wish you had taken advantage of a similar opportunity a dozen years earlier, at the time of the Nazi takeover, when Hitler was standing on his Berlin balcony soaking up the adoration of his SA and of all the hundreds of thousands of other Germans. You could so easily have just pushed him over the parapet; you were always stronger than he was. What a wild photo opportunity that would have been for all the famous newsreel cameramen of the time. Hitler appears nobly and graciously on his balcony, bowing over the balustrade, and suddenly one catches a glimpse of your ugly puss behind him; all at once he leans forward, you grab him by his ankles and, whoops!, down he tumbles into the midst of his own people, where he always claimed to be happiest anyhow. Naturally, the only thing left of you would be little shreds and pieces lying around*] *here and there. History would have come to quite a different conclusion about this man Hitler; and Papen, Schleicher, and Hindenburg would have had you, or what was left of you, guillotined. . . . Instead, you merely stood there, gaping like some tragic rooster. Right to the very end you re-fused to catch on to anything. . . . And now you stand in the hall of the castle, spouting like some schoolmaster:*] What powers have not already sat upon the throne here in this castle during the past millen-nium! So many have arisen, only to plunge again: the Mongols, the Tartars [*was this supposed to be some kind of tutorial in history you were offering me from your prison cell?*], the Lithuanians, the Russians, the Poles, the Austrians, then the Poles again, then the Germans again, and then came the Russians once more and the Hungarians, the French. The Swedes had come and gone repeatedly, Karl XII and August the Strong, and . . . and . . . and [*"and the worst of all, the most barbaric, the most homicidal, that was me" is what you could have said at that point, instead of those three vapid "and"'s and this trite fillip you tacked on:*] yet serene, proud, and haughty, the castle looms over the eternally young Vistula."

Father, comparing the diary from your younger years with these latter-day ruminations, I see that your vocabulary has not improved one iota.

While records and files were being diligently incinerated outside, you blathered on: "In the cathedral near the castle, this holy Polish site, the Polish kings were crowned throughout the centuries. Tombs stand in long rows in the broad crypts of this great cathedral. It was there that my son Niklas enjoyed his games of hide-and-seek and tag, as he was being watched over by those benevolent, child-loving SS troopers who have been so unjustly reproached for their allegedly horrible crimes. [*Yes, okay, the last sentence isn't yours—I take it back, and continue with your text:*] I had had the tombs carefully insulated and protected against possible bombing attacks. [*Believe it or not, I can't find your medal with the Polish eagle for this courageous act of yours; where is it? How could you have had the nerve to take such liberties with Himmler and Hitler watching? Imagine going*

*ahead on your own and having those things carefully wrapped up. Con-
gratulations on your bravery.*] I stood then before the altar with the
black shroud which the Poles had hung there on the occasion of
their loss of freedom almost one hundred fifty years before. [*I am
really surprised that you didn't remove it quickly in 1939, you brave
liberator!*] This shroud accused me, too. [*Well, I'll be . . . it did? Even
after you had served Poland so well with your freedom-loving decrees against
hunting down hedgehogs and marmots and little hoofed creatures? I just
don't believe you. The shroud accused you? Surely you're not going to let
the cat of truth out of the bag now, are you?*] As a final gesture, I
stood before the closed marble tomb in the first niche near the
main portal, the tomb of the last of the Jagiellons, carved by
Veit Stoss, and I reminded myself of how on the seventh of
November, 1939, I had settled into the castle and made it my seat
of government, of how, with a powerful emotional shock I long
studied the masterfully detailed features of the old Polish king
on his sarcophagus. [*That's what's so great about you, that the little
things of life so move and "shock" you—not the attack on Poland, not
the war against France and England, not the persecution and annihilation
of thousands of human beings in the concentration camps even before 1939,
but this stone head of the last of the Jagiellon kings. How touching.*]
Professor Cybichowsky, the Polish gentleman who was guiding me
at the time [*and whom you later did not even consider saving from
liquidation—I'm not groping in the dark, am I?*], stood long in silence
next to me, gazing at this marble countenance. The king was
sleeping. [*What shit, Father; this description is a load of pure shit.*] His
face gave evidence of the terrible torments of his life, and at the
same time had that look of tranquillity that comes with the knowledge of finally being released from existence. It was then that this
Polish gentleman said to me in a dignified and quiet voice: 'Thus
did our kings die in sorrow, nearly all of them. It is a burden of
fate to be king in Poland.' [*You must have sighed deeply at that point;
it was probably at that very second that you felt you had become king in
Poland.*] And as I was about to take my leave, I found myself

standing once more at the little gallery that encircled the sarcophagus, and I thought what a truly terrifying office it was to rule
from this castle."

Hey, hold on there. Two months earlier, in November 1944,
you had written to Mother: "Excitement everywhere, yet here I
sit like a paladin in my castle and calm the others down with my
composure and self-control." That's what I call having a cool eye
for the world situation.

You ascended from the scene of your "emotional shock" at the
tombs of the Jagiellons, riffled through a few more files to be
burned, and sorted out the art treasures with Palézieux, the ones
you absolutely had to take along with you to Bavaria. And then
there transpired something that you describe in your book of
memoirs with a lie: "I had the flag of our Reich lowered. I took
it with me and returned to the Fatherland. The Government
General had now become history." What a beautiful use of the
pluperfect.

The fact of the matter was that you yourself, in a deliberate
and melodramatic way, climbed to the tower and solemnly lowered
the swastika. You never let anyone upstage you in productions in
which you wanted to star. On January 17, 1945, you stood alone
up there and with a misty-eyed gaze cast your eyes one final time
at the view of the Marienkirche, the halls of the drapers' guild,
the area where the ghetto and the Plaszow concentration camp
stood; then you furled the flag and, reeking of smoke, you de-
scended. You must have stunk horribly of smoke, because the day
before had been dedicated to the great conflagration of records in
the castle courtyard. God, how grotesque. This act of incineration
is the first and only indication of your guilty consciences. With
this act you suddenly admitted that everything, but really everything you had done there, had been criminal.

Your personal standard was lowered, too, the standard, as is
customary with "kings," that used to flutter up there in the breeze
whenever you were in residence. I remember it well—and its

counterpart that fluttered over the Schoberhof as a signal to the nearby peasants that the Herr Minister was condescending to dwell amongst them briefly. Unfortunately, I have never been able to verify the rumor that during your divorce battles, and in particular after your confrontation in the salon car, Mother had this flag flown whenever you dropped in on the Schoberhof, but always had it lowered to half-mast by one of her ladies-in-waiting sympathetic to her predicament.

With the flag under your arm, off you went to Upper Silesia, to Seichau, to Count von Richthofen. Another member of that party was Leonardo da Vinci's Signorina Galleroni. She traveled— hardly in keeping with her social position—in one of the trucks. To be sure, she still found herself in the best of company, with a choice selection of the most valuable art objects of Poland. And of course that was no art theft, Father. How did you explain it to the GIs after your arrest? You phrased it so beautifully: "I took along certain objects of art so that they would not be plundered in my absence."

You really could be witty sometimes. You invaded a country with your thugs, you settled in, you murdered a major part of its population, and when you fled, you saved its art treasures from their own owners. Up to the very foot of the gallows you vehemently denied ever having stolen so much as a single art object for your own private pleasure. The first question an American officer asked you at one of your pretrial hearings was both apt and ironic: "Are you interested in art?" What followed could not have been very comfortable for you. You squawked and protested that you had had all Polish art treasures registered so they wouldn't fall into Göring's hands; and naturally all your official quarters had to be properly furnished and decorated. But as far as you as a loyal Bavarian were personally concerned, the only important thing was your personal collection of books on Munich.

In Seichau you delivered yourself of another terrific piece of writing, one that belongs in every letter-writing manual as a model for those who have just lost an empire. The letterhead, still in big fat capital letters, proclaims "The Governor General" and is followed by the classic succinct address "Cracow, Castle." The address had been crossed out in this instance, but you didn't do anything about correcting that title of yours—a very interesting point of law, by the way. Is a Governor General without any ground under his feet still a Governor General? After "Dear Brigitte" comes your husbandly reassurance: "This letter is to tell you that I got out of Cracow at the last moment, both alive and well."

Now that's a good beginning, and demonstrates, incidentally, your principal concern: self-preservation. After her first sigh of relief, Mother must have immediately begun to worry about all the other good German people up there in Poland who were responsible for the refined aspects of administration (the grubby business of slaughter was taken care of by the others, Himmler and those Krügers of yours), but you quickly put her at ease: "I was able to save all our German people [*the Polish subhumans were now back in their own separate category again, is that right?*]. It was a terribly serious undertaking." Then there follows a lot of unimportant details about other people who had to make it back to the West and who would be visiting Mother, and greetings, and kisses, and then two first-class concluding sentences: "I shall have many interesting things to tell you. All the things have been saved."

So that was it. Six million Jews dead, two and a half million Poles dead, a devastated land, and for you that all adds up to "interesting things to tell."

On a second sheet (this time with no letterhead; after all, you had to be a little sparing now with personalized stationery) you append: "The day before yesterday we were still able to hold our big government meeting at the Castle in Cracow!" Oh, glorious time of the old GG, whither art thou gone? You gave the postwar Germans another tried-and-true prescription with that last sentence of yours, one that follows the motto "Never forget the heyday of the Third Reich with its grand and glorious and also its solemn hours, with its true German comradeship. We shall bury those whom we had to sacrifice, but let us continue to cultivate the wonderful bygone days." (For example, your recollection of June 26, 1944: "Yesterday we had a wonderful production of the opera *Ariadne auf Naxos*.")

The rapid advance of the Russians, to be sure, robbed Mother of a potential memory, one she would have loved to share with me after the war. Much too late you had suggested something to her: "It is necessary for you at this time to organize one or two receptions for the ladies at the castle." Let the ladies wait. They are still waiting today. They're also still waiting for their beautiful corselets. I can sometimes see Mother in my mind's eye, roaming like a madwoman through the ruins of the destroyed Warsaw ghetto and crying out through clouds of smoke and fire: "Where are my corselets? I need new corselets again. I'll even pay a zloty. . . ." And out of the ruins, skeletal yellow arms reach out in her direction, each holding a corselet; Mother walks between them as if reviewing the troops, until Stroop* grabs her and brings her back. As a favor to you, he doesn't mention the story of the crazy Frau Governor General in his chilling report about the quelling of the Jewish revolt.

Here, I think, is a touching poetic example of your blasted life. The postage stamps you had printed for the Government General aren't worth a bean to collectors today compared with the counterfeit stamps with a portrait of you on them that the British circulated in 1942. (They did it, no doubt, with the expectation that Hitler would have you wiped out when he saw your face instead of his on the GG stamps.) As a counterfeit you are worth over five thousand marks today. My congratulations, Father.

To sum up: The whole bunch of you got the hell out of Cracow on January 17, 1945. Even though you had behaved so generously toward the victims of your invasion all those long years—as you

---

* The German commandant in Warsaw.

nobly testified in court—nevertheless you spent the days before
the evacuation burning files in the beautiful courtyard of the castle.
That doesn't make much sense, does it? So why did you do it? Is
it because those records could never have produced a shred of
evidence about any heroic behavior on your part directed against
Himmler and in the interest of the Poles?

Be that as it may, one thing is clear. You certainly did not hand
over any art treasures to any Polish officials of the city of Cracow.
Instead, you shipped them off to the West, first to the castle of
Count von Richthofen in Seichau, using up all that sinfully expensive gasoline that our Wehrmacht, still bravely engaged in
defending Polish soil against its owners and their allies, so desperately needed.

Then, if your intention was always to keep orderly and legal
records, why did Palézieux, your man responsible for art objects,
take your adjutant aside in the dark of the night like a conspirator
on a small-town stage and whisper that he had to help him repack
and divert those crates filled with art in the dark of the night and
thus let them quietly disappear from the inventory? The adjutant
turned out to be an honorable fellow that night and wouldn't go
along with it. Palézieux had been specifically acting under your
orders. In fact, the Poles did get most of these things back eventually—except for that portrait of a young man by Raphael. It's
absolutely crazy, Father, when you think of it: Raphael paints a
picture for you four hundred years ago, and it finally lands in
Upper Bavaria in our house in Neuhaus on the Schliersee. It has
never been seen again. It's probably hanging in some farmer's
kitchen, having been swapped by Mother in 1946 for some eggs,
butter, and a pork roast. Mother understood as much about art
as you did about the truth.

Come to think of it, it's quite remarkable that most of the Nazi
big shots used to live permanently in their houses in the country.
No doubt they needed to air themselves out to mask the stench
of their political lives, the way you did on the shores of the

Schliersee. And yet how happy you were to return to your own empire after your airing-out, to your own castle, to your own Poles. With a grin on your fat face, you often used to blurt out a clever little saying you had made up—"*Ostluft macht frei*," "The air of the East makes one free"—quite aware that a parallel motto stood over the entrance to Auschwitz: "*Arbeit macht frei*," "Work makes one free." How that cynical humor of yours used to wow the folks. But then, after the defeat, when you were nothing more than Hans Frank, you switched over to groveling and whimpering. But that didn't work anymore.

The Herr Governor
General Continues
on His Way

You arrived in Neuhaus on the Schliersee—not in quite so poor a state as when you had first arrived in Cracow six years before. No field was too small now, no house too humble: you immediately founded a new Reich, this time in the former Cafe Bergfrieden in the Josefsthal, the "Auxiliary Headquarters of the Government General." Was this where you planned to arrange for a reconquest of your former empire? Pretty grotesque, Father. What was the first thing you did there? You polished up your diaries by falsifying them, those official diaries from the GG—at least the last five volumes of them, all neatly wrapped in their files, which you still had the time to tamper with, with the aid of your most faithful secretary, Frau K.

What an ending—the cheapest sort of forgeries one can imagine. And what a hopeless task it was, what with the sheer bulk of your brutal attacks against the subhumans in East and West; it was an impossible undertaking. Were there even worse ones that you had already destroyed? What a pair of forgers sitting there in Cafe Bergfrieden, your peaceful mountain retreat—a Governor General run down at the heels, trying to clean up his act by editing his old speeches, and loyal Frau K. Again, the noose was the perfect solution for you. If only I could believe that you can really hear me now. I've outgrown my superstition with Ouija boards and table levitation by this time. And Aunt Martel is dead, and no chairs are vibrating, no cupboards are tipping over as I write this.

Your personal authority began to suffer mightily, too. One day your personal valet, Nickl, for years the man responsible for keeping your uniforms neat and tidy, was standing there as you were giving him an order. Nickl looked you straight in the eye and uttered his first democratic sentence: "Kiss my ass!" He turned around and walked out—just left the Governor General standing there. How that makes me laugh, you pathetic dummy. Well, from then on Lilly had to look after your underwear a little bit more. You settled in; gasoline was requisitioned for the few cars still at your disposal; drivers and other personnel were withdrawn from the final battle—you needed them. That, at least, had one positive aspect to it: you probably saved their lives by dragging them down with you to perform their duties in your realm of shadows. There you sat, trying desperately to preserve the dignity of your office. Even your own personal adjutant was still at your side. But why? What was he supposed to do for you, go fetch the milk from the farmer's daughter?

Sometimes you came to visit us at the Schoberhof, though mostly you were with your beloved Lilly in Bad Aibling. But your breathing space began shrinking as the Bavarian countryside came more and more under the Americans' control.

On April 30, 1945, the news took your Nazi breath away: the Führer had finally fallen. Poppa Hitler's little Adolf was dead.

Soon you could catch your breath again. Dönitz was his successor. And what do you, the faithful liegeman, do then? You assemble the tattered remnants of those still loyal to you. You don't quite dare to announce your little plan to them out in the open, in front of the house in the Josefsthal. Instead, you do it inside. You make them swear an oath of allegiance to the new Führer of the Deutsches Reich. Jesus, Father! Would you have gone on doing insane stuff like that forever? An oath of allegiance like that? Grotesque; sickening and grotesque.

Then the day came when we were standing out in front of the Schoberhof and could see the Americans through our binoculars smashing through the pathetic tank trap erected between the Schliersee and Neuhaus, a few crisscrossed tree trunks—they just shoved them aside and continued in the direction of Neuhaus. We were well prepared for our liberation. Mother still had her strength, and she made good use of it. The women of Neuhaus were swiftly summoned to the Schoberhof, and there started sewing and hemming white flags of surrender. The weather was beautiful, so the women were sitting outside stitching where in the old days a Bavarian band in native costume used to play for you on special Nazi holidays.

You stood there posing like a country squire in your lederhosen with embroidered suspenders, green vest, and Bavarian brogues, as you played the role of the jovial landowner.

On May 2 and 3, with your adjutant at your side, you watched from the vantage point of your high path in the woods and saw how American tanks, with their hatches closed, slowly drove toward Neuhaus. You just stood there in your glorious leather coat, the one that reminds me so much of one of those Gestapo overcoats, and you said to your companion: "Just look at those scared rabbits; they're frightened that they've finally caught the scent of our impregnable Alpine fortress." And then you continued on your walk down toward your office. On the afternoon of May 4 you drank your coffee, ate your cake, and said: "I am unquestionably the last Minister of the Third Reich who is still able to enjoy his coffee hour as a free man."

Coming home on his bicycle along this same forest path, someone saw an American jeep driving along the valley and heading directly toward your office. Those GIs had mustered the courage to do this only because on the previous day old F., a local farmer and carpenter, had ridden defiantly past your Auxiliary GG Headquarters on his Haflinger horse right into the face of the American tanks. Maybe you had seen him on his mission and in your kitschy way had begun to think of yourself as Jesus in the Garden of Gethsemane and of old F. as Judas. There you were, waiting as in the Scriptures for the henchmen, so that your destiny might be fulfilled. Farmer F. had attached one of his wife's white sheets to a gigantic pole, and she was screaming after him that he better bring that laundry the hell right back and not give nothing to them damn Americans. But F. was undaunted, and he surrendered the Josefsthal to the U.S.A., including also the erstwhile Nazi big shot Dr. Hans Frank, recipient of honorary doctorates from the universities of Bologna and Bucharest and of honorary citizenship of Leipzig. (Hey, Daddy, do you suppose those honors might still be worth a free streetcar pass for your son today?)

You knew your arrest was coming, so before you retreated into your cafe headquarters you said goodbye to Mother. Standing in the main room of the Schoberhof, you slipped her some cash, a whole bundle of bills. I later learned that it was fifty thousand reichsmarks. So the final act of your conjugal bliss was the handing over of loot. How touching. Thus parted a cheap little couple who had always put themselves above the law. Or we could look at it this way: you were paying Mother off, as if she were some whore. Not a kiss, not a single affectionate word between the two of you, sticks in my memory. Maybe you did have a quick embrace outside, beyond my unfortunately limited field of vision and awareness. I don't really remember. Why was I born too late?

The jeep with a policeman from Schliersee, the American Lieutenant Stein, and two more soldiers in it, stopped at the garden gate. Your "Polish Government General/Upper Bavaria" was now a mere two hundred square meters in size. Stein came in. You were sitting in the living room with your adjutant, your chauffeur, and your secretary, drinking coffee. Stein asked: "Which one of you is Frank?"

Pretty shitty, eh? That's what I call really humiliating. You were proud to have been number one on Roosevelt's war criminal list, and now you're just another unrecognizable face. Stein would certainly have recognized Hitler or Goebbels or Göring right away. It must have been pretty embarrassing for you, in front of the three others at your table. Did you rise from your chair? Did you set down your cup as you replied, "I am"? Stein: "You're coming with me. You're under arrest."

You went out. And now something happened for which I will be eternally grateful to you, because it finally sealed your doom. You surrendered to the lieutenant all your official diaries from the GG, all forty-two volumes of them, with the transcripts of all your speeches, your trips, receptions, government meetings, conferences. That must really have hurt. How conceited you were later in Nuremberg, boasting about how you had handed them over voluntarily, claiming that those diaries would provide exculpatory evidence about your activities as Governor General, about how friendly you had been toward the Poles, how hostile toward Himmler. My God, did you ever mess that one up. The prosecution made more than ample use of those documents. Today they serve to jog my memory whenever my wrath begins to flag. All I need to do is leaf through them for a while. "The Cracow professors gave us a great deal of trouble; it was terrible." (That's you speaking as Governor General and friend of Poland.) "If we could have taken care of things from this end, everything would have come out differently. I therefore urgently request that you no longer commit anyone to a concentration camp in the Reich, but instead proceed with the liquidation here." The evening you wrote that you were probably compiling another list of profound books on philosophy that you wished to order; or perhaps you went to your State Theater in Cracow to see *Faust*, a play you knew practically by heart, of course.

How content you must have been on October 8, 1940, a day on which your stenographers noted down these sentences at an administrative session: "If I should go to Hitler and tell him, 'Mein

Führer, I have killed one hundred and fifty thousand Polacks!' then he would say, 'Good—as long as it was necessary!' "

At ease with yourself and the world, you also uttered this memorable patriarchal sentiment: "As for the rest, we are not in the least concerned about the welfare of this country. We are not in the least concerned about whether the Poles become richer or more secure, or if they lose all their property or not."

How brutal can you be, my dear man? Those sentences of yours are just as evil as the murders committed by the SS.

The prosecution at Nuremberg based its case on revelations like these; but even your own lawyer, Seidl, helped himself with generous servings from your diaries. Of course, he tended to draw his material more from the end of your diaries, those volumes from the later years, the ones in which you managed to fake new material. That was hardly surprising, for the more successful the Soviets were in battle, the more gruesome it became for German soldiers, the closer the front came, the more you seemed to discover your true humanitarian feelings for your Poles, and write them down—you bloody, sanctimonious patriot/father of the GG. As if those hypocritical efforts of yours could have turned wrong into right, blood into nourishment, or ghettos into pretty public parks where the Poles and Jews could wave enthusiastically as you drove past in your open limousine.

Sometimes I see you and Mother before me like a couple of seedy old vaudeville troupers, singing the scenes of your life together in screeching voices, Mother in her stolen furs, you festooned with Raphaels and da Vincis. Mother croaks the ballad which tells the story of how she prevented that guy from killing me. You know the one, you've heard her tell it—the time Mother mustered all the strength at her command and ordered them not to shoot us.

"I Have Carried Out My Orders"

It happened during those days of anarchy at the end of the war. Shortly before, you had paid Mother off with those fifty thousand marks. The Reich was a goner. The GIs had arrived to liberate us from the Nazis. *They* showed how much they liked little kids, when they were sober; but they had discovered our wonderful and well-stocked wine cellar at the Schoberhof. Without worrying about the proper temperature of the wines, about decanting cloudy bottles, about studying the vintages and labels, they simply opened their throats and guzzled away, while we were lined up against the wall of the house, looking as if we were about to break out singing the Polish national anthem any minute. (Did you actually ever see any of those Poles being shot?) One day we were standing next to the front door, into which in your typically modest way you had had your initials cast in metal and gilded, each a couple of feet high. They can still be seen there today. We had been shoved up against the wall to the right of the door. I had obediently raised my shockingly skinny little arms high above my head. Mother stood next to me, her mouth a tight, thin line, with a look that promised no good. In front of us, I can still see it today, was one of our uninhibited liberators, filled to the gills with Bordeaux. He seemed determined to gun us down with his rifle then and there— an intention that aroused me in a strange way. He wanted to do it because—and this was something new to me—we were clearly members of a family filled with criminal intent and potency. But he had made the same mistake you used to make: he underestimated Mother. Instantly she let loose with her sirenlike howl and then began to give him a piece of her mind, the way she used to deal with our Polish workers. Despite the linguistic barrier, she finally succeeded in reminding him, I guess, of his own American supermom. Whatever, we escaped with our lives.

For a young kid the idea of actually being shot down is something hard to get a conscious hold on, it seems to me, whenever I think back on that scene. It really wasn't that I was afraid. My mother had experienced through this episode only a tiny, scarcely measurable part of that terror . . . well, you know what I'm talking about.

Some of the other equally tanked-up GIs got our happy would-be executioner out of his shooting range; the situation calmed down and then gave way to an arrangement that might well seem familiar to you. They let us live; but in exchange for that, they plundered a number of the same things we had once plundered.

They presented a pretty comical sight as they marched off. Some of the GIs had divided up Mother's doll collection; this tough bunch of soldiers was loaded down with Käthe Kruse dolls dressed in little ruches and batiste frills. Mother was as mad as a pack of rabid dogs. I liked her on that day. For the time being, the Americans left our furniture behind; it was too hard to transport by jeep. All our furnishings had an appropriately nouveau-riche bulk and dimension.

Back to you. Lieutenant Stein was sitting in that jeep. They sat you down next to him. A GI stowed the forty-two volumes of your diary on the seat next to him, and the driver stepped on the gas. (Did your adjutant and your secretary wave bye-bye in bewilderment as you drove away?) The jeep drove through Neuhaus, Schliersee, Hausham, Agatharied, and headed toward Miesbach. For the last time, and seated on rougher springs than you had been used to in your "state carriages," you were driven through your beloved valley. In my imagined scenario I was already awaiting your arrival at the prison courtyard in Miesbach. There the POW guards, enraged beyond any words by the horrors of the liberated concentration camps they had just seen, formed a double line of vengeance, anticipating your arrival, and when you got there they beat you so severely from both sides of the gauntlet and for a distance of about seventy feet that later that night you tried to slit your throat with some sort of totally inadequate implement that had been left by an oversight in your cell. Or did this pathetic attempt of yours to evade responsibility happen only on the next day, in the truck that took you to the main POW collecting point at Berchtesgaden? In my mind's eye I observe you from the far end of the gauntlet. I'm always standing there. I see you rolling your eyes in terror as you pass between the rows of soldiers. In a moment you are to experience serious physical pain for the first time in your life. Now, as a kick propels you into the gauntlet, you receive the first blows of their fists, the gouging of their elbows, the pistonlike punches in your kidneys. The soldiers let you stagger forward, and I have to smother my uprush of pity, as I always do, by recalling images from the concentration camps—or that photograph in which a laughing German soldier with a kick of his army boot "helps" an old Jew in Cracow onto a wagon headed for Plaszow or Auschwitz. It is then, always, that I grant you the pain you deserve, your humiliation, your staggering and stumbling, your being jerked to your feet again and again, the blood running from your nose, mouth, and ears. Someone who witnessed your arrival in Berchtesgaden wrote, "They brought in Dr. Frank. He looked as if he had been beaten to a bloody pulp."

You lie in your hospital bed; you look terrible. Once again you have made an attempt on your life; you have slashed your left arm open, this time with a better implement. With your right hand you write: "Since my arrest on May 4, 1945, I have lost all courage to go on living, and see the future as black and threatening." Boy, how right you were; how amazingly correct your diagnosis. Who is it who enters your heart and mind at this point? Your beloved God, the German God of your youth, for He will forgive everything, whatever it is you might say to him now in your immortal verses:

"O Lord! / Now we are alone together, / Only you and I! / Thus it was when I was born, / So it is now that I depart! / Admit me now to Your Heavenly home, / Oh, I beseech you, hear my prayer! / I bring but woe and shame, / And return now to Your heights! / My soul trembles within. / It yearns for You. / It knows I am in torment, / And broken through and through. [*Well, I wonder if that renders your trial superfluous?*] / My play is done, / I'm bound for home. [*This little two-line verse hung in every German home after 1945. With it, millions of murders were quickly reduced to the level of a stage play.*] / I relinquish now my role / Of happy earthly toll. [*That's a ridiculous change in meter. Stop it.*] / The one you choose me to play, / To speak and learn and say, / My strength has reached its borders, / I have carried out my orders. [*It's time again to congratulate you. Those lines have become your most famous ones. They have guaranteed success a million times over: "I acted only on orders." You are not always quoted verbatim, to be sure, probably because of your difficult meter. But no matter: since 1945, four republics have been founded on these two lines of yours— Germany, West and East, reunited Germany, and Austria.*] / Bestowed with all honor once craved, / I yearn now alone for my grave. / O Lord! / Your earth is a single wound. / But to blessèd health I'm now bound. / Heavy toil, heavy tasks forgone, / And all mercy and grace forsworn. [*Father, your rhyme scheme there is infernal; it won't do—even logically it makes no sense. Why not? Because it can hardly be said that we marched through Poland like a procession of Carmelite monks, seeking grace and mercy. You simply must be more realistic.*] / Our myriad gain / Is but torment and pain— / Only torment and pain."

The village populace of Neuhaus continued to greet "Frau Minister" most subserviently right up to the middle of May—although there was a slight tendency toward a modification of behavior, and certain signs of negligence and other lapses were not to be overlooked. But the whole thing changed in a flash after the capitulation and its painful consequences for the Frank family. It was as if we, the Franks, had never been anything better than what we were now reduced to. They just left us in the dust and began to orient themselves toward the new people in power. What a lack of character, wouldn't you say, Father? Or could it be that your beloved Bavarians lacked character earlier, during the days of Hitler, and were now bona fide human beings again?

The only exception around was Farmer Asenjürgl. He still sat there in his undemocratic way, straight as a ramrod, and shouted down greetings from his manure cart—"Good day, Frau Minister." He kept it up to the time of his death. That remained our sole consolation. Things were no longer easy, seeing as how the Polish workers you used to ship us in installments absolutely refused to obey Mother any longer. They wanted to go home instead. Imagine.

You were gone; the village was still there; the Americans settled in, couldn't be budged; the Catholic Church still couldn't make up its mind. Neither a German government nor a Bavarian government was yet in sight, one that could be counted on to cover up any and all crimes in whatever way it could. It was a dangerous time for the Franks, Father. I grew skinnier and skinnier: little me, still on the lookout for Netty's golden-yellow dumpling soup, and full of tuberculosis; the golden-haired son of three fathers who used to play his games with a full tummy, a satisfied lad, never far from the Cracow ghetto or from the Plaszow concentration camp. Jesus, Father, we had no difficulty seeing ourselves as the victims now. And that gave the Franks a little boost. Our bad conscience was quickly assuaged by personal suffering. Mother would put a little note into my hand which said that we, the Franks, actually had nothing more to eat, and I would be sent begging from house to house. It was so embarrassing for me without a nursemaid, without any servant at all. When I got home, the only thing I had to show for it was half a loaf of bread, a gift of charity. I have completely forgotten who gave it to me. I've suppressed the very memory.

Things began to change in our favor when the Catholic Church again took hold in Bavaria. Cardinal Faulhaber sent his chauffeur with a twelve-cylinder ecclesiastical buggy over to Neuhaus. (In the meantime we had had to move into a somewhat less magnificent house.) The chauffeur drove up, as confident as if the Franks were still members of the league of big shots. And the vast maw of the Catholic Church coughed up delicacies compared to which the American Care packages were little more than pathetic alms. The sign of God was understood in Neuhaus. People began to greet us again; not only that, we were elevated, we were invited to visit the Cardinal in his Munich palace. How painfully I was reminded of those cornucopia years in Poland when a lovely dumpling soup appeared in Faulhaber's dining room, a broth of the same perfect golden-yellow color with fresh chives in it. Had Netty, even in her role as a cook, converted from the Franks to the Cardinal, following the political trends of the day? In my memory I still see an abundance of gilding and fat cherubs' legs. I looked around to see if I couldn't discover Johann, too, our servant from Cracow, or perhaps my beloved Lydia, who was good enough not to wish to wreak vengeance on me for the fate of all those Polish children who had lost their lives through your good offices. No, the only thing that was there from the past was Netty's dumpling soup—and a kindly old man who, as he slurped his spoonfuls, extolled your good works, your battles, and your faith and piety. Mother sighed deeply, at the same time taking a good look around to assess the value of all those furnishings. The Cardinal, as Mother said on our way home, knew what was what.

You claimed to have maintained at least casual contact with Faulhaber even during your Nazi heyday. But it ended up being of no use to you at all. Your appeal for papal clemency fell through, whereupon you threatened at Nuremberg to "blow the whistle."

But you didn't do it. What had you planned on blabbing? The secret agreements between the Nazis and the Church? Well, it's good you didn't try that; it wouldn't have fit in too well with your pretense of piety. Furthermore, Faulhaber would certainly never have served me Netty's lovely dumpling soup again after a low blow like that.

Unfortunately Faulhaber died.

His successor didn't wish to serve us any more dumpling soup.

With the Cardinal's death Mother's gentle reproach against him died, too. She used to insist while he was still alive that he be more energetic in supporting your escape to South America (a place so friendly to the Nazis), which Bishop Hudal in Rome had offered to arrange for you.

According to rumors in the family, everything had been prepared for you. Why didn't you go, Father? I'll get the story behind that someday. Meanwhile, my bet is that whatever it was, no honorable motives kept you where you were.

It's strange how certain colors stick in my memory, Father. It's still so vivid, that intense dark green which still passes slowly before my eyes today, as it did at that fateful moment. It was 1945. You had already been arrested when the American soldier came to the Schoberhof and ordered Mother to give him the keys to the Horch—or was it the Maybach? Mother started to bewail the loss of her last status symbol, recalling the elegant days of "Tell your Mother her car is waiting." Then she put on that stubborn and determined pout of hers—the one that frightened more people than just you. The car was still in our garage. The soldier was big and tall, a bit of a nebbish; I was still small. I followed him; he was very serious and probably didn't feel all that sure of himself. He opened both garage doors and I went in after him—or, no, I stayed in the doorway and watched. He got in the car and started up the motor, which if you remember purred so gently that one could hardly hear it. Then, as slowly as a great ship, it emerged and seemed endlessly to glide past me, that wonderful, dark, almost black-green color. That glorious car was one more of the many things you had sold out for. There I stood, between the corner post of the garage and this green apparition, sobbing over the fact that finally everything was now gone: those cozy car blankets, exciting visits to the ghetto, hand kisses for the ladies. I was in a rage.

I grew up dripping from the bucketfuls of pity that were constantly being poured over me, as if I were the one who had been hanged. It was probably why Mother was the only one of us who acted strange and creepy when she came to the children's home in Schäftlarn on October 18 and cheerfully suggested we go out for a walk. It was two nights after your death by hanging. She hugged me unnaturally hard, something I never liked, and said to me: "Your father is gone. He is no longer alive. He is dead." I had been anticipating this visit for quite some time; I could tell from our farewell session at Nuremberg that quite soon you would be shuffling off your mortal coil. So I just clammed up. Mother grew silent, too, and just looked down at me. "Look at me," she said. "I'm not even dressed in mourning, because he died happy. He even wanted to die. You can see that I'm not crying, either. *Why aren't you crying?*" Her words came out in a confused and offended tone of voice. And they were threatening.

Father, there is such a thing as a compulsive expectation that insists we must adhere to certain conventional forms of emotional behavior. If the father must die, the child must cry. Filial piety is never permitted to be consumed in the fires, not even in the fiery furnaces filled with murder victims. I was unable to appreciate that. Mother did not try to describe to me the reasons for your happy death. She couldn't say, for example: "Listen to me, my boy, it was right and just for your father to have been hanged, and why that should be is something I'm going to tell you about here on this bench, where we'll have a pretty view of the Schäftlarn Monastery. Everything began with the fact that your father had all it took to become a really terrific human being, but he didn't want to, because it was probably too demanding, it would take too much energy. And so he used those terrific gifts instead to further his career, without any concern for morals or ethics. And I? I supported him in that. I even urged him on, now and again. . . ."

Of course nothing like that was said. I was just supposed to cry. But the hell I would. I didn't give a damn. Instead, I was treated to an extra-special sausage sandwich, a kind of consolation prize, at the children's home.

Ever since that time there was a rift between Mother and me.

After your death you were often with us. But conjuring up your spirit from the great beyond came to be a little more difficult after Uncle Julius threw himself under a train on the Munich-Holzkirchen line. That was because our medium was Aunt Martel, his wife. And so, whenever we sat at the round table with our hands stretched out, our fingers touching, forming a big circle, and Aunt Martel began her spirit-conjuring moans, and Mother would cry, "Hans, is it you?," it always turned out—as we could tell from the weak knocks on the table spelling out his name—that it was only Uncle Julius again. Mother would then fall asleep, disturbing the séance with her loud snoring, but still leaving her hand in the circle, until her violent snores drove Uncle Julius away.

Even when the two of you were alive, you and Uncle Julius didn't like each other. As far as Mother was concerned, he was nothing more than a poor old brother-in-law, and the only interesting trait about him was his dueling scars. While he was still alive and you were dead, he would perhaps sit there quietly studying his local train schedules. At that time our telepathic communication with you was still splendid. You appeared regularly to your loved ones after our coffee and pastries. You consoled us by telling us how happy you were in the other life, that you had now gotten over the injustice of your death, that we would soon be rich again, and that the Bavarian government would soon give us back the Schoberhof and the little summer house on the Ammersee and your Minister's pension. My eagerly interjected question "And the Horch, too?" was strangled with a hiss by Aunt Martel—whereupon you would vanish. Aunt Martel could mediate any of our claims for pensions, but she couldn't get back any automobiles for me.

What annoyed Mother and me was your lack of poetic imagination. We looked with envy upon Uncle Julius, who appeared one day in Munich to his widow (after she had begged for a special sign of his presence in the other world, kneeling for two hours at the grave of Father Rupert Mayer). To be sure, he appeared as a butterfly, but at least he appeared. Aunt Martel had sat down on a bench in the English Garden—and on gossamer wings Uncle Julius came fluttering to her. What a reunion that was, the way he fluttered around her, a little kiss here, a little kiss there; and then, exhausted from his ardent emotions and joy at seeing her again, he settled down on her black handbag.

How I needed you—how I could have used you even as a cabbage moth. With eyes full of hope and longing, I would gawk at dogs, cats, cows; and even when we used to go fishing without a license in the Schliersee I would gape at the fish and they would gape back at me, like you in your official photos. But they were not you. Nor were you the dachshund that belonged to an old lady in Neuhaus, whose name I can't remember any longer. She lived up on the Dürnbachstrasse, had peach trees in her garden, and owned Waldi, or some name like that. Anyhow, for weeks I believed that he was you. "Come here, Waldi. Daddy, is it you?" I lay on my stomach in that little old lady's garden, trying hard to make contact with you—I had a few questions I wanted to ask. But that stupid dachshund was not you in your new shape. And so one day I took about fifty firecrackers, tied them together, and blew you sky high. It ripped your stomach wide open and you howled for God to take mercy, but the howls grew fainter and fainter as I ran away.

And to think that your life in the great beyond had had such an auspicious beginning. On the night of your death a miraculous event occurred. It revealed that even a criminal who had returned to the bosom of the Church can be endowed with truly magical powers. Mother was sitting with her elite little group of death-watchers in the kitchen of the small apartment that had been assigned to us as a replacement for our old GG quarters. Everyone knew that Mother would be the Widow Frank in a few hours; and I was tensely awaiting the feeling of becoming a semi-orphan that night, the fifteenth to the sixteenth of October, 1946. Mother had taken me to stay at a children's home; the grown-ups wanted to celebrate this death among themselves. They say that Aunt Martel suddenly became very excited and that, lo and behold, shortly after 1:00 a.m. (she swore for the rest of her life it was true), a chair that had stood there without moving all at once began to stir. First you invisibly tipped it backward and then again forward and finally you pushed it under the table, as if you had just arisen from the Feast of Life. After I heard that story, I saw you in my mind standing there with a bloody face, the severed rope still around your neck, your eyes closed. They said you wanted to draw our attention to you with all that shifting of the chair. What is it you wanted to say to Mother, to Aunt Martel, to all the others seated there in a group? That there was no God where you now were? That all your Catholic drivel during your time in prison had been in vain? Tell me, do you know anything at all about what was going on?

There seems to have been something going on that night you shuffled off. "Now Hans has suffered through it, the worst has passed, Brigitte," said Aunt Martel, after you had let go of the chair again. And when they later compared the time of that event with the newspaper report, it confirmed that this chair-tipping episode had happened at the very moment when the trapdoor under your feet was sprung. The joy about those two simultaneous events rendered any mourning over your death superfluous.

Well, maybe you had nothing to do with all of that, and Aunt

Martel was just up to one of her clever tricks. And by the way, that spooky chair in question was not one of those big, heavy ones you had stolen, but just a poor frail object, like one of those ordinary people have in their kitchens. It was already there in our new little apartment; we had not been prepared to bring along any of the things from the Schoberhof we'd swiped during our glory years.

I've never been able to read that last book of yours more than a page at a time, the one you wrote in prison. It's not because of Mother's opinion, either. (She had crossed out passages in it, complaining about "this constant yammering about Adolf Hitler and God and the little baby Jesus and about what a poor little sinner he [*you, not Jesus*] was—that really gets on my nerves.") No, it's because all I find in it is one endless passage after another, insufferable in their disgusting vanity. By the time you began to write all this stuff down in your Nuremberg cell, you had already seen the films of Auschwitz and Treblinka in the courtroom; you had already heard the testimony of a concentration camp commandant [at Auschwitz] like Höss; everything was familiar to you. In fact, you had long since known all about the atrocities in the concentration camps, even though you firmly denied it before the Tribunal. Despite all this, there wasn't the slightest hint of that frankness and honesty which I have tried, all my life, to discover in you. No, again it was not there; it was nowhere to be found in that last book of yours, *Face to Face with the Gallows*, not even in the final sentences of your so-called memoirs.

It is in this book that you finally pull out all the stops. You pile one outrageous and sentimental bit of crap on top of another. It's enough to make a pig puke. "Farewell, farewell forever, you people of Poland and you land of Poland! God be with you and grant you happiness!" Up to this passage, your saccharine composer-friend Richard Strauss, his mouth dripping with musical honey, would have been just the perfect one to furnish the accompaniment. But the sentences that follow were intended more to whet the appetites of the *Heimatvertriebenen*, the associations of exiles from the East, and to make them swallow your nonsense hook, line, and sinker— and then adapt it as the preamble to their constitution when they formulate their vengeful plans for the future: "But now," you mutter to your Polish friends, "now you have committed horrible sins in your thirst for revenge against our people. Silesia, Pomerania, and Danzig have been German for a thousand years. You can never own them. The horrible mass murders you have committed against our people will come back to punish you one day, just as Hitler has been punished. Return to goodness before it is too late! That is what I pray for you."

Father, these stubborn and unrepentant Poles simply did not want to listen to you until now; and even the Lord God, into whose ears you whispered your prayers about the lost territories of the East, is just as stubborn. Is God, contrary to the expectations set down in your private diary, not a German after all? Maybe not even so much as a Pomeranian?

One thing is certain for sure: the Lord God did indeed hold his hand of blessing over all the former GG boys. They, at least, didn't leave us in the lurch after the war. To be sure, they were not too eager to go out walking with Mother in public in Munich, but all of them were certainly faithful about buying copies of your gallows book. That was only good manners. Those memoirs of yours, written in your cell at Nuremberg, have brought in well over two hundred thousand D-marks for us. And that meant the resurrection of the Frank family. Mother managed to evade paying a penny of tax. Your very own wife even published the book herself, with her own "Brigitte Frank Publishing Company," after the original publisher didn't prove successful enough with it to satisfy her. Yes, you see, you always underestimated her. She was one self-assured businesswoman, that woman who hooked you all those many years ago.

This manuscript, written in your cozy Nuremberg cell, was emblazoned with a lofty and ringing dedication—in borrowed words, of course. I didn't have to search long for the identity of that poet out of whose ass you retrieved those words. Of course, I lack your solid, humanistic education, that schooling from which so many bloodthirsty future murderers came. However, I can appreciate that people like you would imagine at the end of their criminal careers that they would be understood only by the loftiest and most sublime of poets. It was Goethe, of course. You took your dedication from the poem "To Werther" in his *Trilogie der Leidenschaft*. That wicked old conformist and collaborator had the whole thing perfectly set out for you; and, as you well knew, he could write much better verse than you: "[*Wer*] *verstrickt in solche Qualen, halbverschuldet,* / *Gab ihm sein Gott zu sagen, was er duldet*" ("To him entrapped in such torments and partial guilt / His God has given voice to utter what he must endure").

It must be pointed out, however, that in Goethe's original the words are "May a god give," not "His God has given." But by that time you had been playing the role of the pious Catholic for quite some time and perhaps had been practicing night after night in your cell with Father O'Connor the moment when you were going to utter your "Jesus, have mercy on my soul." You would stand on the bed, O'Connor would pretend to be the hangman and would count out "One, two, three"—and you would jump off the bed and shout out, "Jesus have mercy on my soul!"

"Once more, Frank. Now put the towel over your face—that's the hangman's hood. Straighten your neck more. Remember, your head is going to be snapped backward. . . . Arms behind you—for God's sake, Frank, they're tied behind your back! . . . Now don't bend your knees. . . . One, two, three—jump!" "Jesus, have mer—" "You began too late, Frank. The rope is only ninety-five centimeters long, so please start saying that a little earlier. Otherwise, you're going to swallow half the words."

Well, you finally got it right. The thing that annoys me most about your Goethe dedication are the words about "him . . . in *partial* guilt." I just can't swallow that. What was wrong with you? Did you suffer brain damage somewhere along the line? Did Hess and Himmler attack you one evening in Munich on the corner of Schellingstrasse and Barerstrasse and then beat you up so severely that you were forced to join their cause? Or did Hitler stroke the nape of your neck until you began to purr like a good Nazi kitty-kat? *Partial guilt!* One way or another, you managed to put up with yourself. None of those other Nazi rats would have stopped you from finishing yourself off. No, as always, you got that quotation completely wrong—not for the fun of it, but for the sake of your salvation, and also mine.

Old Comrades

Mother set about introducing your manuscript to the German nation. She did it with the same boundless energy with which all her life long she had scooped up furs and corselets, her doll collection and her jewelry, Polish workers and geese. How heartrendingly she wept that day in 1951 as she leaned against the wall of the Ecclesiastical Library in Munich. It was on that day that Heaven, always a little fascistically oriented, arranged for her— O Jesus, have mercy!—to have access to the registers where the addresses of all Catholic priests in what was left of Germany were listed. Mother wept, and at that moment I loved her.

The priests were followed by Evangelical pastors, by professors and legislators, by mayors and industrialists, by merchants and bankers. I grew up surrounded by a sea of the most beautiful letters in response to her entreaties, the most glorious words and phrases exemplifying the way a nation could deceive itself, a nation again (or still) under the leadership of people like you—you lachrymose supplicant for divine mercy, you cliché-mongering windbag. That's what you were, right up to the end of your life. The play was done, they all went home. And what did they do there? With no memory, no regrets, no real human emotions, they simply went back to work. Mother sent letters of solicitation throughout the country that was basking in the sunshine of its economic miracle. She was determined to sell your book.

Old comrades from the glorious days of the GG reacted spontaneously. One of the faithful wrote to Mother: "Considering the burden of my past, we didn't know whether it would be good for you if we got in touch or not. But now times seem to have changed so much that there is really nothing for you to worry about in this regard." He wrote that in 1952, the year in which it became possible for me, because of who you had been, to be such a successful hitchhiker. And I can tell you, the man was right.

Mother wasn't quite fast enough in getting into contact with the leading banker at whose bank you had once been in a position to make such impressive deposits back in those early years. He had already had his "attention called to the book by a friendly source," and had already "given it a home" in his library. And as if that weren't enough, he continues: "Incidentally, I have already told numerous acquaintances about this work." Thank you, sir— that led to further sales and profit for us.

Frankly, Father, Mother's promotional letters for your book were so good that they deserved a much better piece of writing than the one you came up with. Your buddies from Cracow days let fall many a melancholy comment. Heinz H. J. wrote: "I am put in mind so often and with such poignant recollections of my own activities in Cracow. They were so rich in artistic experience and so filled with success. And it is in great part thanks to your husband's enthusiasm for cultural expression, his ever-ready intervention on behalf of the Philharmonic, and his great connoisseurship in the arts of Poland." That figures. Profoundly absorbed as we Germans were in our artistic enjoyment, we simply had no time to pay attention to what was really going on there—all the yellow stars on those sleeves, the so-called Extraordinary Peace-Keeping Operation of annihilation, the daily firing squads obliterating the Poles.

Erich L. praises you in a 1952 letter to Mother: "Your most

worthy and honorable husband was a great European in the truest sense of the word!" Well, well. Did your moronic prattle somehow slip unharmed past the terms of surrender in 1945 and then spread victoriously over the map of the new Federal Republic? Or did Herr L. call you a European because you, a German, tyrannized over another European country?

Old G., one of the former directors of the railroad system, which so boldly administered the endless transport of Jews to the death camps, was also delighted by your gallows book. He tells us in 1953 about his own terrible fate, a fate that overshadows that of any Jew: "After having waited for three years, I was called back again by my former management in 1948 and finally landed the directorship of the Federal Railroad System. For over half a year now, having retired at the age of 67, I discover that my life now suits me very well after an eventful career." There you have the end product of our great German past: "an eventful career." Do you see the Beautiful Madonna retching? I do.

The esteemed chief inspector of a nearby district court, Herr Z., writes in 1953: "Perhaps there will be an opportunity for the former GG'ers to get together sometime, especially after so many other reunions of old-timers have taken place by now." Father, whenever two or more GG'ers are gathered together in your name, would your spirit dwell among them?

Nor does Dr. D.V. (LL.D.) attempt for a second to conceal his strong emotions in writing to Mother that same year: "In grateful recollection of those professionally rewarding years which I was privileged to spend at the Ost Institut in Cracow, I ordered a copy of the book as early as last November." And there is a Herr H.G. who "does not regret in the least my own activities in the GG, in both my professional and personal life." And here is yet another lovely sentence with which an old GG'er prefaces an address list of potential book customers for Mother: "First and foremost, I direct you to the gentlemen in the Federal Ministry of Food and Agriculture."

A general reports to Mother: "How often the old times in Cracow are the subject of our conversation whenever two of us sit down together or in a group of good friends from those days."

Dr. F. writes nostalgically: "Your lines seemed to me to be a greeting from a distant world." Yes, Father, those who were now busy building Germany's future all still clung to Germany's glorious past.

It was symptomatic of the general tenor of the times when later, sometime after your death, the Alfred Beck publishing house praised the first edition of your memoirs, *Face to Face with the Gallows*, in personally addressed promotional letters to German jurists with the words: "The author of this unique document, created under remarkable circumstances, was, like you, also a legal scholar and practitioner."

You're smiling? Me too. There was only one lone target of this direct-mail campaign who reacted in a democratic way, one person who stood up and objected to that comparison: Dr. Erich List, whose full name I am pleased to record here, wrote in 1952: "I, and I hope I am not alone, totally reject the insinuation that I am 'a legal scholar and practitioner of the law' like Frank. I should never wish to lay claim to the questionable honor of having been someone like that. . . . What we must prevent here is yet another attempt to smother our convictions about justice and morality which have so painfully and at such great cost been reborn from the chaos. . . . The representatives of legal organizations must stand up as one and in a single voice protest this."

They didn't, Dr. List, and they don't now. I have countless letters, each outdoing the last in unctuous enthusiasm about the nostalgic garbage produced by my father. No, today's legal profession in this country is not much to write home about. Father, here's one instance in which we see eye to eye: our legal minds still don't give a good goddamn about whether they ought to fiddle around and prop up our democracy or whether to work toward its collapse. The most important thing is, keep the language sufficiently clean, logical, and abstract—just as you so memorably outlined in those splendid points you made at that ministers' meeting in Munich.

Then I discovered that you must have had a real connection with the Lord God. Mother received a letter dated September 28, 1953, from the Monastery of Metten, in which the monks wrote: "We shall be reading the book at table in the monastery. His Holiness the Abbot will doubtless be ordering a copy." Jesus, have mercy! What a career! Up above, they were arranging for forgiveness for you—forgiveness for the old anti-Semite, liar, cheat, and murderer. Because the Catholics didn't find anything to have to forgive you for, you, my dear Father, got on the best-seller list at the abbeys.

We were very proud of you—although Mother figured out right away how much more profitable it would have been if every brother had his own copy of your book to read in the privacy of his cell.

As far as the German farming community and its possible interest in your book were concerned, a certain Herr L. had to put us off with a promise for the following winter: "The farm owners I approached in connection with your concern, all of them old party members, were indeed interested, but in the summer they have no time for reading."

On the other hand, a large hardware factory in the Palatinate made an outrageous demand. Can you imagine, they wanted to have a copy sent for their approval so that they might "make up our minds about a possible purchase"? Mother gave it a try anyhow, but she never heard anything from them again. I'm so sorry, especially for you.

Sometimes Mother got a bit sidetracked. The big Aktien Brewery in Mainz refused to order copies of *Face to Face with the Gallows* because, as a managing director or perhaps even the chairman of the board explained, "copies of the book have already been ordered for me and for my firm, and they have now arrived."

On the other hand, Senator K.'s excuse was pretty thin: "With my failing eyesight, I must unfortunately deny myself the pleasure of reading such a long book." Mother commented that he should have taken a leaf from the monks' book in Metten and had the thing read to him at table. Her promotional letter was ingeniously worded, for even on those occasions when the book was not purchased a little contribution of money was usually sent anyhow. And when that didn't happen, she suggested another solution. She had already supplied her letter with a brief reference to her starving little boy, who, already approaching fifteen, was nevertheless depicted as a four-year-old. She told them in what "desperate economic straits" we were. The upshot was that we were flooded with donations of goods. I drowned in cotton underwear for little boys, tiny coats, wee shoes, all of which Mother took to charity thrift shops, where she made a slight profit.

And you had your own successes with your readership. Dr. H.S.F. (M.D.): "On the basis of this book, my earlier image of your husband's character had to be revised from the ground up, and much in his favor." Do you suppose the good doctor might have told his patients something like the following: "You have lung cancer, terminal case, but there's just enough time left for you to get a copy of *Face to Face with the Gallows*. You can order it quickly from the Brigitte Frank Publishing Company, Neuhaus am Schliersee, Dürnbachstrasse. Next patient, please." At least that's the way Mother and I pictured it, and then we enjoyed a good laugh together. Orders came in from the Loden-Frey Company in Munich; and a certain Herr E., the assistant head of some government department, even sent an inspired idea to us from a trip to France, suggesting "how a special promotion of this work might be made possible." Mother thought, "Probably a compulsory purchase plan for the officials in his office—what else?" It didn't work out,

though. Nevertheless, she was soon jubilant over the devoted loy-
alty of the SS, when she received an order for the book from a
staff musician of the Waffen SS who "at one time had been a
guest of Dr. Frank at the castle and [has] fond memories of this
visit." I wonder if you might have noticed him at the time, Father?
I expect he was standing off to one side, concealed behind some
pillar or other, and thus unable to trumpet his SS protest. Even
a Supreme Court Justice found your book to be a source of great
satisfaction and sustenance to him. He wrote to Mother, with his
"most devoted regards," and asked her to send him a copy. For
a long time Mother puzzled over whether she had ever met the
man. I guessed he might have been one of those who used to
sneak me a chocolate candy (perhaps on one of those walks in
that little hedge of evergreens you had planted at the
Schoberhof) in the hope that his kindness would secure him an
appointment with you, a very private one, that could benefit him
in his future career.

Winifred Wagner helped out with her rich supply of acquaintances still faithful to the memory of Hitler. Incidentally, she found
in your book "the best character study of Hitler that I have ever
read." The lady doesn't seem to have read much. But naturally
she had been taken in by your shrewd lawyer's (or in this case,
author's) tricks, and she registered wide-eyed admiration for your
powers of recall and your amazing clearheadedness considering
your precarious situation in the Nuremberg Prison.

For a long time, much about you remained a puzzle to Mother.
On one occasion, she paced back and forth, then sat down again.
The strain of perplexity could be seen in her face as she tried to
recall what you had been up to and when. She muttered over and
over again, "Now, who can that have been?" Once, we received
a letter containing this sentence: "Herr von E. told me that he
had a close friend who is much better off now than he has been
in some time, and that this friend had expressed to him the desire
to learn how to get in touch with you, so that he could express

his gratitude for the assistance he had once received from your good husband."

Let me at least fantasize about it tonight, Father—about what that assistance you gave this man might have been. Do you suppose it's possible that in this letter, now thirty-three years old, I might discover what I have so long been searching for? A single good deed performed by you, a sign that in the fetid swamp of your life somewhere, somehow, sometime, a tiny flower blossomed. Time and again I have gone through the mountains of paper that I have accumulated about your life and Mother's, but I have never found anything of the sort. It can only be that someone has confused you here with Karl Hermann Frank, the one who was publicly hanged in Prague.

And even if it was you who helped this man, how big a deal could it have been? You probably just helped him out of some mess in connection with a smuggling operation. Perhaps on one of your quick trips through the ghetto you told your driver to stop the car when you saw this man standing at the curb in his SS uniform, sad and abandoned. It was probably because some Jewish girl he had forced into bed with false promises about saving her family's life had been ferreted out at the last minute by Krüger and dragged off to a concentration camp, and there the poor man stood now with a pair of bursting German blue-balls in front of her wrecked and empty house.

Mother shook her head once more, and then with her letter opener slit the next envelope that had arrived at our house, another missive from the emerging political reality of the Federal Republic. With delight she read greetings from Herr W. together with his urgent request to send order forms for copies of *The Gallows* (our shorthand title for your book) to the following unquestionably dyed-in-the-wool democratic gentlemen: "Assistant Chief S. of the Federal Ministry for Finance, Dr. von R. of the Federal Interior Office [*heavens above, Father—what would have happened if the Reich budget office had ever taken a close look at your GG? I can see you making the sign of the cross down there in your cauldron even now*], Dr. P., in the Federal Ministry for Food and Agriculture. . . ."

The Gallows must have taken Bonn by storm. Mother and I would often sit in front of the television set, watching the evening news and exchanging knowing glances whenever we caught a report of the latest deeds on the political scene. There you were again; we could recognize you, your phony language, your cowardly behavior. Such cozy family evenings those were for us, with you joining in once again, at least in spirit.

Mother couldn't get the image of Winifred Wagner out of her head. She had instantly grasped the importance of Bayreuth for the new party in power. It seemed that the differences between the old and the new regimes weren't all that great, and so she wanted to work out a little advertising campaign exploiting old Winifred's complimentary words about you—maybe something like this: "Winifred Wagner is another who appreciates what was good about the Third Reich. And if you want something that's even better, read this book. The memoirs of Reichsminister and Governor General Frank about a time which warmed the cockles of all our hearts. In fact, it even incinerated quite a few (though, of course, the actual number is still a matter of contention). Read Dr. Frank's *Face to Face with the Gallows*. He didn't deserve the gallows. But you deserve the pleasure of reading his book." Winifred approved the use of her name, but she underestimated its impact: "You must bear it clearly in mind that I am still one of the dishonored outcasts and pariahs, and that people consider my name to be a red flag and a terror in every sense."

In Mother's promotional endeavors on behalf of the book, she occasionally stumbled across heartrending stories of personal tragedy. Frau S.Z. wrote her that "we members of the former Government General are still the victims of fate." She was embroiled in a battle to get her husband's pension, but there were great difficulties, "since he had to leave his documents of employment in his desk drawer at the office in Lemberg [she means Lvov] when he fled the Russians on 7/19/44." I can see it now: Herr Z. packs up everything in a mad rush, tears down the stairs to his car with its full tank of gas for his getaway. Already he can hear the first shouts of the Russians: "Gimme *urri*, gimme vatch. Tick-tock, tick-tock." (The sound of that word *urri*, "wrist-watch," was synonymous with the word "Russian" for me as a child.) Herr Dr. Z., one of his strong hands clutching a treasure or two from Lemberg as he sits in the backseat of his car, slaps himself on the forehead with his other hand, for his powers of word association were unusually keen, like that of all Germans (e.g., Jews = scum = gas = soap). Something is sending him a signal. He slaps his forehead when he hears the words "tick-tock, tick-tock," and Dr. Z. then thinks of "dick-dock . . . dock . . . document . . . my documents—my documents of employment!" Immediately he begins to anguish over his postwar pension. He had trained himself to believe that his career in Poland could never be questioned or denied on legal grounds. Mother and I had a good laugh inventing that little scenario. We began to suspect that the war had been so obstinately prolonged only because the Germans hadn't completely finished getting all their "documents of employment" together.

We were also amused by the case of a Herr W.W., a man who probably never had any particular difficulties with his salary or pension. Instead, he had the upright conscience of a good German, someone for whom journalists were a horror but who was persuaded that you, Father, were a notable witness to history and worthy of being taken seriously: "Immersed as we are today in this flood of journalistic scheming and lying, every piece of authentic evidence [*your book!*] is important when it comes to accounting for the past and asking ourselves why our efforts were doomed to failure." Well, he probably found plenty of evidence for that in *The Gallows*. Hitler and Himmler . . . now there were the guilty parties. "The play is done, I'm going home" is something Herr W. could easily have said himself. But what puzzles me is

Czechs, Slovaks, or German concentration camp inmates. Instead he writes Mother: "May the Lord console you for all the tribulations you have suffered and be ever present to lend you His helping hand."

Father, there were days when the mailman brought so many letters from priests and priors, from Ursulines and God knows what other orders, that our house began to look like a warehouse for stockpiling indulgences. Mother and I could confidently look forward to life everlasting. Once and for all, a cozy corner in Heaven was reserved for us through the prayers of those who had formerly prayed for Hitler's welfare with their "Heil"'s—a pleasant little nook where Hitler himself might occasionally drop in with a new Monopoly set under his arm and challenge us to a game in that awful voice of his. (You'll be interested only in buying Cracow's Park Place and plastering it over with hotels.) If they were so concerned for you, you two-bit firecracker of a Nazi, that they let loose such a storm of intercession and prayers on your behalf, can you imagine what a full-scale, no-holds-barred tornado there must have been for your real super-murderer, Hitler? It must have been a veritable cyclone, roaring up from the folded hands and ardent throats of those sanctimonious supplicants.

The Provincial Secretary of the Munich Franciscans requested thirty to forty promotional brochures, together with order forms and prepayment slips for copies of your *Gallows*. (Between the lines of his letter you can almost see the cute twinkle in his eye.) "Pending the approval of my superiors," he wishes "to forward them at the earliest opportunity to our various monasteries in Bavaria—a request surely not likely to be denied." Wink, wink go his eyes. That dash of his was divinely inspired.

The Herr Provincial Secretary ends his letter with a formula that I had never seen before: "With Priestly Franciscan Greetings." I suppose that some phrase for ending letters had to be devised to replace the, alas, now forbidden "Heil Hitler."

Hand in glove with the Church, the German business world

was busy building up the Federal Republic in the spirit of your *Gallows*. There is probably not a company library in which your book did not find a home on its shelves. I grew up in an atmosphere of almost total admiration for your life. Mother no longer felt in the slightest burdened by your crimes. It would have pleased you to read again and again in the letters of those placing orders that the "feeling of comradeship of the old Cracowers" had remained intact in the Federal Republic. One man who had gotten a job with the German Research Council (which means that by now you have probably wangled your way into German research; congratulations, Father) poured out his foolish but honorable heart on the topic of his new position: "My work is very interesting, even if it is not as splendid and responsible a position as my former one, of course." What he meant is his job in Cracow, his job in that invaded and illegally occupied country, the country where people were shot to death every day, abducted to death camps every day, the country where orgies of tortures and the gassing of countless human beings took place every day. A "splendid and responsible" job. It makes me want to puke again.

I've been sitting here nearly all my life and I simply cannot understand any of it. I cannot comprehend you or people like you. I look at us Germans and I am frightened. I see letters that they wrote in your spirit, and I think that we have already gotten back as far as the letter C again in our alphabet of heinous acts. There are two people inside each German: One of them is well-behaved, hardworking, a solid citizen. That is the official version of the respectable German. But beneath it, behind it, as if made up of negative ions, there are the authentic Germans, a people of murderers. And the murderers are growing in number, day by day. I see every German being followed by his own negative shadow. The official German carries his attaché case, is beautifully dressed, speaks English and French, goes to the opera and to soccer matches. The other one has a face like yours in your cauldron, is full of an increasing rage at a world that will not acknowledge him for love

or money, and he is flirting more and more with the idea of putting
on the butcher's apron again, delights again in your phrases about
"mincemeat" and "vermin." *Ach*, he says to himself, if only I could
let loose again against all this vermin crawling around. Yes indeed,
I am frightened of these shadow-Germans born of your spirit. "A
greeting from better times," one could say. That's what Mother
wrote to people who she thought were of the proper orientation.
And they were happy to write back, like a Herr P. who spoke of
your execution as a "murder," which he "felt to be not only a
deeply tragic event but also a disgrace to our nation."

Sometimes Mother was capable of committing certain errors—
no, not as far as interpreting people's sympathies was concerned,
but errors in identity. For example, a certain company, Henschel
and Son, steadfastly denied ever having known the two of you and
refused to order even one or, because "and Son" was part of the
title, two copies. Someone in the company wrote: "I have shown
your letter to both Herr Dr. F. Henschel and Herr W. Henschel.
Neither gentleman has any recollection of you. I assume that you
must be confusing them with Herr X. Henschel, who was most
recently an attaché in Japan. . . ." "Yes, he must be the one!"
Mother probably exclaimed.

On repeated occasions Mother would flip back through her
recollections of the time when she was Lady of the Reich, and
remember who it was she happened to be standing next to, who
spoke a casual word to her, or who it was who walked past her
with a little nod and greeting. That happy (or unhappy) person's
life wasn't safe until he had purchased a copy of *Gallows* for his
bookcase. What a poetic symbol for the new Germany that book
was. The Federal Republic grew up, so to speak, in the shadow
of *The Gallows*, your secret best-seller, promoted so assiduously and
so successfully by your representative on earth, Mother. Who
wasn't a member of that chorus of jubilation? Oh, yes, there was
one, that famous historian. He must have really caught on to you
and your book. For once, Mother could afford a disdainful smile

after reading his letter to her: "It is no empty talk on my part when I tell you that at times I was shaken by the tragedy of your husband's entire path through life, right up to the moment of his death." But that could have pleased you; it means that you are not the guilty party, that the tragedy hovering over your entire life was what numbed and deadened your exercise of free will. Dame Tragedy, time for you to enter the picture.

If the purchasers of the book thought they had thereby ceased to be objects of the Frank family's merchandising zeal, they were quite mistaken. For as you know, Father, you had also written letters to your loved ones at home from your Nuremberg jail, each one of them more bombastic and oozing with more schmaltz than the last. So Mother now brought out your *Letters from Nuremberg*, at ten marks per copy. Once again she succeeded in producing a terrific promotional letter: "Dear Herr So-and-So, You were kind enough to have procured a copy of my husband's *Face to Face with the Gallows*. Since I was able to offer that book only on a private basis and unfortunately do not have at my disposal the addresses of additional potential purchasers [*Mother was right, Father. Germany was already drowning in copies of* The Gallows], I no longer have any income from sales. For that reason I am now compelled by my financial straits to issue in a little private printing the letters written by my husband while he was imprisoned at Nuremberg, along with a few personal reflections, and to offer it for sale to the select circle of those who own a copy of his book."

Mother was perfectly well aware of the idiotic pretentiousness of your letters, and so she did not emphasize their historic, let alone literary, value. Instead, she appealed to the economic plight which compelled her to ask for the ten-mark payment in advance of delivery. Not bad, eh?

Mother wrote to the printer in reference to layout and design: "I would think that the letters should be set so that each of them has a page to itself, in order to enhance the appearance of the text somewhat. That way the book would present a more attractive image, don't you think?" Business prospered. Mother wrote to an acquaintance: "If only I had more time. I'm at my typewriter every day at the crack of dawn." And not only she. All of them were together again, Aunt Else and Aunt Martel, Aunt Margot and Aunt Irene, the clique of good old girls who had once surrounded Her Ladyship, but were now sitting in her postwar circle trying to turn a little profit for themselves. But Mother did have her principles. Every one of the promotional letters had to be typed by hand, had to have a personal salutation—no mimeographs and no mass mailings. Once, in that chilly way she had of giving orders to her house servants during those "wonderful years," she instructed Aunt Irene to "press harder when you're typing so they can see the imprint in the paper and feel the indentations on the back."

It wasn't long before your *Letters* was holding its own all over Germany along with *The Gallows*.

Since that time, this country has been thrilling to your immortal, heroic sentences, such as: "Dear Brigitte, How are you?" Now there's an inspired opening for you. There you are in your well-heated cell, regressing to a state of childish behavior. In your next sentence you succeed in composing something that would make even Ignatius of Loyola envious of your genius, even though, to be honest, we couldn't make head or tail of it: "My thoughts are dwelling now in the tranquillity of religion and with the eternal verities of a worthy life." Damn it, if you had only written us what those verities were supposed to be. They're lacking in my life, I'll tell you. Maybe you could have helped me out. What is that, an "eternal verity of a worthy life"? Fidelity? Love? Forgiveness? Belief in God? And how does one think about fidelity, for instance, in the tranquillity of religion? Did you slowly spell the word out to yourself, first forward, then backward? Or did you babble something like this: "Well, then, I wasn't faithful to Lilly— Our Father—I wasn't faithful to Brigitte—Who art—I wasn't faithful to Gertrude—on Earth as it is in Heaven—I was really

faithful to myself—as I forgive my debtors—fidelity, let's see, isn't
that regret at missed opportunities?—as in Heaven like the debtors
upon Earth—only sows care about fidelity—fidelity, schmedel-
ity—the one true Church—community of the faithful without
regret. . . ."

If your babble didn't sound like that, let's hear from you.

In any case, these letters of yours were swallowed hook, line,
and sinker by the Germans. Then Mother had yet another ace up
her sleeve, *The Cabin Boy of Columbus*, a short novel that you wrote
up there in your castle. (There couldn't have been much going on
in your GG between 1939 and 1945.) Since you were the boss of
the whole shebang, there wasn't an editor in the land who could
prevent you from publishing that little piece of patriotic crap about
the boy before the mast. It seems he was the one who really
discovered America first. Because you thought your GG subjects
and your sycophants in the Reich were a mighty stupid lot as far
as education goes, you wrote in your preface: "The sympathetic
reader would do well to keep in mind the contemporaneous nature
of the plot in judging the style and content of my little work."
(For your artistic productions you always wheeled out your middle
initial, M., as in Michael: "By Hans M. Frank.")

Once I remember Mother enjoying a really hearty laugh. It was
on a New Year's Eve after the war. (Remember the last one you
celebrated at the castle, planning the future of your Reichsnebenland, which was to be lived side by side with your allies the
Russians?) Mother told me that in former years—when you still
had those elegant marble floors under your feet—the two of you
used to just toss your champagne glasses over your shoulders after
toasting each other at midnight, and they smashed to smithereens
on the marble. In 1959, for the first time since the end of the war,
she did it again: drank her champagne, tossed the glass . . . and
laughed. Wouldn't you just know it (kitsch never lets up), it was
her last toss. Three months later she was dead. I had managed to
get rid of her. She died quietly, perhaps even a little bit suicidally.

By this time, *Gallows, Letters*, and *Cabin Boy* were no longer selling. Germany had already been inundated with copies of your tear-jerkers. She died quietly in her hospital bed. Unlike you, she didn't leave behind any memorable final words. Nor did she indulge herself in any obsequious gratitude for the kind treatment she had been shown in the hospital.

The End
of an Innocence

Before I let you die, I have one more meeting with you—in Nuremberg, at the Palace of Justice. Come on in, Father. I've been sitting here for decades waiting for you. I'm seated between His Lordship Judge Lawrence and His Honor United States Judge Biddle. Ever since I was a child I have imagined myself seated there, not next to you in the dock. You're thinner; it makes you look good. Dark glasses protect your sensitive eyes. I interpret them naturally as both something ambiguous and something mythically symbolic. Whoever has beheld the filth that he himself has brought about during his lifetime is doomed to suffer from failing eyesight. Your left hand is still twitching from your bungled attempt at slashing your wrist. On the other hand, your throat wound has healed splendidly.

Actually, you've been sitting here day after day, for more than four months, and today, April 18, 1946, is meant to be your and my day of honor. Year after year I've been giving you a chance to own up to your crimes as a man of law and justice (as you liked to call yourself), a chance today to finally stop that foolish torrent of lies. You have nothing more to lose, only me. But you have much to gain. No, not your life; your counsel for the defense, Dr. Seidl, was quite right—he told me decades later that he never entertained any hope at all for those who were implicated in

activities in occupied countries. But you do have one chance now
to point the way, to show the Germans how they might be able
to live with their guilt. It would be a labor of bereavement and
contrition, so to speak—and it would be performed first by Dr.
Hans Frank.

Let's get down to it. Seidl tried in vain to convince the Tribunal
to hear the witnesses first, and then you. But the court wanted
to hear the accused first. I'm frightened. I'm afraid that Seidl will
try tactfully to develop his case, showing how you lived above all
for culture and the arts in Poland: how you founded a great
philharmonic orchestra with only Polish musicians, and also a
Chopin Museum, for which you bought up the remaining memorabilia throughout (occupied) Europe; how obediently you jumped
into the lap of Prince Bishop Saphieha every day; how you had
plastered the walls of the Czestochowa and Drubski monasteries
with notices announcing that you yourself would protect these
holy places; that, all in all, you were truly a blessing for Poles and
Jews, and that Hitler had sent you to Cracow by mistake. And
that's exactly the way it went. But no one is impressed by the
lethargic dialogue you and Seidl are carrying on together, neither
His Lordship next to me nor your co-defendants. I can even see
a smirk on Göring's face. Father, I beseech you, shout out the
truth. Today is Holy Thursday. You can still save your and others'
immortal souls. Dr. Seidl is asking you: "What part did you play
in the events in Poland beginning in 1939?"

I lean forward. I'm afraid that you're now going to say something
like: "Well, I played a big part in the reopening of the Polish-
speaking High School of the Arts in October 1944." But I couldn't
have been more mistaken. You're sitting there, your arms stretched
forward, grasping the railing of the witness stand. You pause for
one second, look up at me and the presiding British judge, then
at Seidl, and say, just a trifle too loud for my sensitive ears: "I
bear the responsibility. Ever since April 30, 1945, when Hitler
ended his life, I have been determined to reveal my responsibility

to the world as clearly as possible. I did not destroy the forty-two volumes of diaries that bear witness to these events and my part in them; instead, of my own free will, I voluntarily handed them over to the American officers who arrested me." Overjoyed, I slap His Lordship's thigh under the table. Putting two fingers of my other hand in my mouth, I give an enthusiastic whistle. (The GIs brought with them over the big pond that way of whistling.) Father, you're doing it! How will you continue? My eyes are glued to Seidl's lips. Go on, Seidl, ask him about his guilt. And Seidl does: "Witness, are you conscious of any guilt in having committed crimes against the rights of nations or against human rights?"

Small as I still am, I climb up on the judges' bench and lean way over forward so as not to miss hearing every word of your confession, so far forward that my rear end is sticking in His Lordship's face. And what is it you're saying now, you goddamned son of a bitch, you miserable legal maneuverer and manipulator? In an instant you've lost all courage to speak the truth. You say nothing. His Lordship Judge Lawrence releases you from your embarrassment. He says: "That is a question which the court has to decide." My God, Father, what a jerk you are. I fall back into my seat; tears trickle down my (needless to say, entrancing) child's face. So he still is the same father I have known from the beginning, the man who turned his heart into a spider's nest for murderers. Dr. Seidl: "Then I shall pass over the question." But *I* shall not pass over the question. With all the strength at my soul's command I shall try to straighten you up again. Hey, man, it's Holy Thursday, it's the day before Jesus was nailed to the Cross—Jesus, remember? The one that you and Mother and Himmler and Goebbels and my second father, Lasch, quoted all the time, the guy from the Holy Trinity whom they tried to claim for themselves?

Imitate Him. And don't forget me. I'm seven years old. I want to live, longer than the Jews, longer than the Poles, longer than the Ukrainians and the refugees—longer than you. Dr. Seidl: "Witness, what do you have to say regarding the accusations that have been brought against you in the indictment?" It's your second chance now. But I already give up and turn off—even before I hear your answer. It's too late. I know that once you've climbed aboard that choo-choo train of yours and gotten up a head of steam and begun to ingratiate yourself, the only thing that could ever straighten you out again is a sharp blast from Mother's whistle. But Mother isn't here, and so you say: "To these accusations my only reply is to ask the Tribunal to decide upon the degree of my guilt at the end of the full trial." "Quite, quite; mumble, mumble; hmmm, hmmm," mutters His Lordship next to me. And in a whisper I voice my agreement: "Imagine Your Grace ever sentencing my father at the beginning of his trial. The whole procedure, of course, was planned so that all the decisions would be rendered at the conclusion. It all shows over again what a sneaky witness that father of mine is." His Lordship agrees with me. Our little conversation must have given you pause, even though you couldn't hear it. For suddenly—just as Seidl is about to proceed to his next question—you continue: "I myself, speaking from the very depths of my feelings and after the experience of the five months of this trial, want to say that now, after I have gained a full insight into all the horrible atrocities that have been committed, I am possessed by a deep sense of guilt."

There's a jolt of activity on the justices' bench. I hug and kiss the Russian judge, fly into the American judge's arms; I can't contain my ecstasy. My father has confessed! Finally, something like a trace of sympathy for humanity issues from your depths. The journalists in the press section wake up. Seidl, as he told me later, was totally perplexed. But he gets hold of himself and quickly shifts tactics: "What were your aims when you took over the post of Governor General?"

Your answer: "I was not informed about anything." I freeze, stiffen.

That's a strange answer. It's exactly as if Seidl had asked you,

"Witness, what time is it?" and you answered, "Yes, the flowers on my brother's grave smell so sweet."

It's all over—all over again. For a few seconds you had begun to make use of your second chance. But then you babble on and arrive at the following remarkable sentence: "My aim was to safeguard justice without doing harm to our war effort." I admit that now I began to cry again. Just a minute ago you were speaking about your deep guilt. And now you're already running away again. From now on, whenever they prove that you had committed a crime you can feign surprise and according to your formula say: "But it was done in the interest of our war effort and was consequently justifiable." It continues in that vein for quite some time. You complain verbosely about how powerless you were. The people who were really responsible for everything were Himmler and Krüger and Koppe and the SS, and you say that none of them had checked their annihilation orders with you in advance. Then you begin to get increasingly snarled up in trivial matters, both you and Seidl. Asked about the size of your GG, you say, "One hundred seventy to one hundred eighty thousand square kilometers," and add in your slimy way: "I request that you do not try to pin me down to the exact number of thousand square kilometers." But His Lordship really lets you have it at that one, and asks what you could possibly be thinking of: naturally you are to be pinned down to every half square kilometer, and the tone of your answer was getting fairly close to contempt of court, and if you are incapable of telling the members of the Tribunal the precise number of square kilometers, His Lordship will immediately have the guillotine rolled into the courtroom. . . . Yes, yes, I know, none of that is true. I just wanted to complete the picture of that sniveling manner you demonstrated yet again on this Holy Thursday.

We hear nothing about your courage in bullying and ranting at that Polish theater director. Remember him? The man who would be damned if he would print in his program a picture of that blockhead of yours and your drivel? Nothing of that steely German manner that you served up to Count Ronikier. And certainly nothing more of an open, frank, and honest confession of guilt. Did you hear me whimpering like a little kid? I simply could not believe my ears.

His Lordship and I, crouching beneath the bench, have just been chuckling over your hypocritical remarks on the size of the GG, when I hear Seidl saying: "Did you ever in any way participate in the annihilation of the Jews?" And with a quick intake of breath I hear you in your answer actually giving me and you and Germany one more chance: "I say yes; and the reason I say yes is because, having been so affected by the five months of this trial, and particularly after having heard the testimony of the witness Höss, my conscience does not allow me to cast off the responsibility solely onto small people. I myself never set up an extermination camp for Jews, nor did I ever support the existence of such camps; but if Adolf Hitler personally has inflicted that dreadful responsibility on his people, then it is mine, too, for we have led the battle against the Jewry for years; and we have indulged in the most horrible utterances—my own diary bears witness against me. And, therefore, it is no more than my duty to answer your question, in this sense and in this connection, with 'yes.' A thousand years will pass and this guilt of Germany will still not be erased."

Here I must make a double paragraph break. *You did it*. You have walked through the portal of guilt. The judges squeeze my hand; I gaze down upon you with love; the only thing that can follow now is the obvious: You will unload now, you will describe your complicity in these crimes, your addiction to fancy automobiles and private railroad cars, your painful fawning and obsequiousness toward the real holders of power, your personal enrichment and also that of your family because you were unable to stop them. Finally you will explain what happened to those 200,000 eggs. The longer your testimony lasts, the more your accursed life will oppress

you. The reliving of it will crush you horribly. And at the conclusion, at the very end, I will grant you permission to weep. You
may even shudder in your fit of sobbing, as if you were having an
epileptic attack. You have my permission to begin to babble a
prayer out of the blue and beg for mercy—even though His
Lordship and I will calmly and with human understanding forbid
you to do that. And so I sit here, as I have been sitting here year
after year ever since, and I wait and wait for further confessions
from you.

Dr. Seidl was completely surprised. Later he told me, "I saw
clearly how the journalists were up and out of their seats, for that
was a truly sensational moment when one of these people admitted
his guilt." And so it was logical that he, Seidl, a young and aspiring
lawyer, but also very clever, wanted to save you. So he instantly
threw the next question at you: "Witness. What was in your
capacity as Governor General your policy regarding the conscription of laborers for the Reich?"

One can detect Seidl's consternation in the somewhat confused
and unexpected way in which he asked that question. You are still
completely self-absorbed, completely preoccupied. Your guilt is
reverberating in your soul. Absentmindedly you ask: "I beg your
pardon?"

Dr. Seidl repeats his question more distinctly. I hold my breath,
and for a change it's my eyes that are popping out of my head.
A faintly murmured "Daddy" passes my innocent child's lips. And
you? *And you?* What passes your lips?

The transcript of the proceedings reveals the following: "Frank:
'My policy is laid down in my decrees. No doubt they will be put
forward as evidence against me by the prosecution, and I consider
that it will save time if I answer that question later, with the
permission of the Tribunal.'"

It's all over, all over, all over. His Grace calms me down and
says that my father is quite right. He will have to come clean and

make a complete confession during the Soviet prosecutor's cross-examination. But I sense that bad things are to come. Your sentence about "a thousand years will pass" is still resounding in my head while you are answering Seidl's next question and claiming again that the first time you ever heard the name Maidanek was in connection with "foreign news dispatches." Then you told about the rumors you had heard, saying that the "stench of the rumors seemed to be penetrating the very walls"—very beautifully expressed, Father. You know better, both of us know better. In fact, you knew exactly what was going on. You had made very clever use of the information earlier, as leverage in your divorce case, dear man. But anyhow, you say again that it wasn't until 1944 that you learned the first details about the lovely home life in the Maidanek camp. Dr. Seidl: "And therefore you didn't know of the conditions in Treblinka, Auschwitz, and the others? Did Treblinka belong to Maidanek, or is that a separate camp?"

Frank: "I don't know that. It seems to have been a separate camp. Auschwitz was not within the territory of the Government General. I was never in Maidanek, nor in Treblinka, nor in Auschwitz."

Too bad you were never there. It would have been so perfect if they had sent you alone into one of the gas chambers after the trial and closed the doors. After Father O'Connor had made the sign of the cross on your forehead, you could have slid down into the darkness, praying fervently—but your prayers would soon have been drowned out by your screams of mortal terror. You would have heard the muffled plop of the first Zyklon B gas pellet; you would frantically have tried to escape from it, but you would have smashed up against the concrete wall. (On the other side of that wall are written the innocent words "Shower Room.") You know that the gas rises from the floor to the ceiling and fills the room from below. You are five feet nine inches tall, six feet on your tiptoes—not tall enough, it's not enough. If it had been my choice,

I would much prefer this way of death for you; it has the advantage of being slower and more agonizing than death by hanging. Well, either way. Just hearing you declaim the following makes me want to see that rope around your neck right now: "One has to take the diary as a whole. You can't go through forty-two volumes and pick out single sentences and separate them from their context. [*Father, how can I possibly reinterpret your statement about turning the Poles and Jews into mincemeat to mean that all Poles, including the Black Madonna of Czestochowa, are invited to visit your Chopin Museum? I've tried it, and believe me, it doesn't work.*] As for the rest, however, I would like to say here that I do not want to argue or quibble about individual phrases. It was a wild and stormy period filled with terrible passions [*is that tantamount to saying that your anti-Semitism and the extermination of whole races of people turn out to be a "passion in a stormy period"? Remarkable*], and when a whole country is on fire in such storm and stress, and a life-or-death struggle is going on, such words can easily be used." That explanation is pretty pathetic—in fact, it's lamebrained and stupid. You sense that yourself and continue (although Dr. Seidl tries to interrupt you): "Some of the words are terrible; I must admit myself that I was shocked at many of the words I had used." But it's all over. I can now give up, on both of us. Yet you proceed to set still another example for investigative commissions of all kinds to emulate in today's Germany, the succession state. It's as if all of our politicians today, infected by your example, had already been seated in the audience at Nuremberg, digesting your answers and turning them into rules for contemporary political behavior.

As documentary evidence for the prosecution, Dr. Seidl reads you the transcript of a conference that you had in 1939 with an officer serving under the Supreme Chief of the Administration Ober-Ost. Dr. Seidl: "It says here: 'During the first conversation which the Chief of the Central Department had with Reichsminister Dr. Frank on October 3, 1939, in Posen, the latter explained the task that had been given him by the Führer and the economic-political principles on which he intended to base his administration in Poland. According to that, it could be done only by ruthless exploitation, by the gutting of the country. Therefore, it would be necessary to conscript manpower to be used in the Reich. . . . ' and so on. That's a close approximation. I have summarized it, Mr. President."

Frank: "Those utterances were surely not made in the way that they are put down here."

Dr. Seidl: "But you do not wish to say that you never spoke with that man?"

Frank: "I cannot remember it at all. It has escaped my powers of recollection."

What a great sentence. For years it was my pièce de résistance, I suppose because it's so crazy. Whenever Mother caught me in a lie I would say: "Mother, it has escaped my powers of recollection," and then she simply had to laugh. She couldn't contain herself and would say—"Ah, God knows, he was quite a character." She would say it cheerfully, meaning you, of course, even with a trace of tenderness in her voice.

God damn it, Father, and God damn me, too. This all took place on Holy Thursday, the day they scourged your newly discovered Jesus. And there you are at that very hour, denying a meeting whose location, whose date, and the names of whose participants are being put in evidence for you. How appropriate. How contemptible.

Now I'll leave you alone for a bit with all that claptrap you're spewing and turn some pages. I'll skip past some of the material concerning you in this tremendous reprint edition of the *Proceedings of the Nuremberg International Military Tribunal*. Its words have become again the latest German political prose, however you slice it. It's my house bible, and wherever I am, whatever page I open it up to, I find nothing but German cowardice, German bellyaching and whimpering. It's my private guidebook on how to lie, a primer for the new Germany. I skip over and come now to Chief Justice Smirnov, the Soviet prosecutor, a man not much to my taste because he doesn't have the brilliance of his Western partners—no big surprise considering the system of justice in that country. But in the course of his cross-examination there is a dialogue that has an almost grotesquely comical effect on me. At the same time, it is so shabby and so far removed from your confession that morning, when you were still able to speak about those one thousand years of German shame. The Russian speaks only Russian. Over your ears (which always reminded me of flesh-eating plants) is a set of earphones that provides you with a simultaneous translation. A real screw-up artist must be sitting at the controls in the interpreters' booth (someone who certainly wouldn't have kept his job very long if he had had to deal with the ingenious technology of the gas chambers). Anyhow, he's partly to blame for an amazing bit of confusion that arises between bench and dock.

Smirnov: "Will the defendant tell us who was the actual leader of the National Socialist Party in the Government General?"

Frank: "I can't hear anything. I can't hear anything at all."

Smirnov: "I am asking you . . ."

Frank: "I hear nothing." And on and on.

The two of you finally make contact, and after Smirnov discovers that you were nominally, but not actually, Party Member Number One in the GG, he says: "You didn't hear of the existence of Maidanek until the year 1944, is that correct?"

Frank: "In the year 1944. [*At that point you must have smelled danger, because you now work that cure-all word "officially" into the next sentence.*] The name Maidanek was brought to my attention officially for the first time by Press Secretary Gassner."

In spite of your clever dodges you are already in the trap. Smirnov now places before you your own report to Hitler of May 1943: "I shall read you an excerpt from your report and I should like to remind you that the report is dated May 1943. Excuse me, it is from June 19, 1943. I quote." And then he quotes endlessly the wrong passage but finally gets to the right one. Smirnov: " 'A large part of the Polish intelligentsia, however, would not let itself be influenced by the news from Katyn and held against Germany alleged similar crimes, especially Auschwitz.' I shall now omit the next sentence and continue quoting from your report: 'Among that portion of the working class which is not communistically inclined, this is scarcely denied; but at the same time it is pointed out that the attitude of Germany toward the Poles is not any better.' Please make note of the next sentence: 'I have reports that there are concentration camps in Auschwitz and Maidanek where likewise the mass murder of Poles is taking place systematically, as in a production line.' "

Now you're sitting in a pile of shit, O Father, O Father of mine. And to think that only this morning you had been speaking so beautifully about your responsibility and your profound guilt. You can just imagine what's coming now, Father; and sure enough, as if Smirnov had been studying Perry Mason, he gets right to the point and asks you complacently: "How can one reconcile this passage from your report which mentions Auschwitz and Maidanek, where systematic mass murder was taking place, with your statement that you heard of Maidanek for the first time at the end of 1944? Well, your report was dated June 1943, and there you mention not only Maidanek but Auschwitz as well."

Well, Herr Reichsminister, Herr Governor General, Herr President of the International Court of Justice, how is the true German supposed to reply to that? As comrade to comrade, naturally. Candidly, openly. But evidently all you have at hand is more of that cowardly crap which you use for your answer now: "With reference to Maidanek, we were speaking about the extermination of Jews. The extermination in Maidanek became known to me during the summer of 1944. [*Along with your courage, your control of the German language is also sinking perceptibly, Father.*] Up to now the question of Maidanek had been mentioned always only in connection with extermination of Jews."

Thus does the onetime brilliant lawyer phrase his answer when he himself is sitting in the dock, the man who was so adroit at fighting on behalf of Hitler. You're pathetic, Father. Naturally Smirnov perseveres, scornfully. Perhaps he was even grinning a little: "Consequently I must understand you to be saying the following—I refer to the text submitted to you: In May 1943, you learned of the mass murder of Poles in Maidanek, and in the year 1944 you learned of the mass murder of Jews?"

Your turn to answer, and by now you're no more than a miserable little heap of grammatical confusion: "I beg your pardon? . . . 1944, about the extermination of the Jews in Maidanek, yes, the official documents have been delivered to me in the foreign press, yes."

At this point, after a bit more give-and-take, Smirnov succeeds in evoking from you your saddest performance in the witness stand so far. The whole thing revolves around your "Ordinance for Combating Attacks Against German Economic Buildup in the Government General." This ordinance is really one of your masterpieces. Savor above all the wonderful Paragraph One once more: "Non-Germans who—with the intention of preventing or disrupting German construction activities in the Government General—violate laws, other ordinances, or official decrees or directives are to be [*well, what? scolded? chased away?*] sentenced to death." Now, that's what I call working in the interests of the war effort, Father.

Paragraph Six is also clever: "The verdicts of the Drumhead Court Martial of the Security Police are to be carried out immediately." But just a little while ago, in your exchange with Seidl, you had been boasting obsequiously about your authority to grant amnesty, from which Smirnov struck the spark that finally lit your funeral pyre.

Smirnov: "I ask you to tell us who the members of this Court Martial, this 'Standgericht,' were?"

Frank: "The Security Police, yes."

(Father, here goes his first little bomb.)

Smirnov: "But you were telling us of your hostile attitude toward the SD, the Security Police. Why ever would you have given the SD the right to deal oppressively with the Polish population?"

Father, look out, he has another ace up his sleeve—he's going to trick you into sliding right down his gullet with that sweet talk of his. Those words of warning were on the tip of my tongue but they were not in my heart. I was totally and completely on Smirnov's side; I even went tsk, tsk with my tongue when you answered so foolishly: "Because that was the only way I could exert any influence over the verdicts. If I had not promulgated this ordinance, then there would have been no possibility of control, and the police could have simply acted blindly."

I know why you are already no longer paying attention, why you have that cringing look on your face, the look you had years ago in Lammers's private salon car. This is another one of those "comradely interrogations" when you close down all your cerebral functions and can only squeak like a rat in mortal terror. Shabby behavior for a man with such a sense of responsibility.

Smirnov: "You spoke of the right of amnesty that was entrusted to you. Perhaps you might direct your attention to Paragraph Six of this ordinance. I would like to remind you of this paragraph: 'The verdicts of the Drumhead Court Martial of the Security Police are to be carried out immediately.' I should like to remind you again that there was only one possible verdict: death. How could you change it if the condemned person was to be shot or hanged immediately after the verdict?"

Now, here it comes, the most potent answer of your life. And how hopeless it is, how ridiculous. A gale of laughter should have swept through the courtroom when you defiantly replied: "Nevertheless, the verdict had to be submitted to me for my approval."

I now leave an empty space to let that last comment take its effect:

Smirnov: "Yes, but the verdicts were to be carried out immediately, were they not?"

How often in my life I have imagined coming down from the judges' bench, crouching inside you, becoming you, seeing myself as you there—torrents of shame, of embarrassment, wanting to crawl away. Spouting off at the mouth, you had begun your testimony with confessions of guilt—and here you are again, as weak and flabby as ever.

Afterwards, in your cell, you begin to secrete those pious phrases of yours; they ooze into your letters to Mother and me. Father O'Connor should have slapped you senseless during the noon recess. I see you all around me, and I don't know what to say now other than to quote your reply to Smirnov's insistent question. Here it is: "That is the general instruction which I had issued in connection with the power given me to grant reprieves, and the committee that dealt with reprieves was constantly in session. Files were sent in. . . ."

Father, you have forfeited even this one last and final chance. And then, the following fall, 1946, you robbed me of even those few hopeful sentences you uttered the previous spring, the time you came close to a confession of guilt. In your revised version you pointed the way for our next generation to deal in its own special way with overcoming the past, our celebrated *Vergangenheitsbewältigung*. In your summation, months later, before the Tribunal withdrew to consider its verdicts, you uttered these slimy words: "I must still rectify one of the statements that I made here earlier. In the witness stand I spoke about the one thousand years that could not erase the guilt from our nation on account of Hitler's behavior. However, not only the fact that the behavior of our enemies toward our people and our soldiers has been so carefully excluded from the proceedings of this Tribunal, but also the gigantic mass atrocities of the most horrible kind [*well, there you go again with your beloved superlatives; now you're the same old fellow once again, only this time freshly baptized as a Catholic*], which, as I have now learned, were committed against Germans, above all in East Prussia, Silesia, Pomerania, and in the Sudetenland by Russians, Poles, and Czechs, and are still being committed—all this has completely canceled out, even today, any possible guilt on the part of our people and nation."

And now the arm of God reaches down from Heaven, the arm in whose millions of little hairs screaming bodies are entrapped like Captain Ahab on the body of Moby Dick, and His arm is plunged into your mouth, down through your throat, through your stomach. And there God's fingers grab hold, and then He, Supergod, begins to pull His arm back, slowly, very slowly, and He turns you inside out, skin side in, with a squishy sucking sound, so that I, amazed by this spectacle of flesh, come down to you from the judges' bench and watch your organs wriggling on your outside; your face has disappeared inside your head. Your eyes are gone. I come closer and see your heart anchored to its tough arteries and veins; it's beating like crazy. You are turned upside down and inside out now, hanging head downward. Your heart is beating in my face. And I open my mouth and bite into it, into your heart, I take bite after bite, until I swallow you and your last flood of lies, until that pumping heart of yours goes limp and you collapse like a bag in the witness stand, a horrifying mass of tattered flesh— while I, an eternal zombie, no doubt about it, leap away from you. I will be trying to leap away from you for the rest of my life.

A NOTE ABOUT THE AUTHOR

Niklas Frank was born in Munich in March 1939 and lived for much of the Second World War in the lavish residences of his father, the Governor General of Occupied Poland. He studied history, sociology, and German literature at the universities of Munich and Kiel, and beginning in 1963 wrote film scripts (with Volker Schlöndorff among others) and film criticism. Since 1968 he has been a journalist, since 1979 with *Stern* magazine, most recently covering German politics and foreign affairs. This book was originally published, in slightly different form, in Germany (as *Der Vater*).

A NOTE ON THE TYPE

The text of this book was set in Perpetua, designed by the British artist Eric Gill (1882–1940) and cut by The Monotype Corporation, London, in 1928–1930. Perpetua is a contemporary letter of original design, without any direct historical antecedents. The shapes of the roman letters basically derive from stonecutting, a form of lettering in which Gill was eminent. The italic is essentially an inclined roman. The general effect of the typeface in reading sizes is one of lightness and grace. The larger display sizes of the type are extremely elegant and form what is probably the most distinguished series of inscriptional letters cut in the present century.

Composed by PennSet, Inc., Bloomsburg, Pennsylvania
Printed and bound by Fairfield Graphics, Fairfield, Pennsylvania
Designed by Virginia Tan